Multivariate Archaeology

Multivariate Archaeology

Numerical Approaches
in Scandinavian Archaeology

Edited by Torsten Madsen

Jutland Archaeological Society Publications XXI, 1988

Distributed by Aarhus University Press

Multivariate Archaeology
Numerical Approaches in Scandinavian Archaeology

ISBN 87 7288 047 3
ISSN 0107 2854

Translation: Peter Crabb
Keyboarding and coding: Torsten Madsen
Lay-out, cover and drawings: Elsebet Morville

Typeset by Uni-C, Århus
Printed by Narayana Press, Gylling
Type: Baskerville 10/11

Published by:
Jutland Archaeological Society
Moesgård
DK-8270 Højbjerg

Distributed by:
Aarhus University Press
Aarhus University
DK-8000 Århus C

The publication of this book has been supported by:
Nordisk Kulturfond
and
The Danish Research Council for the Humanities

Contents

Preface

In June 1981 a research course in multivariable statistic methods was held in Tromsø, northern Norway. The course was arranged by *NAVF's EDB-senter* in Bergen together with *Institutt for samfunnsvitenskap* and *Institutt for matematiske real-fag* at the University of Tromsø. The students at the ten days long course were 18 archaeologists from Denmark, Finland, Norway and Sweden, and the instructors mathematicians and archaeologists from the two institutes in Tromsø.

To some of the participants, the course proved very useful, and it meant a great step forward in the dissipation of multivariate analytical methods in Scandinavian archaeology. Not least in Denmark, the impact of the course was noticeable. The complete set of computer programs used in connection with the course was transferred to the computer centre in Århus. Together with other programs it was joined into a package held together by a Pascal-programmed shell that made it relatively easy to handle. Today, we find these analyses used by many students as standard analytical methods in connection with their theses.

The growing popularity of the methods at the Institute of Prehistoric Archaeology at Moesgård (University of Århus) made it natural that a first Scandinavian symposium on applied multivariate methods in archaeology should be organised from here. It was held in November 1984 at Sandbjerg Slot in southern Jutland with the participation of 16 archaeologists from Denmark, Norway and Sweden, and funded by *Nordiske Forskarsymposier*.

The symposium succeeded in demonstrating that the methods could be moved from a theoretical level into practical archaeological use, and it was agreed at the end of the meeting that it was imperative that there should be a follow-up publication. Unfortunately, as often seen, good intentions are not always enough. The present book, appearing almost four years after the symposium, is not to be considered as the proceedings of the symposium. Only half of the participant at that time have contributed to the book, and others not present at the symposium have joined.

The book as it appears does, however, attain its goal. It demonstrates how, through the use of multivariate, statistical methods, archaeologists can analyse and handle complex archaeological data materials with a speed, stringency and precision that can hardly be obtained by traditional more or less intuitive methods.

The problems treated by the various authors range widely in time and space and they cover the major issues in archaeology - chronology, typology and distribution. A suit of numerical methods is used, but especially one - correspondence analysis - dominates. The versatility of this method is clearly demonstrated, and it is to be expected that it will become one of the major analytical methods in archaeology in coming years.

Publication of this book has been funded by *Nordisk Kulturfond* and *Statens Humanistiske Forskningsråd*, to whom I am grateful for their support. Further I am thankful to Poul Kjærum, Jutland Archaeological Society for accepting it for publication in the society's monograph series. Graphics and layout are due to Elsebeth Morville and the English revision has been carried out by Peter Crabb, to both of whom I am grateful. Typing of manuscripts and subsequent typesetting in TEX was performed by the editor.

T.M.

Multivariate statistics and archaeology

By Torsten Madsen — University of Aarhus

THE ARCHAEOLOGICAL RESEARCH PROCESS

European archaeology has always been considered to be a humanistic discipline, with all its sympathetic insight into the life of the human beings with which it deals. Yet the archaeological data material has no humanistic touch - a collection of dead items bound together by context information. It can be qualified according to context, and the logic of the contexts can be outlined, but it has no inherent humanistic content that can be read as one reads a book.

This disparity in quality between the aim and the means of attaining this aim very often leads to schizophrenic studies in archaeology. On the one hand, we find formalised analyses of artifacts and context information without the slightest reference to 'the Indian behind the artefact', and on the other, far-reaching tales are spun, often without a sound base in the data material. For most archaeologists, this schizophrenia is neatly organised. In one chapter they painstakingly deal with the artifacts and their setting. They describe, measure, compare and summarise, with or without the help of statistics. Then, in the next chapter they discuss and draw conclusions in historical terms about extinct human societies.

Sometimes the schizophrenia is so perfect that hardly any of the painstaking analyses are used for any purpose at all in the concluding chapter. One cannot help wondering what all the descriptions were for.

Some archaeologists do not suffer notably from this disease. They either simply discard the conclusions in terms of human society, and lose themselves in the rigoristic world of 'stamp collecting', or they completely forget about the archaeological record, and become in Flannery's words 'born-again philosopher' (1982).

It is tempting to speak ironically of this unhappy state of affairs. However, it does conceal a very serious problem. What is the nature of the link between the archaeological record and the interpretations in terms of human culture and history?

The archaeological research situation involves two very different realities. One is the reality of prehistoric societies. This is a reality that can no longer be observed even though it is the target of archaeological research. The other is our present reality, which we can observe. The archaeological record is an integrated part of this present reality, and it remains part of this reality no matter how intensely we observe it. We cannot observe the past. There is no logical link that takes us from the archaeological record back into the past, and there is no way we can draw conclusions by rules of logic from the archaeological record to the nature and organisation of past societies.

Yet the archaeological record is real, and basically part of a past reality. This means that there are logical links from the past to the archaeological record, and if only we knew the past, and knew the nature of all the successive transformations that shaped the archaeological record (Schiffer 1972, 1976), we could predict it in great detail. Thus we can state that the archaeological record is structured by the past even if it is part of the present, and consequently there must be a correspondence in structure between the two. This we may use as a guiding principle to evaluate propositions concerning the past, and indeed it is the only link we have to past reality.

Initially, we may separate two obvious levels on which archaeologists work. One is the level of current reality, where we can observe, analyse and categorise with great precision. The other is the imaginary level of the past to which we ascribe qualities and causal relationships. The latter is as much a part of our current reality as the former, and the justification for claiming that our modelling on this level has relevance for the past depends on our ability to show that the structure of the propositions we put forward do not violate the structure of the archaeological record. It is worth noting that we can never prove a statement concerning the nature and organisation of past societies to be true beyond doubt. In simple cases we may feel very certain that our statements are right, even to the degree where we may be tempted to claim that we have drawn a logical conclusion from the archaeological record. With more complex models and general explanations, we can never claim to be certain, and in my opinion these general statements are in fact more a revelation of our current views upon present world realities, than they are statements of facts concerning past realities.

One important point should not be forgotten here. Although we cannot prove anything to be true, we certainly can falsify statements concerning the past. In theory, at least, we can outline the implications of a statement and compare these implications with the actual archaeological record. In simple matters this works quite well. In connection with complex statements, however, one may seriously doubt our ability to draw the right conclusions.

As mentioned, the two levels on which archaeology has to operate can be seen to be pursued independently by many scholars, and most archaeologists have a tendency to keep them separate in their works. However, only when we exploit the two levels simultaneously and try to maintain a strict correspondence between them can we make sensible progress. This means that, all through dealing with the archaeological record, we should keep our picture of the past and its implications in mind, and all through forming and altering our picture of the past, we should be acutely aware of the realities of the archaeological record. Whenever we acknowledge that the implications of our models for the past do not fit the data at hand, we should modify or completely discard our models. All along we must realise that we never work in a vacuum; we are always guided by preconceived ideas. Thus models and ideas come prior to data, but at the same time our picture of the past has credibility only, when it is not refuted by the archaeological record.

In European archaeology the actual approach to the archaeological research process has always been dominated by traditional positivism. Seemingly, within this approach there are no problems at all concerning the linking process. Knowledge of the past is believed to be a direct additive outcome of information extracted from the archaeological record (Childe 1956; Malmer 1984). If only we gather enough information, and if only we analyse the information thoroughly, we will have all we need for an understanding of prehistoric society. Unfortunately, there is no obvious solution to the problem that arises when two scholars working in general with the same material come to two different views of past societies. As they both add together the same figures, but reach different results, one of them must be wrong. An evaluation of the professional standing of the two adversaries seems to be the only way out (Thompson 1956).

Positivism in this version may apparently work well as long as everything, including the analysis of the archaeological record, is done intuitively. Then nobody can follow the steps in the research procedure. But as soon as formalised data analysis is adopted, problems arise. The obscurity of the linking between analyses and syntheses becomes evident, and as the analyses become more and more technical, the crack widens to a gap. Indeed, the schizophrenic behaviour of the archaeologist becomes painfully clear in the publications.

I certainly hold it true that formalised artifact analysis using various forms of 'exact' descriptions and statistics (McBurney 1967; Malmer 1962; Cullberg 1968 among others), has never increased our knowledge of prehistoric societies one bit more than less formal studies have, but it does indeed create voluminous and unreadable books. Often it is the formal analyses and statistics that get the blame, and heated reactions against this 'technological Frankenstein's monster' can be seen (Hawkes 1968:262). It is not generally realised that it is the approach itself that is wrong.

The hypothetical-deductive method introduced from American archaeology in the sixties and seventies never had any notable impact on European archaeology. This is in some ways sad, because its demands for an explicit linking between the hypotheses concerning prehistoric societies and the realities of the archaeological record give it operational strength, and remove (in theory at least) the possibility of excessive, aimless analysis of data materials. It was, however, presented in the archaeological literature (Fritz & Plog 1970; Watson et al. 1971) as an inseparable part of the deductive-nomological model of explanation, and it was really this model that for various reasons did not suit European archaeologists.

The Hemplian approach to explanation is quickly dying in anthropological research today, if for no other reason than for its lack of ability to produce anything but 'Mickey Mouse' laws of culture (Eggert 1982:141, with reference to Flannery). Hopefully, this may free the hypothetical-deductive method from its association with nomological positivism, and give it a less rigid appearance than it required in that company.

The adoption of a hypothetical-deductive approach has two advantages. It forces the linking process between data and synthesis to be transparent, and it gives a more dynamic goal-orientated exploitation of the data material. It does not, however, give the linking itself greater security, as one might be tempted to believe from the writings of Watson et al. (1971).

The only way that the linkage can be made more precise and secure is through the study of what has been termed archaeological formation processes (Schiffer 1976) or more grandiosely 'middle range research' (Binford 1983). By studying how an archaeological record is formed in present-day context, and how in general terms various elements of a living society influence this record, a better understanding can be reached of how a true archaeological record with roots in the past might have been created, and what this indicates in terms of a living society.

The study of archaeology, then, consists of three separate levels, which can be pursued individually, but should preferably not be. One is the theoretical level, where mentally modelled reconstructions of prehistoric societies are made, where cultural relations are specified, and where cultural changes are explained. This level logically has precedence over the others, but it cannot exist meaningfully unless it is constantly linked to the archaeological record.

The second level is the linking process. It consists of statements and arguments of how the archaeological record was formed, with direct reference to a conscious model of the past society in question. The logic of this process runs from the model to the archaeological record. Yet, it is not merely an intellectual exercise, as one might believe from deductive positivism. Empirical knowledge can and should indeed enter the linking arguments. Such a knowledge has definitely always been a part of the linking process introduced through the 'life experience' of archaeologists. However, realising the nature of the linkage it is far more profitable to rely on a formal study of present day formations of the 'archaeological record'. Because of the empirical content of the linking argumentation, the linkage itself seldom appears as a deduction from our models, and there is no reason why it should. The linking argumentation may take any form we wish, as long as we are aware that we cannot make a link unless we have theories and models concerning the prehistoric past; that the logic proceeds from these to the present day context; and consequently that it is wasteful not to explicate theories and models in advance of an attempt to link.

The third level concerns the factual study of the archaeological record in all its many-sided aspects. This is the level where archaeologists really feel at home, and the methods and techniques of this level have been developed to a high degree of perfection. The fun and pleasure of working at this level often make archaeologists forget that it is absolutely futile to work with the archaeological record without an ever present awareness of its relevance to the level of actual theories, models and reconstructions.

STATISTICS AND ARCHAEOLOGICAL RESEARCH

It is an obvious and legitimate question to ask: what has the preceding chapter to do with the use of statistics in archaeology? The present chapter tries to answer this question in some detail, and hopefully it will straighten out some misconceptions concerning statistics as well as place statistics in a more useful framework of application than has so far been the case in Scandinavian archaeology.

To begin with, I will cite Spiegel's account of the difference between inductive and deductive statistics.

If a sample is representative of a population, important conclusions about the population can often be inferred from analysis of the sample. The phase under which such inference is valid is called inductive statistics or statistical inference. Because such inference cannot be absolutely certain, the language of probability is often used in stating conclusions. The phase of statistics which seeks only to describe and analyse a given group without drawing any conclusions or inferences about a larger group, is called descriptive or deductive statistics (1972:1).

Inductive approaches include probability estimation methods based on various theoretical distributions like the binomial, normal and Poisson distributions as well as statistical decisions based on various tests like the well known Chi-square and Student's t tests. It also includes inferences using various forms of regression analysis.

Deductive approaches include all types of descriptive statistics from various simple graphic and arithmetic descriptions of individual variables - alone or two by two - to the complicated multivariate data-reducing analyses which are the main issue of this book.

I would argue that the application of inductive statistics in archaeological research is very problematic. There are two main reasons for this, both of which stem from the nature of the archaeological record. Most inductive statistics require that we know in detail the distributional qualities of the populations to which we apply the inferences. At the same time, they require that we have complete control of the formation of the samples from which we infer. None of these requirements are met in archaeology. Whether we conceive of the 'populations' as a material present in the past, or just as a material present in the earth today, we have to realise that the populations of archaeological material and their distributional qualities are basically unknown. Furthermore, if we speak of past populations, we have no way of knowing the exact history of the formation of the samples. The same, of course, does not necessarily apply if we speak of populations in terms of the hidden part of the archaeological record.

A more fundamental objection against inductive statistics in archaeology may, however, be raised. It is very doubtful whether the archaeological record can be considered to be a sample of anything at all in a statistical sense. That is, the archaeological finds and their compositions cannot be viewed as samples that reveal what some larger background unit looked like. Each find - and each composition - springs from an actual historical event or sequence of events, and thus has a complete 'as it is' meaning by itself. It is a unit of complete information. Even if we speak of excavation samples from, say, a large settlement site, we cannot claim that these are samples in a statistical sense, for the settlement site itself is not a population with some uniform theoretical structure. On the contrary, it is a statistically very haphazard phenomenon, and predicting what the rest will be like from an excavation 'sample' in one part of the settlement is beyond statistics. It is of course possible to devise a sampling strategy that will reveal the structure of the settlement, but then we are not dealing with one, but many samples, and the statistics needed to reveal their information are not inductive, but deductive.

In sociology, there are no problems using inductive statistics, because it is possible to observe the populations and their qualities, and carefully define the extraction of samples in a way that makes it possible to use inference statistics in a meaningful way. As outlined above, the nature of archaeological research does not allow us to observe the original populations from which the archaeological record is extracted, nor can we follow - let alone define - the processes through which the record is extracted. Therefore, a use of inductive statistics in archaeology will for theoretical reasons be a misapplication, and I fear that in most cases it will also in practice lead to erroneous, or rather, nonsensical results.

Deductive statistics, in general, have no a priori assumptions that we cannot control. The specific methods do have limitations that impose restrictions on the data they analyse. However, these restrictions always apply directly to the observed input data. This leaves us in full control to use the methods properly.

It is very important to stress that deductive statistics are descriptive. They have no inferential value whatsoever. We can use them to clarify the contents of the archaeological record, and present it in a form that makes it easier for us to carry out our linking argumentation. They cannot in any way produce the conclusions for us.

Deductive statistics may be used on several levels. We can describe and summarise individual variables, we can describe the relationships between pairs of variables, and we can describe the structure of the interrelations of many variables. Whatever we choose to do, we should never forget to do it with a specific purpose in mind. It is easy to fill page upon page with descriptions using uni-variate and bi-variate statistics, but if we do not intend to use it in the linking argumentation, then why waste time, effort, and expensive pages?

Special problems relate to the methods that deal with many variables simultaneously. Today, the multivariate methods are easy to carry out at a technical level, but they are not so easy to understand as the uni-variate and bi-variate methods. Furthermore, they are easy to misapply if not understood correctly, and if some basic rules are not observed.

The main problem with multivariate analysis lies with the rather complicated treatment that input data are given. If it is not correctly understood what goes on between input and output in these analyses, there is an immediate danger that the output will be used as data for the linking argumentation on false premises.

A further problem is that whereas uni- and bivariate methods in general gives straightforward pictures of the material they analyse, the same is not necessarily true with multivariate analyses. Indeed it is not uncommon to see analyses of genuine data that give very unsatisfactory or even misleading results. It is not sufficient to disclaim it with a 'garbage in, garbage out' shrug, as garbage very often comes out of obviously good archaeological data.

There are two points that I should like to emphasise in this connection. One is that multivariate analyses themselves are not atheoretical. In order to cope with a multivariate situation and represent it in a low-dimensional sub-space, the methods are by nature data-reductive. They subtract the 'unimportant' and leave only the 'important' information for further analysis and interpretation. The principles laid down in the methods to separate important from unimportant and to decide just how comparisons are to be made constitute the essence of the methods. If these principles do not fit the ideas guiding the data selection for an analysis, or the idea of what is relevant in the data material, then it may indeed be very difficult to obtain a reasonable result.

The second point to emphasise is that our ways of thinking in terms of the research process are extremely important here. Were we to adhere to an inductive positivist notion and consequently have a strategy where we collect and describe a lot of material, and then feed everything into a multivariate analytical method, then we would be bound to get a lot of nonsense out. No matter how sophisticated methods are, or may become, they will never be able to make a judgement of relevance between the individual variables. A judgement of relevance has to be made before analysis starts, it has to continue throughout the analyses, and it is entirely the responsibility of the archaeologist. To work with multivariate analysis and obtain good results in the long run means that: you have to define carefully your problem and your intended solution to this problem; you have to stipulate which variables are relevant to the solution, and only carry out analyses of those variables; and finally you should never stop with the first analysis - you should continuously question your preconceived models and the relevance of the data chosen, until you reach a model and a result from the analyses that can safely be linked together. That is definitely the way to do successful research using multivariate statistics. It is also in my opinion the factual practice of archaeological research in general, as outlined in the first section.

In the following I shall look into a few of the multivariate statistical methods and outline the principles by which they work, the areas of possible application within archaeology, and first and foremost the nature and quality of the results they give.

AN OUTLINE OF THREE 'FACTOR-ANALYTICAL' METHODS

Multivariate data may be treated in many different ways. There is an almost infinite choice of techniques, from the very simple to the very complex, that may be applied. Many of these techniques have proved useful to archaeology, and an overall archaeological evaluation of these methods could easily fill an entire book.

In this chapter I shall be concerned with three methods only, all found within the broad and very heterogeneous category called factor analysis. The three methods, principal component analysis (PCA), principal coordinate analysis (PCO) and correspondence analysis (CA), are closely related, since they share the same basic computational principles. Together they form a group of analyses that can handle all types of variables that one may possibly think of in any archaeological material. As they are also the methods used in most of the papers in this book, there is a good reason to discuss their application in archaeology in some detail.

All three methods make use of orthogonal regression applied to a point scatter in a multivariate metric space. As the methods take different types of variables as their input, their ways of reaching a representation in a metric space differ considerably, and consequently, the results from the three analyses are not entirely comparable. They have different qualities, even though the basic computational method is the same.

As not all readers of this book will be familiar with the principles of orthogonal regression in a multidimensional space, let alone its actual computation, a brief outline here may be helpful. Although an understanding cannot be obtained without introducing rather complex mathematics, the use of formulas will be avoided here on purpose, since it would probably scare off more readers than it will enlighten.

First of all, what do we understand by a metric representation in a multivariate space? Consider first a variable that measures some property. It could be a measure of length on a set of comparable items. This would be a measure on a metric scale, and it could be depicted as a scatter of points along an axis (Figure 1). Another variable could measure another property, say width, on the same set of items. This would also be a measure on a metric scale, and we could now depict our two variables in a two-dimensional coordinate system on the paper (Figure 2). If we added yet another variable measured on a metric scale, we could depict the three variables together in a solid-state three-dimensional model, but it would be difficult to make an acceptable representation on a piece of paper. Should we add a fourth, fifth or any number of variables measured on a metric scale, then we are beyond any geometric representation. Yet, arithmetically we may still speak of a metric representation, where each item is represented by one point in a space with a number of dimensions that equals the number of metric variables used to describe the item. Exactly the same rules of metric distance between the items apply in such a multivariate space, as in a normal three-dimensional space.

In order to understand the idea of an orthogonal regression applied to points in such a multivariate metric space, we will have to return to the two-dimensional case. To express the relationship between the two variables of the scattergram Figure 2, we would normally place a regression line through the scatter. This would either represent 'width' expressed as a function of 'length', or 'length' as a function of 'width'. In the first case the regression line would be found by minimizing the sum of squared vertical distances from the points to the line we are seeking. In the latter case the regression line would be found by minimizing the sum of squared distances horizontally from the points to the line. The two lines obtained would not be identical, as they are determined by the variable chosen as the independent.

As we have no interest in giving primacy to a specific variable, the ordinary regression method cannot be used here to express the relationship between the two variables. We need a method that is 'neutral' with respect to the variables, and determined by the scatter of points only. Such a line can be found by minimizing the sum of squared distances perpendicular from the points to the line we are seeking. This line is known as the orthogonal regression line. It will pass through the points in the graph that represent the mutual mean of the variables (the origo), and it is therefore preferable to scale the variables so that they have zero as their mean value (Figure 3).

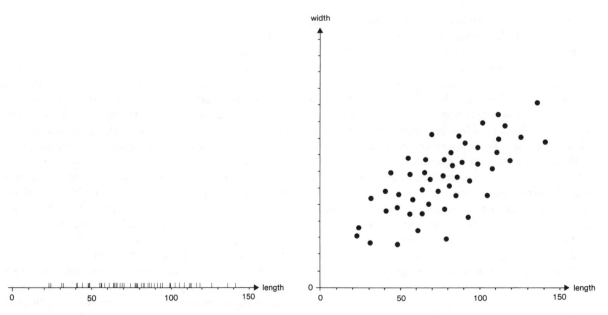

Figure 1. A graphical representation of one metric variable.

Figure 2. A graphical representation of two metric variables.

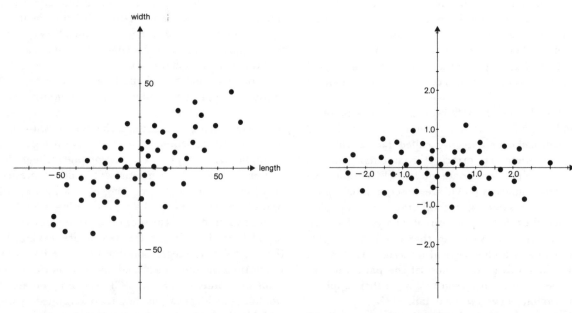

Figure 3. The same data as in Figure 2, but with the two variables scaled to have zero as their mean value.

Figure 4. The same data as in Figure 3, but with the axes rotated in order to let one axis describe the largest possible part of the variation in the point scatter.

Contrary to normal regression, the orthogonal regression is mathematically complicated to carry out, but this need not concern us here. The line obtained will be the one of all possible lines on which the projections of the points have a maximal dispersion along the line. The line thus represents the maximum variation in a single dimension in the scatter, and gives so to speak a maximal 'explanation'.

The remaining variation in the two-dimensional example can be fully explained by a line perpendicular to the first through the origo. Indeed we may claim that we have merely rotated our two original axes of description in such a way that the first describes the maximal part of the variation in the scatter of points, while the second covers the rest (Figure 4). It is important to note that the inter-relationship of the points has not been affected at all. Structure and distances in the point scatter have remained unaltered. It is only the original variables describing the points that have been replaced with others that maximize certain criteria of representation.

It causes no trouble to acknowledge that this two-dimensional example can be replaced by a three-dimensional one. Indeed we can place a line through the point scatter in a tri-axial coordinate system that meets the criteria of orthogonal regression. This line will represent the largest possible part of the variation in the point scatter that can be dealt with in one dimension. Further we can place a second line through the origo perpendicular to the first that represents the major part of the remaining variation, and finally we can place a third line through the origo perpendicular to the two others that covers the rest of the variation.

It is considerably harder to acknowledge that these principles also apply to a four-dimensional or indeed any multi-dimensional case. It makes no difference as far as the method is concerned whether we have three or a hundred dimensions. Arithmetically it works out fine. It is only our geometrical visualisation that is violated.

All three methods to be discussed here are based on orthogonal regression of point scatters in a multivariate metric space, and consequently they share some of the same characteristics in their ways of treating data. Notably, as orthogonal regression is based on minimization of the sum of squared distances from a set of points to a line, it tends to account for variance rather than correlation. This seems in general to be an advantage, but it does also mean that it is rather sensitive to uniqueness in the data, and consequently that careful data screening is a necessity in connection with its application.

The orthogonal regression itself is mathematically extremely complicated. It is performed by what is termed a spectral decomposition of a square (m x m) matrix (singular value decomposition of a rectangular (m x n where $m >= n$) matrix in the case of CA) with a content that properly represents the relationships between the points in the m-dimensional metric space as created from the data matrix.

The decomposition yields a number m non-negative numbers, the so-called eigenvalues or latent roots, and m corresponding vectors, the so-called eigenvectors or latent vectors. These vectors represent exactly the set of m orthogonal regression lines to be found. The corresponding eigenvalues represent the amount of variation covered by the individual vectors. That is to say, the proportion that a single eigenvalue constitutes of the sum of all eigenvalues is equal to the proportion of the total amount of variance represented by the associated eigenvector. The vectors can be ordered by the eigenvalues in falling order, so that the first vector, called the first principal axis, explains the largest part of the variance compared to the other vectors, the second principal axis the largest but one part of the variance, and so forth.

The difference between the three methods of multivariate analysis is outlined in the following.

Principal components analysis

In PCA the square input matrix for the spectral decomposition is the covariance or the correlation matrix between the variables in the data matrix. This implies that PCA can be used safely only with data to which it is meaningful to apply the concepts of covariance and correlation, and this is true with reasonably normally distributed measurement data only. Indeed, if we plot any two variables involved in the analysis against each other in a two-dimensional scattergram, we should find that the scatter of points is more or less an ellipsoid, with only a few outliers. Tendencies for curved point scatters, or scatters divided along two or more lines of correlation are, not acceptable in data used as input for a PCA. Variables that do not follow the normal distribution in general should either be removed from the analysis, or measures should be taken to ensure normality. Likewise, units with extreme values in one or more variables should be removed, since extreme observations will tend to dominate the first axis.

The PCA method is scale-dependent, when applied to a covariance matrix. This means that the actual numerical size of the scatter of values in the variables influences the result. It is thus not immaterial whether we measure a variable, say length, in cm or mm. By measuring in cm with one cipher following the decimal point instead of in mm, we shrink the scatter of this variable by a factor of 10 and reduce the importance of the variable accordingly.

This PCA scale-dependence makes it extremely important that questions of compatibility between variables are always carefully considered before analysis. The numerical scatter within the individual variable should always be catered for according to the importance of the variable, and co-analyses of incompatible variables should never be carried out using a covariance matrix.

A way around the problem with differential scaling is to use the correlation matrix as input. Here all variables become standardised and consequently expressed on the same scale. This solution is probably preferable in many contexts, but as all variables are given equal importance, there is always the danger that small unimportant variables are upgraded in importance beyond reason. The use of PCA then calls for extreme care and consideration, when the data are prepared for analysis.

Apart from the eigenvalues and the eigenvectors, the output from PCA consists of two tables, normally named factor or component scores and factor or component loadings, respectively.

The component scores are the coordinates of the

points (units) on the new set of principal axes defined by the eigenvectors. The component loadings are a set of correlation coefficients between the new principal axes and the original variables. The component scores thus give the position of the points in the multidimensional space seen from another viewpoint than was the case with the original variables. The component loadings tells us to what degree the new principal axes are related to or representative of the original variables.

PCA is normally termed an R-mode type of analysis. This means that basically it analyses the interrelationship between variables. To a certain extent, the component scores can be said to describe inter-object relationships, but they cannot be referred to directly in terms of inter-object similarity.

Principal coordinate analysis

The PCO can with some justification be thought of as a Q-mode PCA of a similarity matrix of some kind. Q-mode here means that it is the interrelationship of the units that is being analysed. This interrelationship is based on the concept of similarity. Many measures of similarity may be used. All those cited by Sokal and Sneath (1973) will do, and perhaps most profitably the coefficient proposed by Gower (1971), that allows for a mixture of variables on all scales in the data matrix. The similarity coefficient matrix is a square symmetric matrix with the units in both rows and columns, and a metric measure of similarity in the individual cells between all units. Properly normalised (by subtracting from each cell the mean values of the corresponding rows and columns and adding the grand mean of the matrix) to secure positive semi-definite properties, this matrix may be submitted directly to spectral decomposition. The result of this will be an orthogonal regression on a (fictive) set of metric variables expressed through the similarity coefficients. The original variables, which need not be metric, do not enter the analysis, and are lost.

The, say n, units analysed are thus thought of as n vectors describing a set of variables in an n-dimensional space, and the axes (vectors) in this space are given by the similarity coefficients (similar to the correlation coefficients in the PCA method). With orthogonal regression, we get a new set of n vectors that describe the same set of variables in a new n-dimensional space, where each new axis represents a linear combination of the original ones.

Next we may investigate how the old axes correlate with the new ones by projecting all vectors in the original space onto the vectors in the new one. In this way we find the position of all units in relation to the set of principal axes, and naturally we

are interested only in the first few principal axes that hold the major part of the information.

As each unit in a Q-mode analysis represent a dimension, and as the units are normally much more numerous than the variables, there often arise computational problems. More than a couple of hundred units can seldom be analysed in one run on most computers.

The use of a similarity coefficient that through composite calculations establishes the units in a metric space of reference has one disadvantage. It is not possible in a simple way, as with the PCA, to 'reverse' the process once the analysis has been carried out, and investigate the variables in relation to the new axial representation. We are not able to see 'what caused what'.

Correspondence analysis

With PCA categorised as an R-mode technique and PCO as a Q-mode technique, the CA may best be classified as a simultaneous R-mode and Q-mode technique. Its origin lies with the study of two-dimensional tables of contingencies, and consequently its extension to cover multivariate cases is also restricted to categorical data. This, however, is the only a priori restriction. As input to CA, any type of categorisation will do. We may use counts, presence-absence registrations, or just registrations of a presence among a series of alternatives. In the latter two cases, presence is noted as 1 while absence and excluded alternatives are noted as 0. The area of application may even be enlarged to cover continuous data by way of proper categorisation of these (Hill 1974).

From this it may be acknowledged that CA is a potentially very useful method. Not only does it work simultaneously on an R-mode and a Q-mode basis, but it also deals with types of variables that are extremely common in archaeology. Furthermore, it does this without assumptions concerning the distribution of the variables. We need not have poisson distribution attached to the error structure as with log-linear analyses of contingency tables, nor do we for that matter need to know beforehand the structure of the phenomenon under study.

Algebraically, CA presents an extension to the PCA (and PCO). Spectral decomposition was there applied to symmetric matrices to yield one set of eigenvectors and one set of eigenvalues. In CA the spectral decomposition, here called the singular value decomposition, is applied to a rectangular non-symmetric matrix, in which case two sets of eigenvectors and one set of eigenvalues are obtained. The one set of eigenvectors will represent R-mode and the other Q-mode. Provided that the data matrix is properly scaled, i.e. it shows similarity between variables and between units simultaneously on a mutual scale, then the vectors given in the R-mode solution and the vectors given in the Q-mode solution will refer to the same principal component space.

Naturally, the two sets of vectors may be found individually, as an R-mode spectral decomposition of the 'correlation' matrix (data matrix pre-multiplied by its transpose) and as a Q-mode spectral decomposition of the 'similarity matrix' (datamatrix post-multiplied by its transpose). This, however, would give the same problem with size as in the PCO method, and as the scaling of the datamatrix prior to analysis makes the spectral decomposition yield vectors referring to the same component space, it is in fact possible to calculate the one set of vectors from the other. We thus need to find the eigenvectors of the minor of the two symmetric matrices only, whether it is the one obtained by pre- or by post-multiplication with the transpose.

The scaling procedure itself is rather complex, and it lies beyond the scope of this paper to discuss it in detail. The first step is to reduce the data matrix to unity by division of each cell frequency with the grand total of the matrix. The sum of all cells thus becomes 1, and we may look upon the matrix as representing a probability distribution of the data. If we call this matrix P, we now enter the row marginal sums and the column marginal sums of P into two diagonal matrices, and subsequently pre-multiply P with the square root of the inverse of the row sum matrix and post-multiply it with the square root of the inverse of the column sum matrix. The effect of this transformation is to stretch, differentially, the column vectors by the reciprocal of the square root of their column sum and stretch, differentially, the row vectors by the reciprocal of the square root of their row sum. Variables measured on disparate scales are thus differentially weighted and, as it were, equalised; similarly for the objects (Jöreskog et al. 1976). The matrix we obtain by this transformation will have the required qualities for singular value decomposition, where the two sets of vectors refer to the same component space.

As stated at the beginning of this chapter, the three methods outlined here constitute a set of methods that can handle all types of variables that we may come across in archaeology. This, however, is not the same as saying that we can freely apply them on any dataset we come across.

To use these methods on actual archaeological data is far from simple, as will be demonstrated in the following two sections, where two specific areas of application are investigated in detail.

In the first section we will look into the study of artefact form based on measurements, and in the second at the classical seriation problem.

POTS FOR GOOD MEASURE

There has always been something fascinating about measurements, and archaeologists really love them. The joy of being able to state the unrefutable fact that a flint axe is 21.6 cm long, give or take half a millimetre, is surpassed only by the joy of being able to state that the exact mean length of say 200 axes is 19.6781 cm. The exactness of the statements, however, does not add to the amount of information gained on prehistoric societies. We receive exact information concerning size, but how does that lead to useful cultural information? In the case of flint axes it may tell us only how worn down an axe became before it was discarded, and only combined with other information can this be of any help.

Measurement data become much more useful when they are used to describe form rather than size. Basically, a description of form means that we take two or more measurements on each item and make comparisons between the items based on these sets of measurements. This of course seems to point straight into multivariate analysis, and from what was outlined in the foregoing chapter it would be natural to apply either a PCA or a PCO to such data.

However, life is not that simple, nor is the treatment of measurement data. If we merely take a series of basic measurements that gives a general outline of the items to be analysed, and take these measurements as direct input for a PCA or PCO, then we are in for great trouble as far as information on form is concerned. Whallon (1982) has demonstrated this very effectively, and has reached very depressing conclusions concerning the usefulness of multivariate statistics in the study of form based on measurements.

He used a series of jars, pitchers, and necked bowls from the Swiss Late Neolithic site of Niederwil to exemplify the problems that arise when continuous measurement data are used as input for a PCA with the hope of finding the base for a workable formal typology (1982:140). As input data, he chose 10 measurements of various diameters and height on the pots, as well as one measurement representing volume. A correlation matrix (1982:Fig 6.2) based on these measurements shows a high all-over positive correlation between the variables. There is thus a high redundancy among them, and obviously this stems from the size of the pots, the measure of volume having by far the highest average correlation with the other variables.

Clearly, size is bound to dominate most analyses carried out with these 11 variables in their raw state, as is the case when they are subjected to a PCA (1982:Fig. 6.3). The first axis accounts for over 83% of the total variance, and it has extremely high loadings on all variables. Indeed, it is the only component with an eigenvalue higher than one, and following normal procedures, the resultant claim should be that the material has only one underlying dimension determining its form, namely that of size. Looking at the outline drawings of the pots, this is quite obviously nonsense, and if one takes the second principal component into consideration, it turns out that it does indeed hold information concerning form, despite its low eigenvalue. A closer inspection of the 1st and 2nd principal components together shows, however, that a proper separation according to form only occurs among the small pots (1982:Fig. 6.11). The reason for this failure can be found by plotting the variables against each other two by two (1982:Fig. 6.12). It then turns out that some combinations of variables do not centre around a simple ratio (regression line) as they supposedly should do. The data at hand are in fact unsuitable for a PCA as they are, and by simply plotting the direct measure of pot size against the ratio between neck height and neck diameter, Whallon can create a division that is much more accurate than the one he obtains by PCA (1982:Fig 6.15).

Whallon states in his general discussion that these problems with redundancy due to size and two or multimodal relationships among primary measurement variables is the rule rather than the exception in studies of artifact form. This makes the use of PCA hazardous if it is not applied with the utmost care. Screening and transformation of the data may indeed be necessary. In general, Whallon seems to prefer not to use multivariate statistics in connection with studies of form based on measurement data. Instead he is inclined to rely on more simple two-dimensional methods.

This depressing example should not prevent measurements on a number of pots being analysed here using a PCA. However, the lessons learned from Whallon will be borne in mind, and hopefully it will be possible to apply the PCA successfully if the proper precautions are taken.

The material to be analysed comes from a study by Eva Koch Nielsen (1983). It consists of 135 complete pots from the Early Neolithic and the earlier Middle Neolithic TRB Culture on the islands east of the Great Belt in Denmark. The pot profiles were placed in a two-dimensional coordinate system with the pots 'standing' on the horizontal axis, and with their vertical symmetry line coinciding with the vertical axis. Eight well-defined points along the profile of the pot were then measured giving rise to 16 separate measurements (Figure 5).

The pots measured comprise three main pottery forms: funnel beakers, bowls and flasks. This was acknowledged from the outset using the standard definitions of these forms, and it turned up very clearly in the two-dimensional scattergrams of the basic measurements also. An example of this can

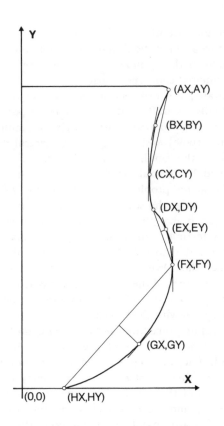

Figure 5. Measurement points of pot profiles used by E.K. Nielsen 1983.

be seen in Figure 6, where the diameter of the rim is plotted against the height of the pot for funnel beakers and flasks. It is obvious that we are dealing with quite different forms, and rather than trying to analyse them together, Nielsen wisely decided to treat them separately, thereby avoiding one of the pitfalls discussed by Whallon.

The largest group of pots in the material is the funnel beakers comprising a total of 102 pots. These alone will concern us in the following. Nielsen continued her investigations by comparing the pot profiles. In order to make these immediately comparable, her first step was to scale all measurements with pot height as unity. She proceeded by calculating a coefficient of agreement between each profile using a squared distance measure. Finally, she created a minimum spanning tree from the matrix of agreement coefficients, using a method very much like the one proposed by Renfrew and Sterud (1969).

The minimum spanning tree formed the basis for her division of the funnel beakers into formal groups, although she did make a visual comparison of the profiles also, and as a result of this moved pots from one group to the other. She ended up with a total of 21 groups which could be assembled into six main groups. Finally, she divided the material into a series of types, which as their base had her formal groups, but which also included the presence or absence of lugs, and various forms of decoration. Thus her final typology was not entirely morphological.

Her typology, when compared to available C-14 dates and information on find contexts, has given much new and valuable information to problems of chronology and group divisions in the Early Neolithic. That, however, is not the issue here. What is of interest in the current context is that by the method she used she did get to the very point of analysing detailed formal variation, and did obtain a result that made sense archaeologically. It would therefore seem worthwhile to try out a PCA on the same data to see how far we may go using that method, and whether it can confirm Nielsen's results.

In order to be able to compare the profiles the way she did, Nielsen had to scale the measurements. Thereby she removed the factor of size from the data. This, in my opinion is the main reason why her analysis was so successful. In order to get a good result from a PCA, it is likewise imperative that the influence of size be removed. In fact, a PCA of the raw measurements (Table 1) yields an explanation percentage as high as 95% for the first component, and if we plot the scores against the third root of the volume (volume is a measure of third degree), we get a correlation coefficient of 0.99. Volume is thus the dominating factor in the material, and its presence prohibits any concern with morphological variation.

One obvious way to scale the measurements would be with the aid of the third root of the volume. This

I have tried with good results, but have nevertheless chosen to use the same method as Nielsen with a minor modification. She scaled all measurements to the height of the pots, but admits that she had difficulties in her comparisons with very narrow and very wide pots. To avoid this, I have scaled all vertical measurements to the height of the pots and all horizontal measurements to the width of the rim. In terms of comparisons of profiles this means that all profiles start and end in the same two points. It may not reduce the effect of size completely, but it turns out to be very effective.

In Figure 7 the scores of the first two components are plotted against each other with signatures according to Nielsen's type divisions. Together they cover 73% of the total variation, and they both have eigenvalues well above one (Table 2). If we take the individual components, then the first component (horizontal axis in the plot) has positive loadings exclusively. Remembering the way the measurements were scaled, this means that positive scores on the first axis indicate that all measurement points are high compared to the total height, and wide compared to the rim diameter. Negative scores on the other hand mean that all measurement points lie low compared to the total height and close to the symmetry line compared to the rim diameter. The second component shows an interesting pattern, since the loadings of all vertical measurements are positive, while the loadings of all horizontal measurements are negative. Consequently, pots with positive scores tend to be flaring with high vertical measurements (particularly the belly measurements), whereas the pots with negative scores have broad horizontal measurements (especially those of the belly) resulting in round-bodied pots.

A closer look at the pattern in Figure 7 in relation to Nielsen's divisions suggests that the result of the PCA is not optimal. It is quite obvious that problems are attached to the 'MN types', which are exclusively distributed along the first component. Probably, the presence of pots of this type possessing high negative scores completely determines this component. As the points of main interest in Nielsen's study lie with the Early Neolithic pottery, and as the Middle Neolithic pottery can be separated from the rest using decorational rather than morphological criteria (which Nielsen used to separate them as 'MN types'), the most logical step is to remove them from the study. Consequently, a new PCA was performed that did not include the MN pots plus a few other pots considered by Nielsen (personal communication) to be very atypical.

A total of 81 pots were analysed this time, resulting in three components with eigenvalues higher than one (Table 3). The scores of the two first components plotted against each other are seen in Figure 8 cover-

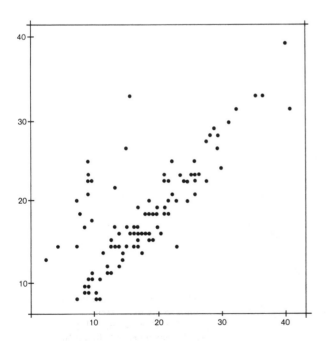

Figure 6. Diameter of rim plotted against height of pot for funnel beakers and flasks.

J	AX	AY	BX	BY	CX	CY	DX	DY	EX	EY	FX	FY	GX	GY	HX	HY
A																
15	4.32	8.65	3.92	7.25	3.72	5.75	3.82	4.95	4.22	4.07	4.32	3.22	3.10	0.92	0.00	0.00
23	11.40	20.00	10.37	17.42	9.60	15.20	9.60	15.20	10.20	13.95	10.37	11.87	8.77	5.35	4.37	0.10
32	8.15	17.00	7.35	15.70	6.65	12.82	7.02	11.42	7.92	9.67	8.20	7.87	5.80	1.95	0.00	0.00
37	10.60	19.20	9.50	17.05	9.03	14.07	9.33	12.33	10.27	10.97	10.43	9.37	7.83	2.67	0.00	0.00
38	7.53	14.20	6.67	11.40	6.40	8.72	6.45	7.90	7.00	6.90	7.17	5.92	5.97	2.75	2.32	0.05
43	6.80	12.10	6.27	10.33	5.97	7.83	6.10	7.30	6.40	6.20	6.55	5.10	5.70	2.00	3.50	0.30
45	8.05	15.60	7.52	12.67	7.20	10.20	7.35	9.52	8.30	7.97	8.60	6.65	7.17	2.55	3.97	0.22
46	8.80	13.77	8.22	12.45	7.70	11.15	7.70	11.15	7.80	10.87	7.90	10.55	6.25	4.37	2.47	0.35
52	7.53	17.20	6.67	15.13	6.00	10.02	6.42	9.02	7.10	8.05	7.40	6.55	6.10	2.95	2.37	0.10
65	8.40	14.82	7.97	13.10	6.85	10.35	6.85	10.35	7.52	8.70	7.75	6.97	6.45	2.80	4.07	0.20
82	9.30	18.70	8.37	16.20	8.00	13.27	8.62	10.27	9.42	9.37	9.70	8.20	7.65	3.75	2.10	0.10
86	6.97	15.90	6.40	14.17	5.87	11.93	5.93	11.77	6.83	10.00	7.30	6.73	6.17	2.70	3.60	0.20
87	6.35	14.20	5.95	11.65	5.63	9.17	5.77	8.77	6.37	7.77	6.65	6.07	5.45	2.52	2.75	0.07
88	10.43	18.20	9.27	15.50	8.93	13.93	9.23	12.47	9.67	11.50	9.90	9.27	8.50	4.05	4.43	0.07
91	8.25	16.50	7.70	14.55	7.25	12.05	7.85	8.95	8.65	7.70	8.95	6.15	7.40	2.20	3.75	0.05
93	7.90	16.20	7.10	14.00	6.80	11.33	7.22	9.27	7.85	8.15	8.12	6.27	6.40	2.40	2.40	0.00
94	8.50	19.07	8.00	16.93	7.73	14.63	8.10	10.87	8.90	9.60	9.27	7.77	7.53	3.10	2.82	0.30
99	4.50	10.20	4.07	7.95	3.90	6.57	4.00	6.10	4.45	5.20	4.62	4.17	3.92	1.77	2.10	0.00
181	7.82	16.30	7.05	14.35	6.75	12.80	6.85	12.07	7.37	10.35	7.57	8.27	6.22	3.37	3.02	0.20
182	5.70	13.20	5.12	10.65	5.00	9.02	5.32	7.50	5.82	6.75	6.00	5.70	4.75	2.10	2.07	0.20
183	8.47	18.90	7.63	15.77	7.40	14.10	7.47	13.43	8.63	11.73	9.12	8.82	7.45	3.82	3.57	0.25
184	6.77	14.20	5.90	11.77	5.50	10.27	5.62	9.77	6.40	8.20	6.62	6.47	5.37	2.52	2.80	0.03
185	5.10	8.10	4.32	5.92	4.10	5.15	4.10	5.15	4.10	5.15	4.10	5.15	2.90	1.47	0.00	0.00
186	6.60	16.50	6.10	14.00	5.90	11.60	6.07	11.40	6.97	10.00	7.40	7.50	6.02	2.77	2.95	0.00
187	9.23	20.00	8.53	18.03	8.03	15.33	8.03	15.33	9.27	13.40	9.60	10.87	7.95	5.02	3.80	0.12
188	8.20	14.10	7.67	12.10	7.22	9.92	7.47	9.42	7.80	8.65	7.92	7.32	6.63	3.00	3.00	0.02
189	3.70	8.30	3.30	6.95	3.10	5.40	3.25	4.20	3.65	3.65	3.85	2.90	2.95	0.90	1.20	0.00
190	5.33	10.20	5.07	8.77	4.87	7.40	5.00	4.90	5.30	4.33	5.43	3.70	4.10	1.27	1.30	0.03
196	8.92	16.10	7.60	13.10	6.80	9.95	7.05	9.22	7.72	7.97	7.95	6.62	5.40	1.75	0.00	0.00
200	5.43	8.20	4.50	6.80	4.20	5.83	4.17	5.60	4.30	5.15	4.32	4.57	3.67	1.97	1.55	0.30
201	6.30	14.00	6.00	12.20	5.17	9.80	5.17	9.80	6.20	8.63	6.83	6.43	5.60	2.80	2.57	0.12
202	5.00	7.60	4.40	6.50	4.00	5.70	4.00	5.70	4.10	5.60	4.10	5.40	3.30	2.30	1.70	0.00
205	14.10	28.30	12.70	23.40	12.40	20.70	12.53	19.70	13.67	17.73	14.05	14.82	11.10	5.77	5.32	0.40
207	4.70	10.00	4.15	8.00	4.00	6.55	4.10	4.80	4.45	4.40	4.55	3.60	3.85	1.45	1.80	0.10
209	12.42	20.40	11.12	16.95	10.60	14.52	10.87	13.17	11.87	11.80	12.27	9.67	8.52	2.52	0.00	0.00
210	4.60	9.70	3.90	8.00	3.62	6.45	3.72	5.67	4.07	4.97	4.20	4.12	3.55	1.85	1.70	0.02
214	6.25	11.00	5.72	9.75	5.47	8.97	5.55	8.77	5.57	8.40	5.60	8.15	4.32	3.17	1.52	0.15
221	12.67	23.10	11.57	20.10	11.02	16.75	11.70	13.92	12.97	12.02	13.23	10.37	10.72	3.90	5.37	0.05
222	13.67	27.00	12.10	22.67	11.57	19.20	11.95	16.87	12.87	14.60	13.13	12.27	10.40	4.90	4.60	0.00
223	12.83	22.00	11.87	18.87	11.57	16.40	11.77	14.97	12.63	13.60	12.87	11.87	10.03	4.73	4.80	0.13
225	4.97	9.00	4.35	7.70	4.10	6.72	4.10	6.70	4.27	6.42	4.35	5.82	3.65	2.57	2.02	0.02
227	7.33	13.90	6.47	11.53	6.10	8.53	6.17	7.93	6.63	7.23	6.85	5.92	5.70	2.65	2.52	0.05
229	4.62	9.60	4.12	8.17	3.92	6.67	3.97	6.00	4.45	5.07	4.65	4.02	3.85	1.70	1.77	0.02
230	10.50	23.50	9.15	19.22	8.50	16.55	8.50	16.55	10.07	14.47	10.65	11.47	8.72	4.85	3.82	0.05
249	8.37	16.40	7.37	13.17	6.92	10.15	7.00	9.57	7.52	8.52	7.72	7.22	6.50	3.25	3.12	0.13
250	18.20	32.50	16.35	30.40	14.75	26.10	14.90	25.30	15.40	23.70	15.55	22.10	12.10	8.00	5.10	0.40
251	13.05	25.20	11.85	21.75	10.70	19.25	11.15	18.75	11.40	17.85	11.45	16.30	8.75	6.40	6.00	0.50
255	17.55	32.50	15.30	29.20	14.60	25.95	14.80	25.35	15.55	23.60	16.00	21.10	12.55	7.60	5.60	0.05
259	9.10	18.40	8.20	15.35	7.85	13.95	8.20	13.55	8.75	12.20	9.00	10.20	6.95	4.15	3.40	0.00
260	6.10	11.30	5.70	9.90	5.20	8.50	5.25	8.30	5.60	7.55	5.60	6.90	4.60	3.05	1.65	0.00
262	8.60	13.80	7.55	11.90	7.20	10.70	7.20	10.40	7.35	9.90	7.40	9.20	5.75	4.15	2.30	0.20
267	6.43	14.50	6.00	11.97	5.80	10.47	6.10	8.97	6.60	7.73	6.75	6.62	5.35	2.57	2.52	0.20
268	9.87	18.10	9.30	16.30	9.07	14.80	9.17	14.07	9.33	13.37	9.43	12.20	7.97	5.23	4.03	0.17
271	14.83	26.60	13.17	23.87	12.57	22.33	12.57	22.20	13.53	19.87	13.73	18.33	11.10	7.50	5.17	0.07
272	4.30	9.40	3.70	7.60	3.40	5.70	3.80	5.00	4.20	4.50	4.40	3.60	3.60	1.80	1.85	0.00
273	11.00	20.60	10.40	18.30	9.60	15.40	9.80	14.20	10.50	13.00	10.90	10.00	8.40	3.60	4.30	0.00
274	5.90	11.70	5.60	10.10	5.07	8.63	5.17	8.40	5.47	7.17	5.63	5.80	4.67	2.27	2.12	0.20
278	15.50	29.50	13.90	24.25	13.40	20.20	13.90	19.10	15.60	16.45	16.25	13.25	12.70	4.80	6.00	0.20
279	10.60	22.40	9.37	18.85	8.92	16.50	9.22	16.10	9.80	14.43	10.20	11.45	8.25	4.55	3.85	0.25
281	4.50	8.60	3.90	7.20	3.65	5.82	3.70	5.12	4.20	4.47	4.45	3.40	3.75	1.45	2.00	0.10
283	10.80	22.40	9.73	19.87	9.07	17.93	9.37	16.90	10.10	15.57	10.32	13.22	8.82	5.85	4.52	0.22
288	13.85	22.60	12.10	19.10	11.30	17.07	11.40	16.13	11.90	13.70	12.03	11.60	10.50	5.80	4.07	0.30
290	12.80	22.90	11.80	19.65	11.47	17.72	11.92	15.37	12.95	13.30	13.25	11.37	10.57	4.67	4.90	0.25
293	12.90	22.00	11.20	17.70	10.70	14.90	11.00	13.30	12.10	11.20	12.40	7.50	10.90	3.40	5.10	0.00
294	10.70	19.90	9.20	16.30	8.80	14.10	8.90	13.75	9.65	12.20	9.85	10.40	7.70	3.55	3.75	0.05
300	10.20	16.10	9.70	13.10	9.37	11.57	9.45	10.02	9.62	9.70	9.75	9.05	6.87	3.70	3.12	0.07
305	9.20	15.10	7.57	11.50	6.72	8.17	6.75	8.10	7.35	7.07	7.57	5.87	6.75	3.30	3.60	0.00
307	12.77	21.10	11.17	17.13	10.27	13.10	10.53	11.10	11.03	10.00	11.23	8.80	9.20	3.93	4.02	0.12
308	8.35	14.10	7.50	10.90	6.95	8.60	7.10	7.80	7.45	7.05	7.45	6.05	6.35	3.10	3.45	0.20
311	9.53	15.00	8.47	12.05	8.07	8.87	8.10	8.30	8.22	7.80	8.25	7.17	6.50	2.67	2.62	0.05
312	6.95	15.90	6.45	12.87	6.17	10.87	6.27	9.92	7.25	8.20	7.42	6.90	6.30	3.17	3.17	0.15
320	14.77	28.00	13.47	23.20	12.92	19.55	13.15	16.67	14.20	14.87	14.57	12.52	12.22	5.97	5.00	0.27
321	4.40	10.20	3.92	8.10	3.75	6.07	3.77	5.57	4.20	5.02	4.45	3.72	3.07	1.05	0.00	0.00
323	16.20	31.20	15.40	26.53	15.03	23.03	15.13	22.27	16.17	19.77	16.53	16.23	13.20	6.60	3.87	0.00
324	6.37	11.60	5.83	9.80	5.57	8.65	5.72	8.15	6.10	7.20	6.30	6.10	5.10	2.12	2.65	0.17
325	20.30	31.50	18.00	27.35	16.15	23.90	16.20	23.45	16.75	21.35	16.97	18.60	13.72	8.05	5.95	0.27
326	4.80	11.20	4.53	9.33	4.40	7.55	4.70	6.52	4.97	6.00	5.13	4.73	4.23	2.03	2.22	0.05
327	11.05	24.80	10.17	21.67	9.92	19.97	10.42	18.60	11.22	16.75	11.57	14.62	9.80	7.22	4.20	0.32
328	10.47	23.00	9.77	19.83	9.27	17.30	9.50	16.62	10.40	14.70	10.85	11.45	9.02	5.32	3.87	0.07
329	12.35	22.20	12.10	19.97	11.85	16.62	12.05	15.17	12.50	14.70	12.67	14.10	9.10	5.35	3.25	0.00
336	7.00	12.10	5.70	9.45	5.32	7.95	5.37	7.80	5.42	6.95	5.45	5.95	4.50	2.60	2.50	0.27
B																
3	9.63	18.73	6.87	14.40	5.52	8.97	5.52	8.97	6.52	8.10	6.90	6.90	5.62	3.72	2.10	0.15
33	14.40	29.20	13.75	26.35	13.50	23.20	13.95	20.20	14.55	19.25	14.75	17.55	12.50	9.05	5.85	0.00
59	11.92	22.10	10.45	17.30	9.90	14.22	9.90	14.22	10.32	12.97	10.45	10.70	8.00	4.57	3.20	0.05
60	8.40	14.40	7.85	11.85	7.60	9.65	7.65	9.15	7.85	8.65	7.90	8.00	6.35	2.85	3.50	0.25
61	13.20	23.10	12.50	19.90	12.10	16.90	12.10	16.90	12.70	15.40	12.80	13.60	11.40	9.20	4.20	0.00
131	11.60	23.00	10.77	19.77	9.90	16.67	10.25	15.27	11.22	13.87	11.70	11.82	9.72	5.22	4.97	0.30
195	9.40	16.30	8.32	13.25	8.05	11.47	8.17	10.37	8.57	9.37	8.70	8.00	7.17	3.52	2.97	0.00
211	7.27	12.80	5.62	10.30	4.52	7.02	4.55	6.60	5.12	5.97	5.35	5.17	4.30	2.30	1.67	0.05
212	8.27	14.70	7.97	13.13	7.60	10.47	7.65	9.27	7.77	8.97	7.82	8.60	6.52	3.92	3.10	0.03
213	6.50	14.00	5.00	11.00	4.00	6.83	4.00	6.70	4.77	6.07	5.07	4.97	4.10	2.10	2.17	0.00
216	7.00	14.70	5.95	12.10	4.57	7.15	4.57	7.15	5.17	6.15	5.42	5.17	4.67	3.07	1.45	0.05
218	8.70	16.00	8.43	13.70	8.30	12.43	8.37	11.90	8.60	11.27	8.73	10.63	6.60	5.13	2.75	0.05
226	6.22	15.30	5.07	9.60	4.60	6.25	4.62	6.17	5.10	5.12	5.30	4.22	4.42	2.12	2.37	0.02
233	9.77	18.90	9.15	15.70	9.00	13.42	9.15	11.85	9.30	11.55	9.37	11.15	7.02	3.72	3.85	0.27
234	10.80	18.80	9.70	15.90	9.03	10.93	9.10	10.87	9.43	10.27	9.60	9.00	7.27	3.53	3.23	0.03
236	9.90	17.20	8.40	13.55	7.70	10.33	7.83	9.97	8.10	9.03	8.20	8.22	6.92	3.80	3.52	0.20
286	12.02	22.50	11.42	19.65	11.27	17.20	11.37	14.97	11.57	14.60	11.62	14.20	9.47	6.80	3.50	0.15
292	15.10	24.20	13.17	19.97	12.27	15.87	12.43	14.97	12.77	14.03	12.92	12.45	10.32	5.72	4.55	0.20
306	20.23	39.40	18.17	34.20	17.53	27.93	18.17	24.03	19.10	22.63	19.50	21.23	14.63	9.47	4.33	0.07
309	11.43	14.40	10.17	11.27	9.77	10.00	9.80	9.83	9.90	9.47	9.97	9.07	8.93	5.17	3.60	0.07
322	11.00	21.20	8.00	16.90	6.20	10.57	6.20	10.57	7.15	9.20	7.45	7.87	6.42	4.72	2.77	0.07
C																
17	7.90	32.80	7.35	27.80	7.02	23.17	7.37	22.75	11.57	19.32	13.47	12.25	10.92	4.15	4.82	0.17
26	4.80	17.65	4.50	15.47	4.25	11.70	4.97	10.72	6.67	9.12	7.22	6.87	6.07	3.07	2.77	0.18
28	3.70	14.30	3.23	11.77	3.20	8.90	3.20	8.90	5.33	6.83	5.93	4.83	5.07	2.30	2.53	0.20
42	2.13	14.60	2.07	14.00	2.32	8.87	3.02	7.50	4.50	6.85	5.20	5.35	3.55	1.37	0.00	0.00
56	7.60	26.70	7.30	23.00	7.00	20.10	7.10	16.90	9.80	13.70	10.60	10.00	8.70	4.30	4.05	0.20
110	4.10	16.50	4.00	14.40	4.20	11.30	5.10	10.42	6.52	9.10	7.05	6.85	5.62	2.50	2.80	0.10
113	4.00	18.50	3.40	18.50	3.70	16.55	3.80	14.75	6.35	11.85	7.00	7.35	5.60	2.30	3.70	0.15
117	6.70	21.50	6.05	19.45	5.70	14.85	5.70	14.85	8.65	12.25	9.30	9.30	7.05	3.20	2.15	0.00
219	4.95	17.60	4.35	14.82	4.12	13.05	4.65	11.87	6.55	9.77	7.27	7.07	6.10	3.12	2.82	0.07
237	1.27	12.90	1.17	11.20	1.57	9.07	2.55	8.22	5.05	6.65	6.10	4.97	4.25	1.42	0.72	0.00
238	4.45	21.10	4.15	18.97	3.95	15.02	5.00	11.30	7.92	8.97	8.72	6.80	7.10	3.37	3.37	0.12
239	3.60	19.90	3.20	16.50	3.10	13.63	4.53	10.60	6.40	8.40	6.93	5.93	5.83	2.20	3.13	0.00
240	4.47	24.50	3.90	21.77	3.67	18.50	4.25	13.55	8.00	11.05	9.40	7.82	6.95	2.47	1.22	0.00
241	4.42	23.40	3.70	19.45	3.42	13.50	4.90	9.95	7.75	8.65	8.52	7.07	6.92	2.87	2.95	0.03
242	4.55	22.00	4.32	19.75	4.10	16.20	4.60	12.40	7.60	10.30	8.72	6.85	7.17	2.57	3.40	0.10
245	4.95	22.00	4.65	20.10	4.37	17.85	5.60	14.00	8.17	11.40	9.17	8.63	7.37	3.73	3.20	0.03

Table 1. 16 measurements as defined in Figure 5 taken on 135 pots. The three groups of pots are: A: funnel beakers. B: bowls. C: flasks. Data after E.K. Nielsen 1983.

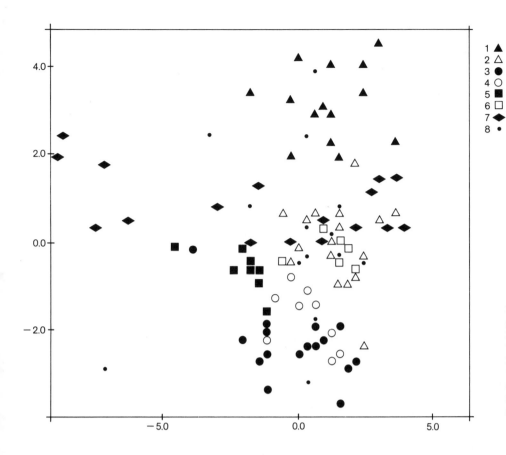

Figure 7. Plot of the first two principal components from a PCA of 102 funnel beakers. The numbering corresponds to Nielsen's type division as follows: 1: type I. 2: type II. 3: type III. 4: type IV. 5: type V. 6: broad-lugged beakers. 7: MN types. 8: type not decided.

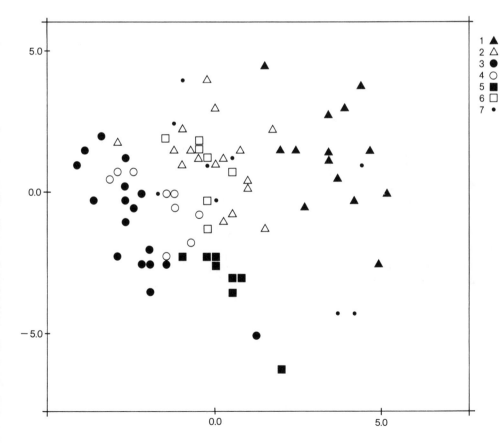

Figure 8. Plot of the first two principal components from a PCA of 81 funnel beakers. The numbering corresponds to Nielsen's type division as follows: 1: type I. 2: type II. 3: type III. 4: type IV. 5: type V. 6: broad-lugged beakers. 7: type not decided.

Axis	E.val.	Expl.%	BX	BY	CX	CY	DX	DY	EX	EY	FX	FY	GX	FY	HX	HY
1	6.62	47.28	0.89	0.69	0.89	0.88	0.87	0.70	0.78	0.67	0.71	0.55	0.63	0.37	0.32	0.15
2	3.65	26.05	-0.22	0.24	-0.24	0.32	-0.36	0.61	-0.60	0.71	-0.66	0.79	-0.59	0.72	-0.17	0.24
3	1.38	9.84	0.10	0.18	0.12	0.09	0.12	-0.03	0.08	0.03	0.06	0.08	-0.34	-0.20	-0.83	-0.66

Table 2. Eigenvalues, explanation percentages and factor loadings for the first three principal axes from a PCA on all 102 funnel beakers.

Axis	E.val.	Expl.%	BX	BY	CX	CY	DX	DY	EX	EY	FX	FY	GX	FY	HX	HY
1	5.22	37.30	-0.44	0.16	-0.53	0.36	-0.67	0.64	-0.86	0.72	-0.87	0.78	-0.73	0.69	-0.18	0.27
2	4.66	33.27	0.74	0.72	0.71	0.84	0.61	0.68	0.45	0.65	0.39	0.55	0.35	0.50	0.29	0.18
3	1.52	10.86	0.14	0.19	0.17	0.11	0.17	-0.03	0.06	0.04	0.01	0.12	-0.47	-0.27	-0.86	-0.58

Table 3. Eigenvalues, explanation percentages and factor loadings for the first three principal axes from a PCA on 81 selected funnel beakers.

ing 71% of the total variation. The two components are in fact the same as before, but they have changed places so that the first and most important component is the one that was second before and vice versa. Moreover, the plot of the scores now shows a clear tendency to cluster, that in part answers well with the division suggested by Nielsen.

The attempt to make a morphological division using basic measurements is thus quite successful, and it is not due to profound morphological differences in the material analysed, as can be seen from Figure 9, where examples of Nielsen's types I, II and III are shown. Especially, the marked separation of type I from II may come as a surprise to many who have been working with the Early Neolithic, and it is of utmost importance for the current discussion concerning chronology and group divisions at the beginning of the Early Neolithic.

Instead of the R-mode PCA that takes its starting point in the relationships between the measurements, we could also have used the Q-mode PCO that takes its starting point in the relationships between the pot profiles. In Figure 10 we see the coordinates of the two first components from a PCO plotted against each other. The input similarity matrix is based on squared distances between the pot profiles, computed in exactly the same way as Nielsen did. A comparison between the results of this PCO (Figure 10) and the foregoing PCA (Figure 8) shows them to be almost identical. Thus, even though it may seem more correct to rely on comparison of profiles (PCO), it turns out that a PCA based on interrelationships between the variables works out just as well. As the latter can handle far more cases in one run on the computer than the former (limited by the number of variables only), and as it is easier to interpret the components in a PCA by help of the loadings, then this method is far to prefer for analyses of this type.

ARCHAEOLOGICAL TIME SERIATION

Time is undoubtedly the most dominating issue in archaeology. It cannot be observed, yet it plays a role in the evaluation of any observation made. Change in past material culture happened on many different levels, and was caused by many different types of agents. It is one of the main goals of archaeology to outline and explain these changes in terms of dynamics and structure in specific prehistoric societies. Yet, in all societies that we are dealing with, we find that part of the changes follows some general pattern for which a specific historic explanation would miss the point.

This phenomenon was first discussed in depth by Hildebrand and Montelius in the second half of the preceding century (Gräslund 1974:167ff). By empirical observation they noticed that artifacts from one period show almost always close affinity in form to those of the immediately preceding period.

In line with the natural sciences of that time, they spoke of an evolution, and their theory was that this

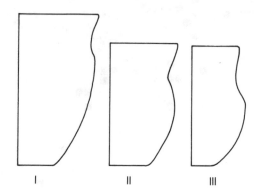

Figure 9. Examples of the three main type groups separated through the analysis Figure 8.

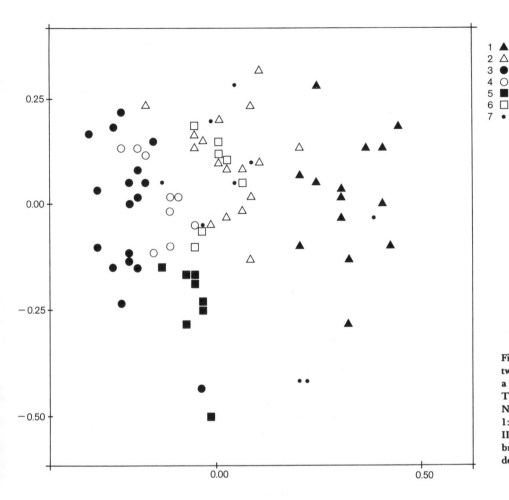

Figure 10. Plot of the first two principal components from a PCO of 81 funnel beakers The numbering corresponds to Nielsen's type division as follows: 1: type I. 2: type II. 3: type III. 4: type IV. 5: type V. 6: broad-lugged beakers. 7: type not decided.

evolution was continuous, unbroken and inherent to the cultural process. One practical outcome of this - and indeed their main concern - was that conclusions on time relationships could be obtained directly from a study of the artifacts without any reference to the find context (Gräslund 1973:19-20).

This was the beginning of the typology concept. Since then this concept has been treated to death by archaeologists, and nothing or very little remains of its original meaning. Indeed there is very little consent as to what meaning the term should be given today.

This is not the place for a discussion of the typology concept. It is sufficient to note that the existence of a continuous development in artifact forms over time is an empirical fact that relates to human societies in general. And further that it is true - with qualifications - for the composition of artifact assemblages also as laid down by human societies. The continuous development is not in itself a 'universal law' since discontinuous breaks may occasionally occur as an outcome of ordinary cultural processes within the societies. Yet, the continuous development that we observe in artifact forms and assemblages must have a background in universal mechanisms inherent to human societies, and more basically in the behaviour patterns of human beings.

No matter what kind of explanation one may offer for these regularities, they are of great practical importance to the archaeologist in his efforts to exert time control over his material. It is these practical aspects that are the issue of the following.

The basic criteria for continuity in terms of qualitative variables were discussed by Malmer (1963). He operated with two types of elements or variables in his criteria. 'Constant elements', were variables with only two states - either present or absent. Those are what I would prefer to call dichotomous, nominal variables. The other type he named 'variable elements', and from his example (degrees of coarseness in an ornament type) it is clear that he was referring to ordinal variables. He does not seem to have considered the type nominal, alternative variables.

Malmer suggested two criteria of continuity based on the two element types that he separated. The first criterion was: continuity is present if in a series of artifacts, constant elements are gradually replaced by other constant elements. In a diagram this may be shown as in Table 4.

The second criterion states: continuity is present if the 'variable elements' have their states replaced in a regular, ordered (= rank order) manner in a series of artifacts. In a diagram it takes the form

21

```
1:  A B C D E . . . .
2:  . B C D E F . . .
3:  . . C D E F G . .
4:  . . . D E F G H .
5:  . . . . E F G H I
```

Table 4.

```
1:  J1
2:  J2
3:  J3
4:  J4
5:  J5
```

Table 5.

```
1:  Wa Xa Ya Za
2:  Wb Xa Ya Za
3:  Wb Xb Ya Za
4:  Wb Xb Yb Za
5:  Wb Xb Yb Zb
```

Table 6.

	A	B	C	D	E	F	G	H	I	W	X	Y	Z
1:	1	1	1	1	1	0	0	0	0	1	1	1	1
2:	0	1	1	1	1	1	0	0	0	0	1	1	1
3:	0	0	1	1	1	1	1	0	0	0	0	1	1
4:	0	0	0	1	1	1	1	1	0	0	0	0	1
5:	0	0	0	0	1	1	1	1	1	0	0	0	0

Table 7.

	K1	K2	K3	K4	K5
1:	1	0	0	0	0
2:	0	1	0	0	0
3:	0	0	1	0	0
4:	0	0	0	1	0
5:	0	0	0	0	1

Table 8.

	A	B	C	D	E
1:	15%	3%	16%	66%	0%
2:	17%	6%	13%	59%	5%
3:	26%	8%	10%	31%	25%
4:	19%	11%	8%	18%	44%
5:	16%	25%	3%	15%	41%

Table 9.

	A	B	C	D	E	SUM
1:	8	2	9	36	0	55
2:	19	7	14	65	5	110
3:	26	8	10	32	25	101
4:	16	9	7	15	37	84
5:	15	23	3	14	38	93

Table 10.

shown in Table 5, which is not an operational form for the type of analyses considered in this paper. One has to transform the information into a series of alternative, two-state, 'artificial' variables to utilise the ordinal scale information (Madsen 1985:12–14). Table 5 transformed into a table of alternative variables preserving the rank order information takes the form shown in Table 6.

Tables 5 and 6 may be rewritten so that the element labels are placed in the column headings, and their values are given in the table as 1 and 0. Tables 5 and 6 together would take the form of Table 7. It should be remembered that the variables W–Z are not real observed variables, but artificial variables presenting the information in the one variable J alone.

The third type of variable, the nominal, alternative variable – not treated by Malmer – could be given the same representation as in Table 5, but in a dichotomous version it would, assuming one variable (say K) with five states, look like Table 8. We can immediately see that although this type in its dichotomous version turns up with as many 'variables' as it has states, it is nevertheless one variable only. There is no, and cannot be any information on continuity in Table 8. Only combinations with other alternative dichotomous variables in a larger table can lead to information on continuity.

The dichotomising of alternative variables takes up a lot of space, as each variable state has to be transformed into a separate 'variable'. It is, however, a necessary operation, if this type of variable is to be analysed by a CA. If one has many alternative variables, it may therefore be more reasonable to use a PCO, which can handle alternative variables directly.

The above should be seen as a formalised representation of the original typological concept. It is important to note that it can be fully given a common matrix representation, which can be analysed by multivariate metric statistics.

Naturally, the typological concept is confined to artifacts, but the principles that govern it can in fact be applied to closed find associations, as demonstrated by Malmer also (1963:30–32). If we have a series of closed finds containing various artifacts that can be classified into types, then we may use Malmer's first criteria of continuity in exactly the same way as we did with the typological series. Normally, his second criteria of continuity do not enter here as long as we are dealing with discrete objects. However, we may work directly on the basic descriptive (classified) elements of the artifacts within the closed finds. Then, of course, the second criteria of continuity are applicable too.

The matrix representation for an analysis of continuity in find associations would be inseparable in structure from one stemming from a typological analysis.

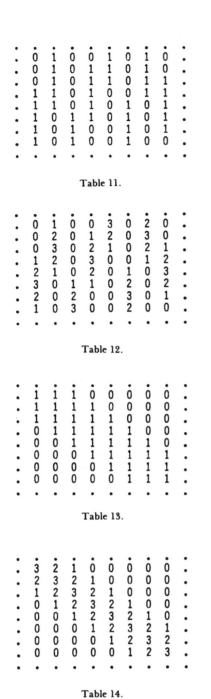

Table 11.

Table 12.

Table 13.

Table 14.

In Scandinavian and European archaeology in general, the concern with problems of continuity has always focused on qualitative aspects. In American archaeology, the focus has mainly been on quantitative aspects, at least since the forties. In the frequency seriation, as the method developed here was named, the basic idea is that the relative frequency of a given type of artifact or artefact element will change continuously with time. And further, that the general pattern will be one of artifact types or element types coming into being at one point in time, growing in relative frequency, reaching a peak, diminishing in relative frequency again and finally disappearing.

Archaeologically, this means that if we have a number of find associations, sufficiently large to allow for a relative frequency representation, laid down over not too long a period of time, and preserved undisturbed, then we may sort them according to the relative frequencies of their types as seen in Table 9. Table 9, however, could stem from a matrix of counts as in Table 10, and Table 10 in turn has in principle the same characteristics as Table 7, ie. they both contain positive integers representing counts of qualities. The only difference is that the counts in Table 10 may reach any positive integer, whereas the counting method in Table 7 prevents integers other than 0 and 1. For a method of analysis like CA dealing with counts, this makes no difference at all. Both tables have a form and content which are suitable for direct input to a CA, although, of course, you cannot mix the two types of counting in the same analysis.

Thus you can turn most types of archaeological variables whether qualitative or quantitative in origin into a type of abundance table suitable for a CA.

If we turn to the PCO, we have an even larger flexibility, since we may take the different types of variables as direct input to the method. Thus the input table for PCO may well contain a mixture of: dichotomous, nominal variables noted as 1 and 0; alternative nominal variables, where each state is represented by a number; ordinal variables, which have been transformed into two-state, alternative, nominal variables; ratio scale, frequency variables, which must be given as relative frequencies.

The PCO is thus more flexible with regard to types of input data, and combinations of the various types, than is CA. But, then of course there are other features in favour of CA, as noted earlier in this paper and discussed again later.

Finally, the third method, PCA, cannot be used for this type of data at all, since the data will tend to be poisson distributed, rather than normally distributed, the latter being a requirement of the PCA.

We have seen that the criteria of continuity used in archaeology may be given a common matrix representation of positive integer counts showing the abundance of column variables (element types or artifact types) on row units (artifacts or find associations). And we have noted that the incidence type of matrix with 1's and 0's is to be considered a special case of the abundance type of matrix, only.

What then are the conditions for a given matrix to yield a perfect representation of continuity? They are: »in each individual column either, *the elements increase to a maximum and then decrease*, or *the elements increase*, or *the elements decrease*« (Kendall 1971:219) (eg. Table 12). If we take the special case of the incidence matrix, then the conditions may be expressed as: »all the 1's in each individual column have to be lumped together without any intervening 0's« (Kendall 1970:126) (e.g. Table 11).

Our interest in continuity need not be limited to the relationship between the units in the rows. Indeed we may be interested in whether there are relations of continuity among the variables in the columns as well. The conditions for this with respect to the elements within each row are exactly the same as with the units. Thus a matrix in which there is a perfect representation of continuity for both the units and the variables would take the form shown in Table 13 and 14.

The operation of interchanging rows and columns in a given data matrix in order to obtain the best possible solution with respect to the idealised matrices Table 11-14 is known in archaeology as seriation.

A vast amount of ingenuity has been invested in the development of methods that can achieve this aim (Marquardt 1978). The problem, however, is not easily solved, since there is no true 'arithmetic solution' to the permutation of rows and columns. Most solutions are iterative. That is you keep interchanging the order of rows and columns (by hand or machine) until you feel that you cannot improve the order any further. A major problem with this type of procedure is that you can always obtain some sort of order which resembles the one you aim at (e.g. Table 11-14), and it is very difficult, not to say almost impossible, to decide from a reordered data matrix whether it is sufficiently close to the ideal to allow you to conclude that the criterion of continuity is being met with. As Kendall has stated in relation to permutations of a matrix:

As long as we work solely with permutations, the method, or any variant of it, will of necessity yield a linear ordering as an answer, and so will be given no opportunity to 'fail'. I attach great importance to methods which are capable of failure, because it is obvious that in some ill-chosen problems a method ought to fail, and thus warn us that we are taking too simple-minded a view of the data. (1971:218)

Kendall proposed the use of a method that could fail. He applied Kruskal's non-metric scaling program (MDSCAL) to ideal data of the type shown in Table 10. The result was a perfect line-up of the units in the correct order, laid out in a semi-circle - or horseshoe. When applied to real data, one may simply judge from the degree to which the units follow a semi-circle how well the criterion of continuity is met with. And naturally, one simply takes the order of the units in the semi-circle as a usable approximation to the optimal order of the row units in the data matrix.

It is exactly the same type of problem-solving with the same benefits we achieve by using either the principal coordinate analysis or the correspondence analysis as a means to seriate matrices.

In order to investigate the seriation potentials of the two methods, I used a series of 50 by 50 ideal matrices as input, some being of the general type seen in Table 13, others of the general type seen in Table 14. No matter which type of matrix was chosen, the result was the same for each of the two methods.

The first two axes of the PCO place the units in a formation very similar to a horseshoe (indeed more horseshoe-like than the formation obtained by non-metric scaling) (Figure 11). In order to understand why the layout of the units on the first two principal axes attains this arced shape, we should remember that the PCO is based on a similarity matrix between the units. The first two principal axis of the PCO can thus be considered as a two-dimensional 'mapping' of the similarity coefficients. Units with a high degree of similarity are placed close to one another, units with a lesser degree of similarity farther apart, and units with no similarity as far apart as possible, yet still so that the inter-point distance of all those units with no similarity is the same. It is the latter that create the arced lay out, because generally speaking we will have a situation where not only the similarity between the tails of the sequence, but also between the tails and the middle of the sequence will be zero. The only way to present this is through an arc, where the interdistance between the end points is approximately the same as between the end points and the middle of the sequence. This of course is a very simplified way of explaining the horseshoe. An elaborate explanation would be more complex and harder to come at (Kendall 1971:227).

When using the PCO for seriation we should note that it is only the units that are sorted, and indeed if we reorder the input matrix according to the sequence order of the first two principal axes, we get a matrix layout as in Table 11 or 12. To obtain an order of variables using the same method we would have to transpose the data matrix so that the variables 'become the units', and vice versa. However, this would be possible only if all variables were of the abundance type (including the incidence case), and then there would be no reason to use a PCO at all. It would be much better to choose a CA.

A CA performed on the same ideal matrices yields a somewhat different type of layout, closely resembling a parabola. In fact it is not a parabola, but it probably would have been, had it not been for the edge effect to be found in any input matrix. Thus Hill (1974:348) has proved mathematically »that when a single natural gradient exists in the data, the later axes may be approximate polynomials of the first« (1974:351). Hill specifically points to archaeological seriation as an issue where this feature of the CA can be of great value, and he gives his share to the seemingly endless seriation attempts on the Münsingen Rain data (1974:350-354). The result he obtains is the best I have seen on the Münsingen Rain as yet.

The parabolic formation we find in Figure 11 consists of 50 points. Yet in reality it represents 100 points, for both the units and the variables are present. Due to the absolute symmetry in the 50 by 50

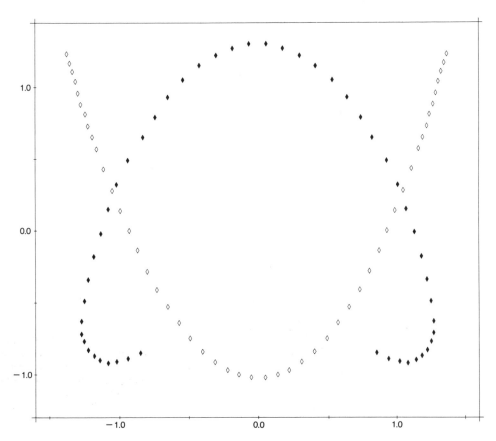

Figure 11. Plot of the first two principal axes from a PCO (heavy signatures) and a CA (open signature) of a 50 by 50 matrix containing ideal data.

matrices that have been used as input, units and variables cover each other exactly two by two in the plots of the principal axes. This, of course, is a situation that is never encountered with real data. However, we always get an ordering of both units and variables at the same time, and the matrix we receive when we use the sequence order from the Ca is of the type Table 13 and 14, where both rows and columns are sorted.

When compared to the PCO, the CA method is much to prefer. It gives a simultaneous ordering of both units and variables, with reference to the same set of principal axes. This means that not only do we get a sequence of units and variables, but when the least tendency for clustering is present (the rule rather than the exception with real data), we can immediately distinquish where the break points are in terms of both units and variables.

To see practical seriation results using the CA, we need only turn to several of the papers in this book. Thus the papers of Bech, Holm-Olsen, Højlund and Nielsen, all give very fine examples of the usefulness of the CA in seriation studies, and finer recommendation of the method than these papers can hardly be given.

Having said this, however, I feel urged to stress a point. The CA cannot work miracles. It cannot (and that is a true virtue) create a seriation if there is no

reasonable degree of continuity in the input data. In that case there will be no good seriation to obtain. Further, it is imperative to stress that continuity is not something that is either in the archaeological record or not. It is something that is in the description of the data given by the archaeologist or not. If a seriation study fails to yield a proper seriation, then it is far more likely that it is the archaeologist who is at fault, than the archaeological record.

The PCO is not used in any of the seriation studies in this book, but several of the authors have in fact used it at an earlier stage. In all cases comparisons with results obtained with the CA fell out to the advantage of the latter, and consequently this method was chosen for the final analyses.

To exemplify the difference between the two methods, on a real-life material and not only on theoretical data distributions, I shall offer an example employing data that I have borrowed from Vankilde (1986). The input data matrix represents counts of 33 Early Bronze Age metal types found in 35 hoards. In Figure 12 the plot of the first two principal axes obtained from the CA is given (which was also the method chosen by Vankilde). In Figure 13, the plot of the first two principal axes from the PCO is shown.

As can be seen immediately, the result obtained from the CA is far better and more precise than those

25

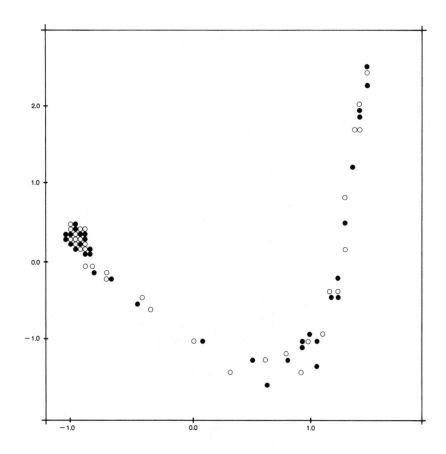

Figure 12. Plot of the first two principal axes from a CA of 35 Early Bronze Age hoards (heavy signature) described by 33 types (open signature). Data after Vankilde 1986.

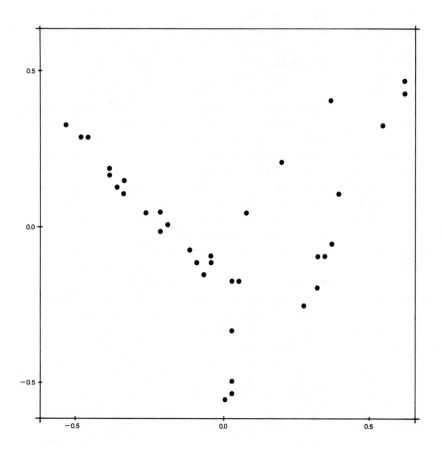

Figure 13. Plot of the first two principal axes from a PCO of 35 Early Bronze Age hoards. Data after Vankilde 1986.

obtained from the PCO. The difference between the two results is clearly due to the difference in treatment of the primary data in two analyses. The pretreatment and weighting of the data in the CA is far better than the completely equal treatment of data irrespective of numerical weight given in the PCO. Thus, whenever possible the CA should be used in preference to the PCO.

A final question should be raised. Can we be sure that a seriation resulting from a CA, a PCO, or any other method for that matter, gives us a true time sequence as a result? The answer must be a clear no. On the contrary we can be certain, time after time, to come across seriations that have nothing or very little to do with time.

As time goes by, continuity appears in the remains of material culture, and provided that we select the proper units described by the proper variables, and analyse these, then surely we get a time seriation. However, continuity in the remains of material culture may be created by many other agents than time, and although time very often is involved in the continuity we see, we must always be alert to other causes.

To see examples, we need only turn to the paper of Holm-Olsen (this volume), where the seriation created is determined by geographical factors, or to Højlund's paper (this volume), where a very fine chronological seriation is penetrated by social differences between two building areas in a most intriguing manner. The lesson to learn from these two papers is quite simple. A seriation can never be assumed to be a time seriation until this has been proved by independent means.

For a closer demonstration of the usefulness of these methods - in addition to what is demonstrated in the other papers in this book - the two final sections are devoted to two classical problems in archaeology. The first problem is that of a typological division based on morphology. The other is the time seriation problem. It is demonstrated here how multivariate statistics may help solve these problems in a more rigorous and controlled manner than otherwise possible.

I hope very much that these examples, together with those given by the other authors in this book may help to convince the reader that not only are multivariate statistics usable in archaeology, but in fact are a means of obtaining better results than can be gained by other means.

CONCLUDING REMARKS

This paper has covered a wide range of issues. It began with a general discussion of the archaeological research process, in order to establish a firm base for the understanding of the role of statistics in archaeology. It continued with an assesment of the usefulness of statistics in archaeology. The conclusion reached here was that inductive statistics are of little use, due to the nature of the archaeological research situation, whereas deductive statistics have a high use potential as a means of organizing and finding structure in the primary archaeological record.

In the following section, three multivariate deductive methods were outlined. These methods are the ones used throughout this book in the various papers, and the primary purpose of the section was to give a brief introduction to the methods and to state their virtues and shortcomings in relation to archaeological data.

Correspondence analysis and pottery chronology

A case from the Late Roman Iron Age cemetery Slusegård, Bornholm

By Jens-Henrik Bech — Museum of Thy and Vester Hanherred

From 1958 to 1964, Professor Ole Klindt-Jensen carried out excavations at the huge Slusegård cemetery on the south-east coast of the island of Bornholm. More than 1,400 graves were excavated during the six years that the investigations lasted. In time they span from the end of the Pre-Roman Iron Age to the beginning of the Early Germanic Iron Age. Compared to other cemeteries on Bornholm, Slusegård stands out as the most important burial site between 100 BC and 400 AD, with an extremely large, rich and well-documented data material.

In 1978 the first two volumes of the excavation report were published (Klindt-Jensen 1978), presenting the site plans and the descriptions of the individual graves and their contents. Due to his premature death, Ole Klindt-Jensen was deprived of the opportunity to crown his work with a final volume to summarise and interpret the evidence from Slusegård. In order to complete his work, a group of researchers has for some years been working on this final volume. The present paper should only be seen as a peripheral contribution to part of the work carried out in this connection, and it is presented here because correspondence analysis of pottery from Slusegård has offered interesting results, relevant to the theme of this book.

A total of 826 pots have been registered from the burials on Slusegård. 700 of these could be determined according to 46 pot types based on morphological and decorational criteria, 18 were separated as unique forms, while 108 were fragmented to a degree where an exact assignment to types could not be made.

Approximately one third of the pottery stems from the older part of the cemetery, i.e. from the last part of the Pre-Roman Iron Age and from the Early Roman Iron Age. The rest is younger, and as only very few pots can be attributed to either period C3 of the Late Roman Iron Age, or the oldest part of the Germanic Iron Age, it is quite a considerable amount of pottery that belongs to the intervening periods, i.e. C1 and C2 of the Late Roman Iron Age. As will be seen later, it is especially material from C1 that predominates.

This difference in frequency through time is primarily a result of changes in burial practice. Among the oldest graves, only one pot is normally found in each grave. During the Early Roman Iron Age this custom gradually changes, and two or even three or more pots may now be found. However, it is only with the beginning of the Late Roman Iron Age that the picture changes perceptibly. A wide range of graves now have a very rich inventory of pottery often composed of beakers, cups, jugs and one-handled and large three-handled vessels (Figure 1). During C2 or at the beginning of C3, the development reverses, and the comprehensive pottery inventory disappears again. The burials now contain one-handled vessels, beakers or vases only.

By way of the changes in the total inventory of the graves it is possible to divide these into seven main, temporal groups. This division corresponds quite closely to earlier chronological schemes for the Early Iron Age. An exception, however, is constituted by phases 4 and 5, which together correspond more or less to C1 of the Late Roman Iron Age. It is even possible to divide both of these two phases further, using formal and decorational changes in the vast pottery inventory. Thus a chronological system of 4a, 4b, 5a and 5b may be proposed for Slusegård. It is the analysis leading to this division that is the subject of this paper.

A manual matrix seriation was originally used to obtain a subdivision of phases 4 and 5. The matrix formed had a selection of graves as units, and a selection of pottery types and supplementary decorational elements as variables.

Slightly more than 30 pottery types can be separated in the Late Roman Iron Age material from Slusegård, but many of these types are found in too small numbers in the graves to have any practical use in a seriation. Further, as trial sortings of the

29

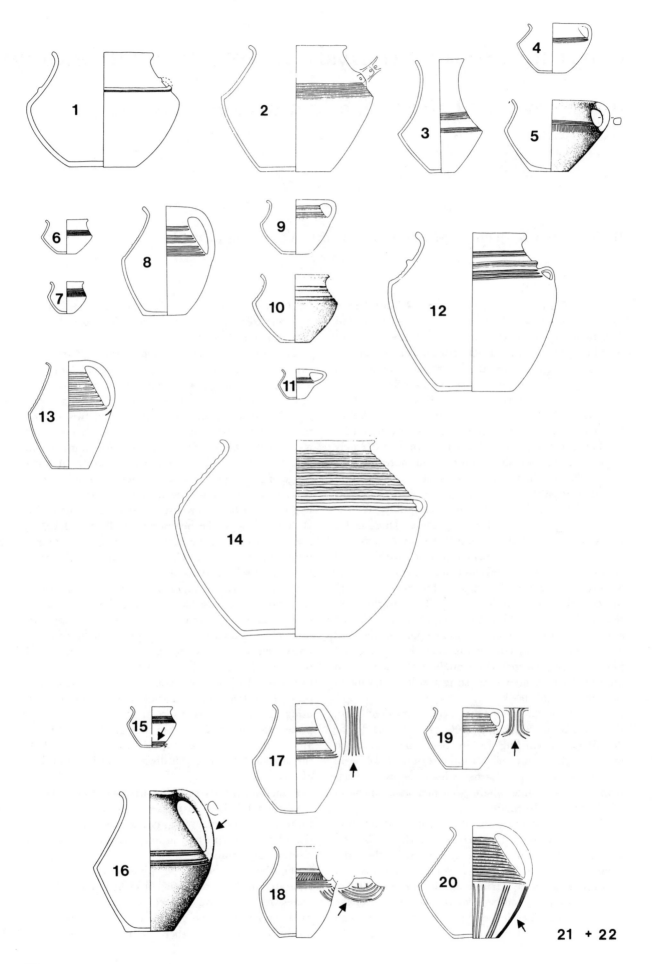

VARIABLES

	Unit	ID	1	2	3	4	5	6	7	8	9	10	11	12	13	14	15	16	17	18	19	20	21	22
★	1	1237	1	.	1	.	.	.	.	.	.	.	.	.	.	.	.	.	.	.	.	.	.	.
★	2	942	1	.	1	.	.	1	.	.	.	.	.	.	.	.	.	.	.	.	.	.	.	.
★	3	783	1	.	1	1	.	.	.	.	.	.	.	.	.	.	.	1	.	.	.	.	.	.
★	4	536	.	1	1	1	.	.	.	.	.	.	.	.	.	.	.	1	.	.	.	.	.	.
★	5	932	.	1	1	.	1	.	.	.	.	.	.	.	.	.	.	.	.	.	.	.	.	.
★	6	71	.	.	.	.	1	1	.	.	.	.	.	.	.	.	.	.	.	.	.	.	.	.
★	7	1158	.	.	.	1	.	1	.	.	.	.	.	.	.	.	.	1	.	.	.	.	.	.
★	8	85	.	.	.	.	1	.	.	.	.	.	.	.	.	.	.	2	.	.	.	.	.	.
★	9	280	.	.	.	1	.	.	1	.	.	.	.	.	.	.	1	1	.	.	.	.	.	.
★	10	538	.	1	.	.	1	1	.	1	.	.	.	.	.	.	.	1	1	.	.	.	.	.
★	11	535	.	.	1	1	.	1	.	.	.	.	.	.	.	.	.	.	1	.	.	.	.	.
★	12	937	.	.	.	.	1	1	.	1	.	.	.	.	.	.	.	2	.	.	.	.	.	.
★	13	1211	.	.	.	.	.	1	.	1	.	1	.	.	.	.	.	.	.	.	.	.	.	.
★	14	20	.	.	.	.	.	1	.	1	.	.	.	.	.	.	.	1	.	.	.	.	.	.
★	15	558	.	.	.	.	.	1	.	1	.	.	1	.	.	.	.	1	1	.	.	.	.	.
▲	16	940	.	.	.	.	.	.	1	1	.	.	.	.	.	.	1	1	.	.	.	.	.	.
▲	17	915	.	.	.	.	.	.	1	1	.	.	.	.	.	.	1	1	.	.	.	.	.	.
☆	18	1234	.	.	.	.	.	1	.	1	1	.	.	1	.	.	1	1	.	.	.	.	.	.
☆	19	224	.	.	.	.	.	.	1	1	.	.	.	1	.	.	1	1	.	.	.	.	.	.
☆	20	1229	.	.	.	.	.	.	1	1	.	.	.	1	.	.	1	.	1	.	.	.	.	.
☆	21	910	.	.	.	.	.	.	1	1	.	.	.	1	.	.	1	1	.	.	.	.	.	.
☆	22	1163	.	.	.	.	.	.	.	1	.	.	1	1	.	.	.	1	.	.	.	.	.	.
●	23	1225	.	.	.	.	.	.	.	.	.	.	.	1	1	.	.	2	.	.	.	.	.	.
●	24	25	.	.	.	.	.	.	.	1	.	.	.	.	.	.	.	1	.	.	1	.	.	.
☆	25	1243	.	.	.	.	.	.	.	1	.	.	.	1	.	.	.	.	1	.	.	.	.	.
▲	26	248	.	.	.	.	.	.	.	.	.	.	.	.	1	.	.	1	1	.	.	.	.	.
☆	27	1254	.	.	.	.	.	.	.	1	.	.	.	1	.	.	.	.	1	.	.	.	.	.
▲	28	1230	.	.	.	.	.	.	.	.	.	.	.	.	1	.	.	1	1	.	.	.	.	.
☆	29	281	.	.	.	.	.	.	1	1	.	1	1	.	.	.	.	.	2	.	.	.	.	.
▲	30	1233	.	.	.	.	.	.	.	1	.	1	1	.	.	.	.	.	.	.	.	.	.	.
●	31	919	.	.	.	.	.	.	.	.	.	.	.	1	1	.	.	1	.	.	.	.	.	.
●	32	1240	.	.	.	.	.	.	.	1	.	.	.	1	.	.	.	.	1	1	.	.	.	.
●	33	236	.	.	.	.	.	.	.	.	.	.	.	1	1	.	.	1	1	.	.	.	.	.
▲	34	64	.	.	.	.	.	.	.	.	.	.	.	.	1	.	.	1	.	.	1	.	.	.
●	35	198	.	.	.	.	.	.	.	.	.	.	.	1	1	.	.	.	2	.	.	.	.	.
●	36	949	.	.	.	.	.	.	.	.	.	.	.	1	1	.	.	.	2	.	.	.	.	.
○	37	1167	.	.	.	.	.	.	.	.	.	.	.	.	1	1	.	1	1	.	.	.	.	1
○	38	1231	.	.	.	.	.	.	.	.	.	.	.	.	1	1	.	.	2	.	.	.	.	1
○	39	5	.	.	.	.	.	.	.	.	.	.	.	.	1	1	.	.	1	.	1	.	1	.
○	40	140	.	.	.	.	.	.	.	.	.	.	.	.	1	1	.	.	2	.	.	.	.	.
○	41	1226	.	.	.	.	.	.	.	.	.	.	.	.	1	1	.	.	2	.	.	.	.	.
○	42	901	.	.	.	.	.	.	.	.	.	.	.	.	1	1	.	.	2	.	.	.	.	.
▲	43	51	.	.	.	.	.	.	.	.	.	.	.	.	1	.	.	.	.	2	.	.	.	.
○	44	240	.	.	.	.	.	.	.	.	.	.	.	1	1	.	.	.	.	.	2	1	.	.
○	45	243	.	.	.	.	.	.	.	.	.	.	.	.	1	1	.	.	1	.	.	1	.	.
○	46	1228	.	.	.	.	.	.	.	.	.	.	.	.	1	1	.	.	2	.	.	1	.	1
○	47	26	.	.	.	.	.	.	.	.	.	.	.	.	1	.	.	.	1	1	1	1	.	1
○	48	43	.	.	.	.	.	.	.	.	.	.	.	.	1	.	.	.	1	1	1	.	1	1
○	49	212	.	.	.	.	.	.	.	.	.	.	.	.	1	.	.	.	1	1	1	.	.	1
○	50	67	.	.	.	.	.	.	.	.	.	.	.	.	1	1	.	.	2	.	.	.	.	.
○	51	1236	.	.	.	.	.	.	.	.	.	.	.	.	1	1	.	.	2	.	.	.	.	.
○	52	907	.	.	.	.	.	.	.	.	.	.	.	.	1	.	.	.	.	.	2	2	1	1
○	53	61	.	.	.	.	.	.	.	.	.	.	.	.	1	.	.	.	.	2	.	.	1	.
○	54	1165	.	.	.	.	.	.	.	.	.	.	.	.	1	1	.	.	.	.	2	1	1	1
○	55	1259	.	.	.	.	.	.	.	.	.	.	.	.	1	1	.	.	.	1	.	.	1	.
○	56	1	.	.	.	.	.	.	.	.	.	.	.	.	1	1	.	.	.	.	2	2	1	1
○	57	33	.	.	.	.	.	.	.	.	.	.	.	.	1	1	.	.	.	.	.	.	.	.

Table 1. Manually sorted matrix seriation of selected burials from Slusegård, Bornhom. The left hand symbols correspond with the symbols used in Figure 2.

← Figure 1. Pottery types (1-14) and decoration elements (15-22) used in the analyses:
- 15: Horisontal grooves on lower part of vessel.
- 16: One handled vessels except cups with decorated shoulder and no ornaments on handle.
- 17-19: One handled vessels except cups with decorated shoulder and different kinds of handle decoration.
- 20: Bundles of vertical grooves on lower part of vessel.
- 21: Cups with handle decoration.
- 22: Three-handled vessels with handle decoration.

matrix proceeded, some of the types could be seen to be too invariant over time, and had consequently to be excluded. In the final version the matrix held 14 pottery types. The same procedure was applied to the supplementary decorational elements, which were reduced to eight elements. Among these, details of handle decorations turned out to be especially useful (Figure 1).

After it had been decided which types and supplementary decorational elements were to enter the seriation, it was also necessary to make a careful choice among the grave units. As a minimum each grave to be seriated should have two of the selected variables present. This criterion reduced the number of suitable graves to 57.

The final result of the manual matrix seriation is shown in Table 1, where form types and decorational elements are shown separately to make the seriation clearer. The general procedure of the manual sorting was:

1. an intuitive sorting to yield an approximate seriation based on a criterion of concentration along the 'diagonal';

2. a decision on the sequence of the variables based on an assumption of their 'chronological development';

3. a permutation of the units based on a computational method suggested by Goldman (1972) that seeks to concentrate the presence registrations of the variables along the 'diagonal'.

The seriation that gave rise to the subdivision of phases 4 and 5 was thus carried out without the help of multivariate statistics. However, as such methods became available at this point in my work with the Slusegård pottery, it was certainly desirable to check the results by independent means and to compare the manually and the mathematically based solution. The method used was correspondence analysis, partly because it is ideal for the type of data at hand, and partly because it has been shown to be able to yield seriations, where these are obtainable (see Madsen this volume).

With the matrix Table 1 as a direct input to the correspondence analysis, a plot of the first two principal axes showed a very nicely ordered V-shaped for-

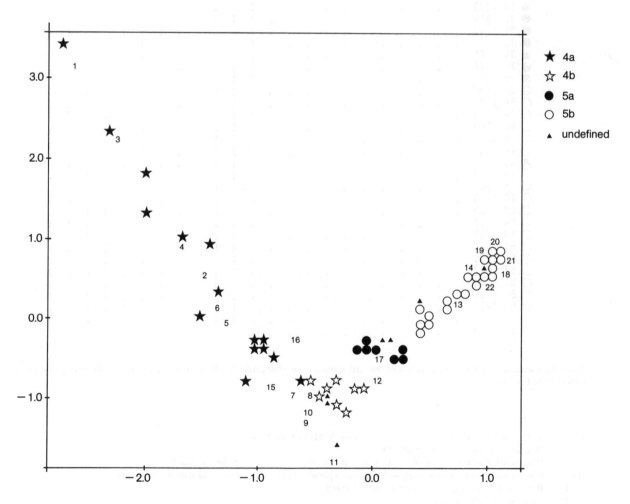

Figure 2. Plot of the first two principal axes from a correspondence analysis of the data in Table 1.

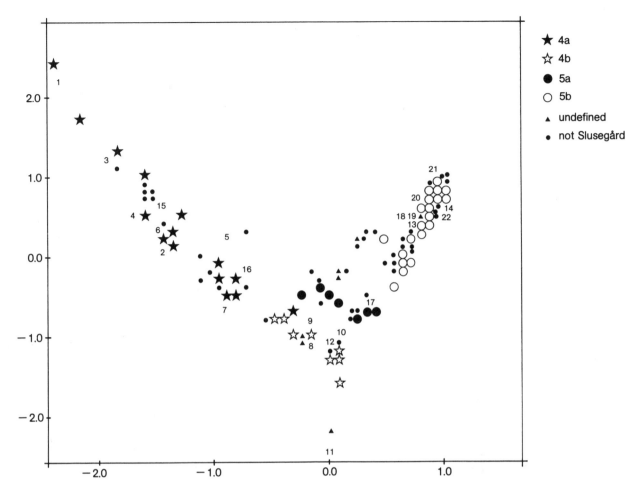

Figure 3. Plot of the first two principal axes from a correspondence analysis of the data in Table 2.

mation of both units and variables (Figure 2). This is the formation obtained when conditions for a seriation are ideal, and the order of both units and variables may be directly read from the plot by following the V-shaped formation from one end to the other (Madsen this volume).

A comparison between the manual seriation (Table 1) and the mathematical seriation (Figure 2) shows very close agreement, and a first reaction may well be that the only advantage of the latter is its extreme speed and ease of use due to its computer-based execution. A few hours of typing at a terminal is all it takes, although it should not be forgotten that the tiresome process of screening out variables and units unsuitable for seriation is not avoided. However, a second glance at the plot Figure 2 reveals a further advantage of the mathematical solution. We are not merely presented with a sequence of units and variables, but also with a scaling in two dimensions where the structure of the sequence is directly visualised. We are given indications of degree of clustering versus continuity, and we are given indications of the strength of the breaks that separate individual groupings. This is very useful, when we turn to the formal

definition of the phase division based on the seriation.

The basic requirement of input data for a seriation, if this has to be credited with any value at all, is that there be a continuous replacement of variables across units. This implies that a formal phase division based on defining types will always create an artificial 'box system' into which the material is ordered. As very clearly shown by the V formation in Figure 2, the requirement for a seriation is unquestionably met in the pottery data supplied, and consequently any defined phase division will tend to create an artificial disruption of a continuum.

The definitions that I have chosen for a phase division of the Slusegård pottery are as follows. Of special importance are the vases of type 3 and jugs of types 8 and 13. Functionally, they are of the same kind, and they seem to replace each other over time. Type 3 is the oldest and type 13 the youngest. The latter may be claimed to define phase 5, while the two others define phase 4. Further, in phase 4 we may take three-handled vessels of type 12 to define the beginning of 4b (this type continues into 5), while a group of types (3, 1, 2, 4, 5 and 6) exclusively belong

	VARIABLES																						BROOCHES				
UNITS	1	3	4	6	2	5	7	8	9	10	12	11	13	14	15	16	17	18	19	20	22	21	A	B	C	D	E
★ 1	1	1	.	.	.	.	.	.	.	.	.	.	.	.	.	.	.	.	.	.	.	.					
★ 2	1	1	.	.	.	1	.	.	.	.	.	.	.	.	.	.	.	.	.	.	.	.					
★ 3	1	1	1	.	.	.	.	.	.	.	.	.	.	.	.	1	.	.	.	.	.	.					
63	.	.	.	.	.	.	.	.	.	.	.	.	.	.	3	.	.	.	.	.	.	.	*	*			
★ 5	.	1	.	.	.	1	.	.	.	.	.	.	.	.	.	.	.	.	.	.	.	.		*			
58	1	1	.	.	1	.	.	.	.	.	.	.	.	.	.	2	.	.	.	.	.	.					
61	.	1	.	.	1	.	1	.	.	.	.	.	.	.	1	.	.	.	.	.	.	.					
62	.	1	.	.	.	.	.	.	.	.	.	.	.	.	2	1	.	.	.	.	.	.					
59	.	1	1	.	.	.	.	.	.	.	.	.	.	.	.	1	.	.	.	.	.	.			*		
67	.	1	.	.	.	.	.	.	.	.	.	.	.	.	1	1	.	.	.	.	.	.					
★ 4	.	1	1	1	.	.	.	.	.	.	.	.	.	.	.	1	.	.	.	.	.	.		*			
★ 11	.	1	1	.	1	.	.	.	.	.	.	.	.	.	.	.	1	.	.	.	.	.					
60	.	.	1	1	.	1	.	.	.	.	.	.	.	.	1	.	.	.	.	.	.	.					
★ 6	.	.	1	.	1	.	.	.	.	.	.	.	.	.	.	.	.	.	.	.	.	.					
★ 7	.	.	1	.	1	.	.	.	.	.	.	.	.	.	.	1	.	.	.	.	.	.		*			
★ 9	.	1	1	.	.	1	.	.	.	.	.	.	.	.	1	1	.	.	.	.	.	.					
64	.	1	.	1	.	.	1	.	.	.	.	.	.	.	.	2	.	.	.	.	.	.					
70	.	.	.	.	.	1	.	.	.	.	.	.	.	.	1	1	.	1	.	.	.	.		*			
★ 8	.	1	.	.	.	1	.	.	.	.	.	.	.	.	.	2	.	.	.	.	.	.					
66	.	1	.	.	1	.	1	.	.	.	.	.	.	.	.	1	.	.	.	.	.	.					
65	.	.	1	1	.	1	.	1	.	.	.	.	.	.	.	2	.	.	.	.	.	.					
★ 12	.	.	1	.	1	.	1	1	.	.	.	.	.	.	.	2	.	.	.	.	.	.					
68	.	1	.	1	.	.	1	.	.	.	.	.	.	.	.	2	.	.	.	.	.	.					
★ 10	.	.	1	1	.	1	.	1	1	.	.	.	.	.	.	1	1	.	.	.	.	.					
★ 13	.	.	.	1	.	1	.	1	.	.	.	.	.	.	.	1	.	.	.	.	.	.			*		
★ 14	.	.	.	1	.	.	1	.	.	.	.	.	.	.	.	1	.	.	.	.	.	.					
71	.	.	.	.	1	.	1	.	1	.	1	.	.	.	1	1	.	.	.	.	.	.					
69	.	.	.	.	1	.	1	1	.	.	.	.	.	.	.	2	.	.	.	.	.	.					
☆ 20	.	.	.	.	.	1	.	1	.	.	1	.	.	.	1	.	1	.	.	.	.	.			*	*	
☆ 18	.	.	.	.	.	1	.	1	1	.	.	1	.	.	1	.	1	.	.	.	.	.		*			
◇ 15	.	.	.	.	.	.	1	1	.	1	.	1	.	.	.	1	1	.	.	.	.	.					
☆ 19	.	.	.	.	.	.	1	1	1	.	.	1	.	.	.	1	1	.	.	.	.	.					
△ 16	.	.	.	.	.	.	.	1	1	.	.	.	.	.	.	1	1	.	.	.	.	.					
△ 17	.	.	.	.	.	.	.	1	1	.	.	.	.	.	.	1	1	.	.	.	.	.					
☆ 21	.	.	.	.	.	.	.	1	.	.	1	.	.	.	.	1	1	.	.	.	.	.		*			
72	.	.	.	.	.	.	.	1	1	1	.	.	.	.	.	.	1	.	.	.	.	.					
☆ 22	.	.	.	.	.	.	.	1	.	1	.	.	.	.	.	.	1	.	.	.	.	.		*			
73	.	.	.	.	.	.	.	1	.	1	.	.	.	.	.	.	1	.	.	.	.	.					
☆ 25	.	.	.	.	.	.	.	1	.	.	1	.	.	.	.	.	1	.	.	.	.	.					
☆ 27	.	.	.	.	.	.	.	1	.	.	1	.	.	.	.	.	1	.	.	.	.	.					
☆ 29	.	.	.	.	.	.	.	1	1	.	1	1	.	.	.	.	2	.	.	.	.	.			*		
▲ 30	.	.	.	.	.	.	.	.	1	.	1	1	.	.	.	.	.	.	.	.	.	.					
● 23	.	.	.	.	.	.	.	.	.	.	1	1	.	.	.	2	.	.	.	.	.	.					
74	.	.	.	.	.	.	.	1	1	.	.	.	.	.	.	1	.	1	.	.	.	.					
75	.	.	.	.	.	.	.	1	.	.	.	.	.	.	1	.	1	.	1	.	.	.					
● 24	.	.	.	.	.	.	.	1	.	.	.	.	.	.	.	1	.	1	.	.	.	.					
76	.	.	.	.	.	.	.	1	.	.	.	.	.	.	.	1	.	1	.	.	.	.					
● 31	.	.	.	.	.	.	.	.	.	.	1	1	.	.	.	1	.	.	.	.	.	.			*		
● 33	.	.	.	.	.	.	.	.	.	.	1	1	.	.	.	1	1	.	.	.	.	.					
● 32	.	.	.	.	.	.	.	1	.	.	1	.	.	.	.	.	1	1	.	.	.	.					
79	.	.	.	.	.	.	.	1	.	.	1	.	.	.	.	.	1	1	.	.	.	.					
77	.	.	.	.	.	.	.	1	1	.	.	.	.	.	.	.	1	1	.	.	.	.					
78	.	.	.	.	.	.	.	1	.	1	.	.	.	.	.	.	1	1	.	.	.	.					
▲ 26	.	.	.	.	.	.	.	.	.	.	1	.	.	.	.	1	1	.	.	.	.	.				*	
▲ 28	.	.	.	.	.	.	.	.	.	.	1	.	.	.	.	1	1	.	.	.	.	.					
81	.	.	.	.	.	.	.	.	.	.	1	.	.	.	.	1	1	.	.	.	.	.					
85	.	.	.	.	.	.	.	1	.	.	.	.	.	.	.	1	.	1	.	.	.	.					
● 35	.	.	.	.	.	.	.	.	.	.	.	.	.	.	.	2	.	.	.	.	.	.					
● 36	.	.	.	.	.	.	.	.	.	.	1	1	.	.	.	2	.	.	.	.	.	.		*	*		
○ 38	.	.	.	.	.	.	.	.	.	.	1	1	.	.	.	2	.	.	.	.	1	.			*		
▲ 34	.	.	.	.	.	.	.	.	.	.	1	.	.	.	.	1	.	1	.	.	.	.			*		
83	.	.	.	.	.	.	.	.	.	.	1	.	.	.	.	1	.	1	.	.	.	.					
84	.	.	.	.	.	.	1	1	.	.	.	.	1	.	.	1	.	2	.	1	.	.					
86	.	.	.	.	.	.	.	1	.	.	1	.	.	.	.	1	.	1	.	.	.	.					
89	.	.	.	.	.	.	1	.	.	.	1	.	.	.	.	1	.	1	1	.	.	.					
○ 37	.	.	.	.	.	.	1	.	.	.	1	.	1	1	.	1	1	.	.	.	1	.					
88	.	.	.	.	.	.	1	.	.	.	.	.	.	.	.	.	.	2	.	.	.	.					
82	.	.	.	.	.	.	.	1	1	.	1	.	.	.	.	.	1	1	.	2	.	.					
80	.	.	.	.	.	.	.	1	.	.	1	.	.	.	.	.	1	1	.	.	.	1					
91	.	.	.	.	.	.	.	1	.	.	1	.	.	.	.	.	1	.	1	.	.	1					
○ 40	.	.	.	.	.	.	.	.	.	.	1	1	.	.	.	.	2	.	.	.	.	.					
○ 41	.	.	.	.	.	.	.	.	.	.	1	1	.	.	.	.	2	.	.	.	.	.					
○ 42	.	.	.	.	.	.	.	.	.	.	1	1	.	.	.	.	2	.	.	.	.	.					
○ 39	.	.	.	.	.	.	.	.	.	1	1	1	.	.	.	.	1	.	1	.	.	1			*	*	
87	.	.	.	.	.	.	.	.	.	.	1	.	.	.	.	.	1	1	.	.	.	.					
90	.	.	.	.	.	.	1	.	.	.	1	.	.	.	.	.	2	.	1	.	.	.				*	
94	.	.	.	.	.	.	1	1	.	.	1	1	.	.	.	.	2	1	.	.	.	.					
96	.	.	.	.	.	.	.	.	1	.	1	1	.	.	.	.	2	1	.	.	.	.					*
○ 44	.	.	.	.	.	.	.	.	1	1	1	.	.	.	.	.	2	.	1	.	.	.					
92	.	.	.	.	.	.	.	.	.	.	1	.	.	.	.	.	1	1	.	1	.	.					
○ 46	.	.	.	.	.	.	.	.	.	.	1	1	.	.	.	.	2	.	.	1	1	.					
○ 45	.	.	.	.	.	.	.	.	.	.	1	1	.	.	.	.	1	.	1	.	1	.					
○ 47	.	.	.	.	.	.	.	.	.	.	1	.	.	.	.	.	1	1	1	1	1	.					
△ 43	.	.	.	.	.	.	.	.	.	.	1	.	.	.	.	.	2	.	1	.	.	.					
○ 48	.	.	.	.	.	.	.	.	.	.	1	.	.	.	.	.	1	1	1	.	1	1					
98	.	.	.	.	.	.	.	.	.	.	1	.	.	.	.	.	1	.	.	.	1	1					
○ 50	.	.	.	.	.	.	.	.	.	.	.	1	.	.	.	.	1	.	2	.	.	.					
○ 51	.	.	.	.	.	.	.	.	.	.	1	1	.	.	.	.	.	2	2	.	.	.					
93	.	.	.	.	.	.	.	.	.	.	1	.	.	.	.	.	.	1	.	.	.	.				*	
○ 49	.	.	.	.	.	.	.	.	.	.	1	.	.	.	.	.	.	1	1	1	1	.					
97	.	.	.	.	.	.	.	.	.	.	1	.	.	.	.	.	.	.	1	.	.	.					
○ 57	.	.	.	.	.	.	.	.	.	.	1	1	.	.	.	.	.	1	.	.	.	.					
○ 52	.	.	.	.	.	.	.	.	.	.	1	.	.	.	.	.	.	2	2	1	1	.	*	*	*		
○ 54	.	.	.	.	.	.	.	.	.	.	1	1	.	.	.	.	.	2	1	1	1	.					
○ 55	.	.	.	.	.	.	.	.	.	.	1	1	.	.	.	.	.	1	.	1	1	.					
○ 56	.	.	.	.	.	.	.	.	.	.	1	1	.	.	.	.	.	2	2	1	1	.					
95	.	.	.	.	.	.	.	.	.	.	1	1	.	.	.	.	.	1	1	1	.	1					
○ 53	.	.	.	.	.	.	.	.	.	.	.	1	.	.	.	.	.	2	.	.	.	1		*			
101	.	.	.	.	.	.	.	.	.	.	.	1	.	.	.	.	.	1	.	.	1	1					
99	.	.	.	.	.	.	.	.	.	.	.	1	.	.	.	.	.	1	.	.	1	1					
100	.	.	.	.	.	.	.	.	.	.	.	1	.	.	.	.	.	1	.	.	1	1					

to 4a. Finally, to separate 5a from 5b, we may take three-handled vessels of type 12 to be indicative of 5a, and three-handled vessels of type 14 of 5b. Some of the decorational elements may also be used here, for elements 18 and 19 can be attributed to phase 5 in general, whereas elements 20, 21 and 22 define 5b.

In Figure 2, the individual graves are attributed to the four phases according to the definitions above, and it can immediately be seen that there is an almost perfect agreement between the division based on definitions and the scaled, descriptive division produced by the correspondence analysis. Only one grave is directly misplaced, and only seven graves of the 57 have escaped phasing by use of the definitions. Problems can be seen to exist between 4a and 4b, where the correspondence analysis indicates a clear separation, but where definitions have placed one grave belonging to 4a in the 4b group, and left three undefined graves in the same area. Apart from this, however, the almost perfect fit must be taken as a strong argument for the usefulness of the criteria chosen to define the phase divisions 4a, 4b, 5a and 5b at Slusegård.

It has been claimed in the preceding that the seriation carried out on the pottery data from Slusegård represents a chronological development. However, even though we have data that can be perfectly seriated, we cannot accept such a claim without proof, since it is quite conceivable that a perfect seriation could be caused by other agents of variation than time.

To prove that we are not dealing with some unique local ordering on Slusegård, we may supplement the data to be seriated with 44 graves from other burial grounds on Bornholm. A correspondence analysis of the 101 graves gives a plot on the two first principal axes (Figure 3) that comes very close to the plot for Slusegård alone (Figure 2). The groupings still fit the selected criteria for a phase division of the Slusegård graves, even if the seriated matrix (Table 2) shows some differences between Slusegård and the other sites.

In the more comprehensive seriation Table 2 we also find the final proof of a chronological cause in the occurrence of five chronologically important brooch types in the graves (Types A-E, Figure 4). Especially brooches of types B and E are important chronological indicators here (between 4a-b and 5b) (Mackeprang 1943:13; Albrectsen 1968:225), but also others fit into the seriation according to a time variation.

As mentioned earlier, the phases Slusegård 4a-5b probably cover the Late Roman Iron Age phase C1

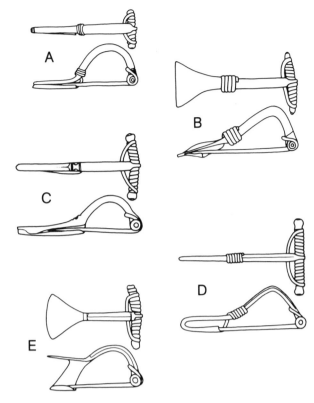

Figure 4. Chronologically significant brooches found in the graves in Table 2.

only. According to the most recent absolute dating, this means that the complete time span of our seriation is only 75-100 years. Each sub-phase is thus only some 20-25 years long, provided they are all of approximately the same length.

That prehistoric pottery in general has a short life span is supported by ethnoarchaeological investigations (Foster 1959; David & Hennig 1972). This may be seen as a point in favour of the feasibility of the short-term phase divisions based on pottery suggested above, even though we are clearly close to what it is possible to achieve chronologically in archaeology. Nor is it in this connection irrelevant that Ulla Lund Hansen in her treatment of Zealandic material from the Late Roman Iron Age reaches a comparably fine division of C1 based on pottery and brooches (1976:128).

← Table 2. Seriated matrix of 101 graves from Bornholm sorted according to the correspondence plot Figure 3. The left hand symbols correspond with the symbols used in Figure 3.

Correspondence analysis applied to hoards and graves of the Germanic Iron Age

Karen Høilund Nielsen — University of Aarhus

During work with the Germanic Iron Age, especially the graves from the later part of the period, and the bracteate hoards from the earlier part of the period, problems arose concerning seriation and classification (K.H. Nielsen 1984a).

One of my objectives was to classify the strings of beads from Late Germanic Iron Age graves on Bornholm. This could be done using either individual beads or strings of beads. Earlier studies have revealed a change in the composition of bead colours through the Late Germanic Iron Age, a change from red/yellow to blue/green (Ørsnes 1966:170; Iversen & Näsman 1978:90).

For this reason, and because the individual bead types have a rather long existence (rectangular prismatic beads with cut corners for instance being known both from the Roman and the Germanic Iron Age), I considered it more appropriate to work with the strings of beads. As colour is the most distinguishing feature of the beads in question, this has been given priority in the analysis. Bead material forms another element in the analyses, whereas shape is used only exceptionally.

To avoid a troublesome, uncertain, manual sorting of the beads, I needed a method of numerical analysis which could identify groups among the strings of beads, and relate these groups to one another, as well as show which factors separated them.

My next objective was to establish a local chronology for the female graves of the Late Germanic Iron Age on Bornholm. The data here were obtained from a series of graves with combinations of generally rather few artifacts, mostly of metal.

Instead of using the existing chronological system (Ørsnes 1966), I preferred to carry out an independent seriation of the contents of the graves based on an assumption of a gradual change in type composition. Once again I needed a suitable numerical analysis method for sorting the graves, preferably one that could reveal whether the change was truly gradual or happened in stages - i.e. whether the graves tended to cluster.

My final objective concerned the Jutish bracteates from the Early Germanic Iron Age. Up till now there has been only loose conjecture on the relative dating of these bracteates. Nobody has so far looked at the type combinations in the finds. Originally, my intention was to investigate whether there was a gradual change in the type composition and whether a seriation or clustering could be used as a basis for an explanation of the chronological and/or spatial distribution. But the correspondence analysis gave a far from clear picture of the interrelationships in the material. Instead, it has led to some methodological considerations on the relationship between seriations based on matrix permutations and correspondence analyses.

CHOICE OF ANALYSIS

The data at hand is of the abundance type, which can be represented in a two-way matrix. The correspondence analysis is a multivariate technique that can handle abundance data, and graphically relate any combination of clustering and seriation in the material (Madsen 1985:179 ff.). Furthermore, it is symmetrical with regard to units and variables. That is to say, they are analysed in the same multidimensional space and can thus be shown in the same plots (see also Bølviken et al. 1982). This makes correspondence analysis easy to interpret. Of special interest here is its treatment of data that seriates well. Linearity in the data forms a parabola in the plot of the 1st and 2nd axes. For less perfect seriations, the points will tend to form clusters in a semi-circle around the centre, and for rather bad seriations one may see only a swarm of points in the plot tending to avoid the centre.

Other analyses such as multi-dimensional scaling (Kendall 1971:215 ff. with further references) and principal component analysis (Madsen 1985 with further references) may also be used and may reveal both clusterings and seriations. However, they

No.	Name	T	A	B	U	Z	A1	M	B1	X	F	L	Y	K	N	G	E	D	Q	H	J	P	C	V	R	I	W	S	
23	Kobbeå 33	.	19	12	.	.	2	.	.	.	.	.	.	.	.	.	.	.	.	.	.	.	.	.	.	.	.	.	
1	Gudmingegård	.	34	20	.	.	.	.	.	.	.	.	.	.	.	.	.	.	.	1	.	.	2	.	.	.	.	.	
22	Kobbeå 2	1	32	24	.	.	6	.	.	.	.	.	.	.	.	.	.	.	.	.	.	.	2	.	.	.	.	.	
15	Lousgård 36	.	62	30	.	2	.	2	.	2	.	.	.	.	.	.	6	.	.	.	.	.	.	.	.	.	.	.	
29	Nr. Sandegård 426	.	37	72	.	.	.	.	1	.	1	.	.	.	.	2	.	4	3	.	4	.	.	.	.	.	.	.	A
14	Lousgård 35	.	59	65	.	.	.	.	.	2	.	.	.	.	.	13	4	6	.	.	.	.	3	.	.	.	.	.	
5	Knarregård 1	.	18	9	.	2	.	.	.	1	.	.	.	.	.	.	.	7	.	.	.	.	1	.	.	.	.	.	
17	Lousgård 40	.	25	27	.	.	2	.	.	.	.	.	.	.	.	10	.	5	.	.	.	.	.	.	.	.	.	.	
28	Nr. Sandegård 397	.	8	55	.	.	3	.	.	8	.	.	.	.	.	14	.	5	.	.	.	.	.	.	.	.	.	.	
4	Nexø Nymølle 2	.	1	41	.	.	.	.	.	.	8	.	.	.	.	.	.	11	.	.	.	.	.	.	.	.	.	.	
16	Lousgård 39	.	18	.	1	.	.	.	.	2	.	.	.	.	.	5	7	.	.	1	.	.	.	.	.	.	.	.	
20	Melsted 13	.	11	28	.	.	.	.	16	.	.	.	.	.	.	14	28	20	.	.	.	.	.	.	.	.	.	.	(A)
3	Strandmarken Nexø 12	.	3	51	.	.	.	.	13	.	39	.	.	.	.	.	19	26	.	.	.	.	.	.	.	.	.	.	(A)
11	Lousgård 16	.	.	1	.	.	1	.	.	15	5	.	.	3	.	6	30	1	.	.	1	.	.	.	.	.	.	.	
2	St. Kannikegård 195	.	1	.	.	.	1	.	1	12	5	.	13	.	2	1	5	.	.	.	1	.	.	.	.	.	.	.	
19	Lousgård 9	.	.	.	.	.	.	.	.	1	4	5	5	.	1	16	2	.	.	.	.	1	.	.	.	.	.	.	
7	Lousgård 6	.	.	.	.	.	.	.	.	.	1	.	.	7	1	9	2	1	.	.	.	.	.	.	.	.	.	.	B
8	Lousgård 10	.	.	.	1	1	.	1	.	.	3	.	10	4	3	22	.	.	.	.	.	.	.	.	.	.	.	.	
6	Lousgård 3	.	.	.	.	.	.	.	.	.	.	.	4	.	3	.	3	7	3	.	1	.	.	.	.	.	.	.	
12	Lousgård 18	.	.	1	.	.	.	.	.	5	.	.	7	.	5	15	1	1	.	.	.	.	.	.	.	.	.	.	
10	Lousgård 12	.	.	1	.	.	2	.	.	2	1	2	.	4	11	3	8	4	.	.	2	.	.	.	.	.	.	.	
27	Nr. Sandegård 6	.	.	.	.	.	.	.	.	1	12	3	.	11	4	9	29	4	3	.	1	.	.	1	.	.	.	.	
26	Nr. Sandegård 4	.	.	2	.	4	1	.	3	15	10	1	16	.	19	61	30	2	.	.	.	.	.	.	.	.	.	.	
21	Melsted b 2	.	.	.	.	.	.	.	.	.	.	.	.	.	.	12	10	.	.	.	.	.	.	.	.	.	.	.	
31	Ellegård	.	.	1	.	.	1	.	.	5	4	.	1	2	4	7	9	3	.	2	1	.	.	.	4	1	.	.	
25	Lillevang-Melsted 4	.	1	.	.	.	.	.	.	.	1	.	4	.	8	.	12	2	5	.	1	5	.	.	3	.	.	.	C
9	Lousgård 11	.	.	.	.	.	.	.	.	1	.	.	1	.	2	.	25	.	.	.	1	5	.	2	.	.	.	.	
13	Lousgård 28	.	.	2	.	.	1	.	.	.	.	.	.	2	1	5	2	.	1	.	1	.	3	5	1	14	1	2	
24	Lillevang-Melsted 2	.	.	.	.	.	.	.	.	3	.	.	.	.	.	3	19	.	.	.	.	.	9	.	.	9	.	9	D
30	Saltuna 14	.	.	.	.	.	.	.	.	.	.	.	.	.	.	8	1	.	.	.	.	.	.	.	3	.	.	11	
18	Lousgård 47	.	.	.	.	.	.	.	.	.	.	.	.	.	.	4	1	.	.	1	.	.	.	18	4	.	.	21	

A: opaque orange
B: opaque red
C: dim yellow
D: white
E: translucent blue
F: opaque green
G: translucent green
H: brown
I: uncoloured
J: other monochrome
K: polychrome blue
L: polychrome white
M: polychrome yellow
N: polychrome green
P: polychrome turquois
Q: other polychrome
R: gold foil
S: silver foil
T: bone
U: slices of shell
V: rock crystal
W: carnelian
X: bronze spiral
Y: bronze spiral on wood
Z: wood on bronze
A1: bronze bead
B1: amber

Table 1. Matrix showing counts of 27 different types of beads from strings containing more than 20 beads in 31 graves (the bækkegård cemetery is excluded).

have weaknesses not found with the correspondence analysis. Principal component analysis requires data with a normal distribution, which abundance data seldom have, and multi-dimensional scaling relies on similarity coefficients, which takes you one important step away from the original data before the analysis is performed and thus make the results harder to interpret.

CLASSIFICATION OF THE STRINGS OF BEADS

The bead material used comes from 90 graves with more than 10 beads per grave: altogether appr. 3,800 beads. Forty-seven of these graves are from Bækkegaard, and they include more than 1,500 beads. The beads from Bækkegaard are, like most of the finds from Bornholm, kept in the National Museum, Copenhagen, but on their arrival at the museum in the last century, became mixed. Thanks to the excavators' notes, the combination of colours in the strings of beads from various graves can be

reconstructed (Vedel 1890), but information on the combination of shapes was lost, and the polychrome beads can be classified only as such.

Thus, in the following analyses, only the colour, the material, and the translucency are used, because they are factors that are easy to relate to the beads from Bækkegaard. Anyway, shape does not seem to have chronological significance.

Two separate analyses of the colour combinations will be carried out. One comprises all finds, the other excludes Bækkegaard. The results from the two can then be compared, to see whether the finds from Bækkegaard agree with those of the other finds. If the two analyses show approximately the same results, it can be considered to corroborate the correctness of the information on colour combinations given by Vedel and also as a test of significance for the analysis of colour combinations.

The first analysis has been performed on strings with 20 or more beads and employing all variables. A total of 31 strings of beads fulfil this require-

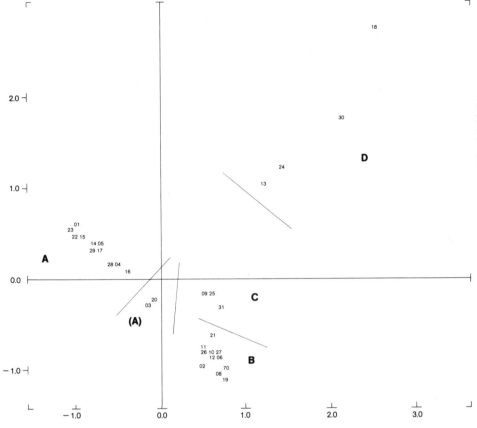

Figure 1. Plot of the first two principal axes from a correspondence analysis of the data in Table 1. The numbers refer to strings of beads from graves. For the lettering see text.

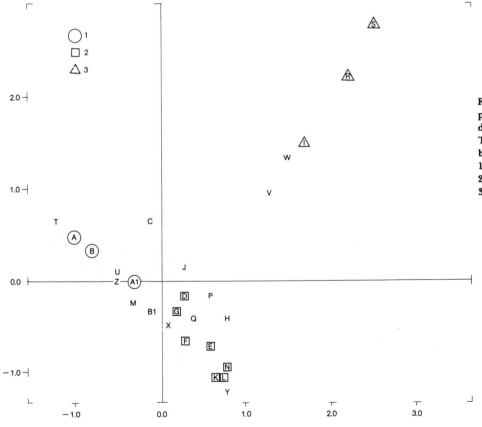

Figure 2. Plot of the first two principal axes from a correspondence analysis of the data in Table 1. The letters refer to the bead types as described in Table 1. Key to signs: 1, reddish beads. 2, white, green and blue beads. 3, uncoloured and foil beads.

ment, and they are described by means of 27 variables (Table 1).

The plot of the first two principal axes (Figures 1–2) reveals a clear tendency to cluster, but also a slight seriation tendency. Five clusters emerge from the plot, one of which consists of two strings only. The composition of beads in these two strings shows a high percentage of amber beads, which is quite unusual for the material as a whole. If we reorder the data matrix following the curved layout of both cases and variables from left to right, we find the pattern shown in Table 1.

The result is that four main clusters can be isolated among the strings of beads, differing very markedly from each other. The first group (A) is characterised by opaque beads of orange and red colours. The second group (B) is characterised by opaque green, translucent blue and polychrome white, blue, and green beads. The third group (C) is characterised by the occurrence of white, stone-like beads, beads with gold foil, and the near absence of translucent blue and opaque green beads. The last group (D) is characterised by the occurrence of beads with silver foil, gold foil, colourless beads, and white stone-like beads in relatively high percentages, and the almost total absence of polychrome beads of all colours.

The second analysis includes the graves from Bækkegaard and some other graves with limited information. The variables have been selected on the basis of the information furnished by Vedel (1890:68–73). We thus have only 17 variables but 67 strings of beads (Table 2).

The plot of the first two principal axes reveals much the same pattern as in the first analysis (Figures 3 and 4). The seriation tendency is clearer in this analysis, but the clustering is no less marked than it was in the first analysis. We may thus divide the strings of beads into three main groups, between which there are two minor groupings. One of the latter is identical to the one that could be separated in the first analysis containing an unusually high percentage of amber beads.

When we compare the results of the two analyses, it is quite clear that the same groups appear in both, althogh there are minor deviations due to differences in the definitions of the variables.

Leaving out the two strings with amber beads, the four remaining groups can now be described in relation to a larger part of the total bead material. The bead groups are named R3a–d and, as before, the strings of beads and the variables are reordered in the data matrix using the order of the plot from left

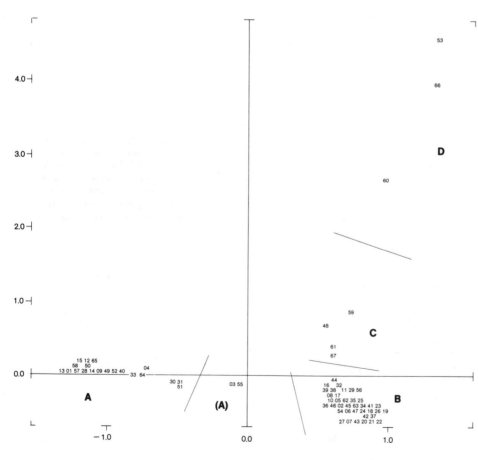

Figure 3. Plot of the first two principal axes from a correspondence analysis of the data in Table 2. The numbers refer to strings of beads from graves. For the lettering see text.

Table 2 — Matrix showing counts of 17 different types of beads.

#	Site	R	A	B	Q	C	N	K	P	D	H	E	F	G	M	L	I	J	
13	Bækkegård 24	.	28	68	.	.	.	.	.	.	.	.	.	.	.	.	.	.	
1	Gudmingegård	.	34	20	.	2	.	.	.	.	.	1	.	.	.	.	.	.	
58	Kobbeå 33	.	19	12	.	.	.	2	.	.	.	.	.	.	.	.	.	.	
15	Bækkegård 30	.	24	80	.	.	.	.	.	3	.	1	2	1	.	.	.	.	
28	Bækkegård 90	.	76	41	.	.	.	.	.	.	4	3	.	3	.	.	.	.	
57	Kobbeå 2	1	32	24	.	.	.	6	.	.	.	.	.	.	.	.	.	.	
12	Bækkegård 23	.	11	87	.	1	.	.	.	2	.	1	2	2	.	.	.	.	
14	Bækkegård 26	.	79	17	.	.	2	.	2	.	2	8	.	.	.	.	.	.	
50	Lousgård 36	.	62	30	.	2	.	2	.	2	.	6	.	.	.	.	.	.	
65	Nr. Sandegård 426	.	37	72	1	.	.	1	2	4	.	1	4	.	.	.	.	.	A
9	Bækkegård 14	.	25	7	1	.	.	.	.	4	1	.	1	.	.	.	.	.	
49	Lousgård 35	.	59	65	.	3	.	2	13	.	4	6	.	.	.	.	.	.	
52	Lousgård 40	.	25	27	.	.	.	2	10	.	.	5	.	.	.	.	.	.	
40	Knarregård 1	.	18	9	1	1	2	.	.	.	7	.	.	.	.	.	.	.	
33	Bækkegård 112	.	35	2	.	6	.	.	.	8	.	.	.	4	.	.	.	.	
4	Nexø Nymølle 2	.	1	41	.	.	.	.	8	.	.	11	.	.	.	.	.	.	
64	Nr. Sandegård 397	.	8	55	.	.	.	11	14	.	.	5	.	.	.	.	.	.	
30	Bækkegård 103	.	18	.	3	.	.	.	.	.	10	2	.	.	.	.	.	.	
31	Bækkegård 104	.	12	6	.	.	.	.	.	.	12	.	.	.	.	.	.	.	
51	Lousgård 39	.	18	.	1	.	.	2	5	.	7	.	.	1	.	.	.	.	
3	Strandmarken Nexø 12	.	3	51	.	.	.	13	39	.	19	26	.	.	.	.	.	.	(A)
55	Melsted 13	.	11	28	.	.	.	16	14	.	28	20	.	.	.	.	.	.	
36	Bækkegård 135	.	1	1	.	.	.	.	.	2	13	10	8	.	.	.	.	.	
2	St. Kannikegård 195	.	1	.	.	.	.	.	1	14	21	1	5	.	.	.	.	.	
8	Bækkegård 11	.	.	.	.	.	.	1	.	39	19	.	3	7	.	.	.	.	
10	Bækkegård 16	.	1	.	.	.	.	.	.	22	.	19	2	.	.	.	.	.	
17	Bækkegård 44	.	.	.	.	.	.	.	.	23	17	.	8	3	.	.	.	.	
46	Lousgård 16	.	.	1	.	.	.	.	16	11	3	30	1	1	.	.	.	.	
39	Bækkegård 157	.	1	.	.	1	.	.	2	6	5	5	.	5	.	.	.	.	
16	Bækkegård 35	.	.	2	.	1	.	1	.	6	10	21	3	.	.	.	.	.	
38	Bækkegård 153	.	.	3	.	.	.	.	1	7	28	9	17	12	.	.	.	.	
6	Bækkegård 3	.	.	1	.	.	.	.	.	9	20	5	.	2	.	.	.	.	
47	Lousgård 18	.	.	1	.	.	1	.	.	10	8	15	1	.	.	.	.	.	
54	Lousgård 9	.	.	.	1	.	.	.	5	2	9	16	2	.	.	.	.	.	
27	Bækkegård 88	.	1	1	.	.	.	.	5	.	42	.	.	.	.	.	.	.	
7	Bækkegård 5	.	.	1	.	.	1	1	27	27	34	.	.	.	.	.	.	.	
24	Bækkegård 76	.	.	.	.	.	2	.	.	5	20	4	1	.	.	.	.	.	
34	Bækkegård 132	.	.	.	.	.	.	.	11	21	12	7	.	3	.	.	.	.	
63	Nr. Sandegård 6	.	.	.	.	.	.	.	1	21	21	29	4	1	1	.	.	.	
18	Bækkegård 50	.	.	1	.	.	.	.	.	17	15	6	.	3	.	.	.	.	
42	Lousgård 6	.	.	.	.	.	.	.	2	9	9	2	.	.	.	.	.	.	B
20	Bækkegård 60	.	.	3	.	.	2	.	.	22	91	2	.	.	.	.	.	.	
43	Lousgård 10	.	.	.	.	.	1	1	1	3	17	22	.	.	.	.	.	.	
21	Bækkegård 62	.	.	.	.	.	.	.	.	13	24	.	1	.	.	.	.	.	
22	Bækkegård 63	.	.	.	.	.	.	.	.	7	37	.	.	.	.	.	.	.	
19	Bækkegård 59	.	.	.	.	.	.	.	.	23	36	5	2	.	.	.	.	.	
23	Bækkegård 66	.	.	.	.	.	.	.	.	10	20	.	3	.	.	.	.	.	
26	Bækkegård 85	.	.	.	.	.	.	.	.	7	19	2	1	.	.	.	.	.	
37	Bækkegård 143	.	.	.	.	.	.	1	.	16	17	.	2	.	.	.	.	.	
25	Bækkegård 77	.	.	1	.	.	.	.	.	10	25	9	1	.	.	.	.	.	
35	Bækkegård 134	.	.	.	.	.	2	1	2	24	16	.	9	.	.	.	.	.	
41	Lousgård 3	.	.	.	.	.	.	.	.	3	7	7	3	.	.	.	.	.	
11	Bækkegård 17	.	.	.	.	.	.	.	.	7	2	24	21	1	.	.	.	.	
29	Bækkegård 93	.	.	1	.	.	.	.	.	19	32	27	7	.	.	.	.	.	
56	Melsted 62	.	.	.	.	.	.	.	.	.	12	10	.	.	.	.	.	.	
5	Bækkegård 2	.	1	2	.	.	1	.	2	6	32	8	1	.	.	.	.	.	
45	Lousgård 12	.	.	1	.	.	.	.	4	4	17	8	4	2	.	.	.	.	
62	Nr. Sandegård 4	.	.	2	.	.	.	.	8	34	29	61	30	.	.	.	.	.	
32	Bækkegård 105	.	.	.	.	.	.	.	.	1	5	5	20	.	.	.	.	.	
44	Lousgård 11	.	.	.	.	.	.	1	.	2	6	.	25	3	.	.	.	.	
67	Ellegård	.	.	1	.	.	.	.	8	11	6	9	3	4	.	.	4	.	
61	Lillevang-Melsted 4	.	1	.	.	.	.	.	8	7	.	12	5	.	.	3	.	.	C
48	Lousgård 28	.	.	2	.	3	.	.	1	5	4	.	2	15	5	1	1	2	
59	Lillevang 2	.	.	.	.	.	.	.	5	3	1	16	.	.	.	1	5	.	
60	Lillevang-Melsted 2	.	.	.	.	.	.	.	6	.	19	.	.	.	.	.	9	9	
66	Saltuna 14	.	.	.	.	.	.	.	.	.	8	1	.	.	.	.	3	11	D
53	Lousgård 47	.	.	.	.	.	.	.	.	7	1	8	.	.	.	.	18	21	

A: opaque orange   E: translucent blue   I: gold foil   M: rock crystal   R: bone
B: opaque red   F: white   J: silver foil   N: wood on bronze
C: dim yellow   G: other monochrome   K: amber   P: bronze
D: green   H: polychrome   L: carnelian   Q: slices of shell

Table 2. Matrix showing counts of 17 different types of beads from strings containing more than 20 beads in 67 graves (the bækkegård cemetery included).

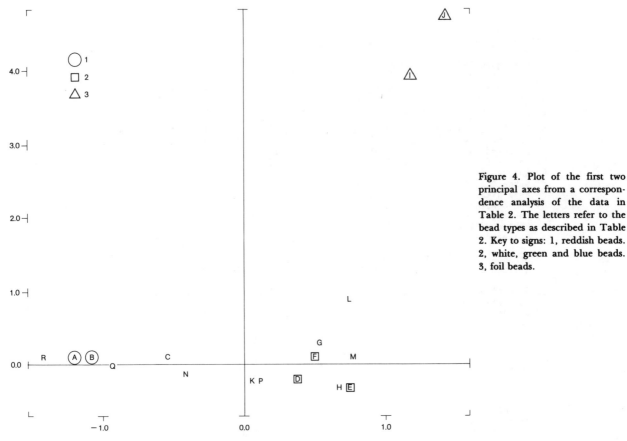

Figure 4. Plot of the first two principal axes from a correspondence analysis of the data in Table 2. The letters refer to the bead types as described in Table 2. Key to signs: 1, reddish beads. 2, white, green and blue beads. 3, foil beads.

to right. The following characteristics apply to the four groups:

R3a A high percentage of orange and red opaque beads.

R3b Polychrome, green and translucent blue beads. White stone-like beads occur rather frequently.

R3c Beads with gold foil and relatively low percentages of polychrome and translucent blue beads. Apart from the beads with silver foil, there is no clear distinction between R3b and R3c.

R3d Beads with gold and silver foil and/or white stone-like beads. Colourless beads were not separated by Vedel, but are probably included in the category 'other monochrome'. Carnelian beads appear for the first time in this group.

The results clearly show that the assumption of a clustering in the combinations of colour in the strings of beads is correct. That the separation of the groups is so clear-cut comes as a surprise, however.

The results also show that the strings of beads can be seriated, although the seriation is not perfect. The

following investigation of the female graves will show whether this seriation - in relation to the other ornaments - is chronological. (Further analyses and information concerning the beads are published in K.H. Nielsen 1988.)

CHRONOLOGICAL INVESTIGATION OF THE FEMALE GRAVES

In the 1880s and 1890s Vedel made the first attempt to establish a chronology of the female graves from Bornholm (Vedel 1886, 1897). In 1966, Ørsnes constructed a more sophisticated chronology for the Late Germanic Iron Age in Denmark and Scania as a whole. My intentions here are to create a local chronology for Bornholm, and to check the results of Ørsnes's investigation. Ørsnes used the combinations of types as a base for his chronology. His actual method is not described in detail, but the results are shown in a two-way matrix. It is important to note that the matrix is not truly sorted using the concentration principle of the values along the main diagonal, as stressed by Robinson (1951) and Kendall (1971 with further references). Rather, it is a graphical presentation of his interpretation. In

```
                                        N M M N Q R N N N R Q N O O N I R I Q K Q K S K D J Q S P G E P E P R R G I G P F H I A E
                                        2 3 3 3 3 2 2 2 3 1 1 2 3 3 3 2 3 1 3 1 1 1   1 2 3 4 3 2 2 2 3 3 1 2 1 1   1 2 1
                                        f     c d c a g c b       e   b     a a d c   b   d           a   b   a       b           a e
 64 Lousgård 29          2 1 . . . . . . . . . . . . . . . . . . . . . . . . . . . . . . . . . . . . . . . . . .
 78 Lillevang 9          2 1 . . . . . . . . . . . . . . . . . . . . . . . . . . . . . . . . . . . . . . . . . .
 83 Lillevang-Melsted 5  2 . 1 . . . . . . . . . . . . . . . . . . . . . . . . . . . . . . . . . . . . . . . . .
 85 Nr. Sandegård u.nr.  2 . . 1 . . . . . . . . . . . . . . . . . . . . . . . . . . . . . . . . . . . . . . . .   G (Vik)
 46 Bækkegård 156        . 1 2 1 . . . . . . . . . . . . . . . . . . . . . . . . . . . . . . . . . . . . . . . .
 73 Kobbeå 20            . 1 . . 1 . . . . . . . . . . . . . . . . . . . . . . . . . . . . . . . . . . . . . . .
 57 Lousgård 28          . . 2 . 1 . . . . . . . . . . . . . . . . . . . . . . . . . . . . . . . . . . . . . . .
 76 Lillevang 1          1 1 . 1 . . . . . . . . . . . . . . . . . . . . . . . . . . . . . . . . . . . . . . . .
 65 Lousgård 47          . . . 1 1 2 . . . 1 . . . . . . . . . . . . . . . . . . . . . . . . . . . . . . . . . .
 92 Saltuna 14           . . . 2 1 . 2 . . . 2 . . . . . . . . . . . . . . . . . . . . . . . . . . . . . . . . .
 81 Lillevang-Melsted 2  . . . 1 2 . . . 2 . . . . . . . . . . . . . . . . . . . . . . . . . . . . . . . . . . .   F2 (2C)
 77 Lillevang 2          . . . 1 1 . 1 1 . . . . . . . . . . . . . 1 . . . . . . . . . . . . . . . . . . . . . .
 36 Bækkegård 105        . . . 1 . . 1 . . . . . 1 . . . . . . . . . . . . . . . . . . . . . . . . . . . . . . .
 54 Lousgård 12          . . . 1 . . . 1 2 1 . . 1 . . . . . . . . . . . . . . . . . . . . . . . . . . . . . . .
 82 Lillevang-Melsted 4  . . . . . . . 1 1 1 1 . . . . . . . . . . . . . . . . . . . . . . . . . . . . . . . . .   F1 (2B)
  4 Gudhjem              . . . . . . . 1 . . 1 . . . . . . . . . . . . . . . . . . . . . . . . . . . . . . . . .
 93 Ellegård             . . . . . . 1 2 1 . 2 . . . . . . . . . . . . . . . . . . . . . . . . . . . . . . . . .
 20 Bækkegård 44         . . . 1 . . . . . . . 2 . 1 1 . . . . . . . . . . . . . . . . . . . . . . . . . . . . .
 40 Bækkegård 132        . . . . . . . 1 . . 1 . . . . . . . . . . . . . . . . . . . . . . . . . . . . . . . . .
  2 St. Kannikegård 195  . . . . . . . 1 1 . . 1 . . . . . . . . . . . . . . . . . . . . . . . . . . . . . . . .
 22 Bækkegård 59         . . . . . . . 1 1 1 . . 1 . . . . . . . . . . . . . . . . . . . . . . . . . . . . . . .
 24 Bækkegård 66         . . . . . . . . 1 . . 1 . . . . . . . . . . . . . . . . . . . . . . . . . . . . . . . .
 51 Lousgård 6           . . . . . . . . 1 1 . 1 . . . . . . . . . . . . . . . . . . . . . . . . . . . . . . . .
 50 Lousgård 3           . . . . . . . . 2 . . 1 . . . . . . . . . . . . . . . . . . . . . . . . . . . . . . . .   E (2A)
 87 Nr. Sandegård 6      . . . . . . . . 2 . . 1 . . . . . . . . . . . . . . . . . . . . . . . . . . . . . . . .
 44 Bækkegård 153        . . . . . . 1 . . 2 1 1 . . . . 1 . . . . . . . . . . . . . . . . . . . . . . . . . . .
 53 Lousgård 11          . . . . . . . . 1 . 1 . . . . 1 . . . . . . . . . . . . . . . . . . . . . . . . . . . .
 43 Bækkegård 143        . . . . . . . . 1 2 1 . . . . . . . . . . . . . . . . . . . . . . . . . . . . . . . . .
  8 Bækkegård 3          . . . . . . . . 1 1 1 . . . . . . . . . . . . . . . . . . . . . . . . . . . . . . . . .
  9 Bækkegård 5          . . . . . . . . 1 . 1 2 . . . . . . . . . . . . . . . . . . . . . . . . . . . . . . . .
 27 Bækkegård 77         . . . . . . . . 1 2 1 1 . . . . 1 . . . . . . . . . . . . . . . . . . . . . . . . . . .
 21 Bækkegård 50         . . . . . . . . 1 1 . . 2 . . . . . . . . . . . . . . . . . . . . . . . . . . . . . . .
 86 Nr. Sandegård 4      . . . . . . 2 . . 2 1 . . . . . . 1 . . . . 1 1 . . . 1 . . . 1 . . . . . . . . . . . .
 55 Lousgård 16          . . . . . . . . 1 . . . . . 1 1 1 . . . . . . . . . . . . . . . . . . . . . . . . . . .
 69 Melsted b2           . . . . . . . . 1 . . . . . . . . . . . . . . . 1 . . . . . . . . . . . . . . . . . . .
 26 Bækkegård 76         . . . . . . . . 1 1 . . . . . . . . . . . . . . 2 . . . . . . . . . . . . . . . . . . .
 56 Lousgård 18          . . . . . . . . 1 . . . . 1 1 . 1 1 . 1 . 1 . . . . . . . . . . . . . . . . . . . . . .
 28 Bækkegård 88         . . . . . . . . 1 . . . . . . 2 . . . . 1 . . . . . . . . . . . . . . . . . . . . . . .
  7 Bækkegård 2          . . . . . . . . 1 . . . . . . . . . 1 . . 1 . . . . . . . . . . . . . . . . . . . . . .
 13 Bækkegård 17         . . . . . . . . 1 . . . . . . . . . 1 . . . . . . 1 . . . . . . . . . . . . . . . . . .
 38 Bækkegård 109        . . . . . . . . 1 . . . . 1 . 1 . . 1 . 1 . . . . . . . . . . . . . . . . . . . . . . .
 52 Lousgård 10          . . . . . . . . 1 . . . . . . . . . 1 . 1 . 1 . . . . . . . . . . . . . . . . . . . . .
 31 Bækkegård 93         . . . . . . . . 1 . . . . . . . . . 1 . . 1 1 1 . . . . . . . . . . . . . . . . . . . .
 42 Bækkegård 141        . . . . . . . . 1 . . . . . . . . . 1 . . . 1 . . 1 . . . . . . . . . . . . . . . . . .   D (1D)
 10 Bækkegård 11         . . . . . . . . 1 . . . . . . . . . 1 . . . . 2 . . . . . . . . . . . . . . . . . . . .
 12 Bækkegård 16         . . . . . . . . 1 . . . . . . . . . . 1 . 1 1 1 1 . . . . . . . . . . . . . . . . . . .
 47 Bækkegård 157        . . . . . . . . 1 . . . . . . . . . 2 . 2 . 1 1 . . 1 . . . . . . . . . . . . . . . . .
 48 Bækkegård 163        . . . . . . . . 1 . . . . . . . . . . . . 1 . . . . . . . . . . . . . . . . . . . . . .
 65 Lousgård 9           . . . . . . . . 1 . . . 1 . 1 . 1 . . . . 2 . . . . . . . . . . . . . . . . . . . . . .
 29 Bækkegård 89         . . . . . . . . . . . 1 . . . . . . . . . . 2 . . . . . . . . . . . . . . . . . . . . .
 37 Bækkegård 106        . . . . . . . . . . . . . . . . . . . . 1 . 1 1 . . . . . . . . . . . . . . . . . . . .
 14 Bækkegård 20         . . . . . . . . . . . . . . . . . . . . . . 1 . 1 1 . . . . . . . . . . . . . . . . . . .
 39 Bækkegård 112        . . . . . . . . . . . . . . . . . . 1 . 2 . 1 1 1 1 . 1 1 . 1 . . . . . . . . . . . . .
 23 Bækkegård 60         . . . . . . . . . . 1 . . . . . . . . . . . . . . 1 . . . . . . . . . . . . . . . . . . .
 11 Bækkegård 14         . . . . . . . . . . . . . . . . . . . . 1 . 1 2 1 . . . . . 1 . . . . . . . . . . . . .
 19 Bækkegård 35         . . . . . . . . . . 1 . . . . . . . . . 1 . 1 . . 1 1 . . . . 1 . . . . . . . 1 . . . .
 17 Bækkegård 26         . . . . . . . . . . . . . . . . . . . . 1 . 2 . . . 1 . . . 1 . 1 . . . . . . . . . . .
 33 Bækkegård 95         . . . . . . . . . . . . . . . . . . . . . . 1 1 1 . . . . . 1 . . . . . . . . . . . . .
 61 Lousgård 39          . . . . . . . . . . . . . . . . . . . . . . 1 . . . 1 . . . . 1 . . . . . . . . . . . .
 30 Bækkegård 90         . . . . . . . . . . . . . . . . . . . . . . 1 . . 1 . . . . 1 . . . . . . . . . . . . .   C (1C)
 35 Bækkegård 104        . . . . . . . . . . . . . . . . . . . . . . 1 . . 1 . . . . 1 . . . . . . . . . . . . .
 25 Bækkegård 74         . . . . . . . . . . . . . . . . . . . . . . 1 . . . 1 . . . . 1 . . . . . . . . . . . .
 32 Bækkegård 94         . . . . . . . . . . . . . . . . . . . . . . 2 . . . 1 . 1 . . . . . . . . . . . . . . .
 71 Kobbeå 33            . . . . . . . . . . . . . . . . . . . . . . 1 . . . . . 1 . 1 . . . . . . . . . . . . .
 16 Bækkegård 24         . . . . . . . . . . . . . . . . . . . . . . 1 . . . 1 . 1 . 1 . . . . . . . . . . . . .
 89 Nr. Sandegård 426    . . . . . . . . . . . . . . . . . . . . . . 1 . . . 1 1 2 1 . . . . . . . . . . . . . .
  3 Nexø Nymølle 2       . . . . . . . . . . . . . . . . . . . . . . . . . . 1 1 . . . . . . . . . . . . . . . .
 34 Bækkegård 103        . . . . . . . . . . . . . . . . . . . . . . . 1 . . 1 1 . . . . . . . . . . . . . . . .
 41 Bækkegård 139        . . . . . . . . . . . . . . . . . . . . . . . 1 . . . . . 2 . . . . . . . . . . . . . .
 70 Kobbeå 2             . . . . . . . . . . . . . . . . . . . . . . . . . 1 . . . 1 1 . 1 1 . . . . . . . . . .
 58 Lousgård 35          . . . . . . . . . . . . . . . . . . . . . . . 1 . . 1 2 3 . 2 . . . . . . . . . . . . .
 74 Kobbeå 6             . . . . . . . . . . . . . . . . . . . . . . . . . 1 . . 1 2 . 1 . . . . . . . . . . . .
 91 Saltuna 10           . . . . . . . . . . . . . . . . . . . . . . . 1 . . . . . 1 . 1 . . . . . . . . . . . .
  1 Gudmingegård         . . . . . . . . . . . . . . . . . . . . . . . . . . 1 . 2 . . . . . . . . . . . . . . .   B (1B)
 15 Bækkegård 23         . . . . . . . . . . . . . . . . . . . . . . . . . . 1 . 2 . . . . . . . . . . . . . . .
 18 Bækkegård 30         . . . . . . . . . . . . . . . . . . . . . . . . . . 1 1 . . . 1 . . . . . . . . . . . .
 62 Lousgård 40          . . . . . . . . . . . . . . . . . . . . . . . . . . 1 2 1 1 . 1 . . . . . . . . . . . .
 60 Lousgård 36          . . . . . . . . . . . . . . . . . . . . . . . . . . 1 2 2 1 . 1 . . . . . . . . . . . .
 59 Lousgård 37          . . . . . . . . . . . . . . . . . . . . . . . . . . 1 . . 1 1 . . . . . . . . . . . . .
 67 Melsted 15           . . . . . . . . . . . . . . . . . . . . . . . . . . 1 . 1 . 2 . . . . . . . . . . . . .
 88 Nr. Sandegård 397    . . . . . . . . . . . . . . . . . . . . . . . . . . 1 2 3 . 2 . . . . . . . . . . . . .
 84 Lensgård             . . . . . . . . . . . . . . . . . . . . . . . . . . 1 . 2 . . . . . . . . . . . . . . .
 90 Gryet                . . . . . . . . . . . . . . . . . . . . . . . . . . 1 . 1 . . . . . . . . . . . . . . .
 49 Knarregård 1         . . . . . . . . . . . . . . . . . . . . . . . . . . 1 . 1 . 1 1 . . . 1 . . . . . . . .
 80 Melsted-Kobbeå 9     . . . . . . . . . . . . . . . . . . . . . . . . . . 1 . . 1 1 . . . . . . . . . . . . .
 45 Bækkegård 155        . . . . . . . . . . . . . . . . . . . . . . . . . . 1 . . . 1 . . . 1 . . . . . . . . .
 72 Kobbeå 4             . . . . . . . . . . . . . . . . . . . . . . . . . . . . . . 1 3 . . . . . . . . . . . .
 68 Melsted 13           . . . . . . . . . . . . . . . . . . . . . . . . . . 1 . . . . 2 . . . . . . . . . . . .
 79 Lillevang b2         . . . . . . . . . . . . . . . . . . . . . . . . . . . . . . 2 1 . . . 1 . . . . A (1A)
 75 Kobbeå 11            . . . . . . . . . . . . . . . . . . . . . . . 1 . . . . . . . . . . . . 2 . 1 1
  6 Møllebakken 2        . . . . . . . . . . . . . . . . . . . . . . . . . . . . . . . . 1 2 . 1 . 1 3
  5 Møllebakken 1        . . . . . . . . . . . . . . . . . . . . . . . . . . . . . . . . . . . . 2 . . 2
 66 Melsted 8            . . . . . . . . . . . . . . . . . . . . . . . . . . . . . . . . . 1 1 1 3
```

Table 3. Matrix showing counts of 44 types of ornaments in 93 female graves from Bornholm. The types are described in the text.

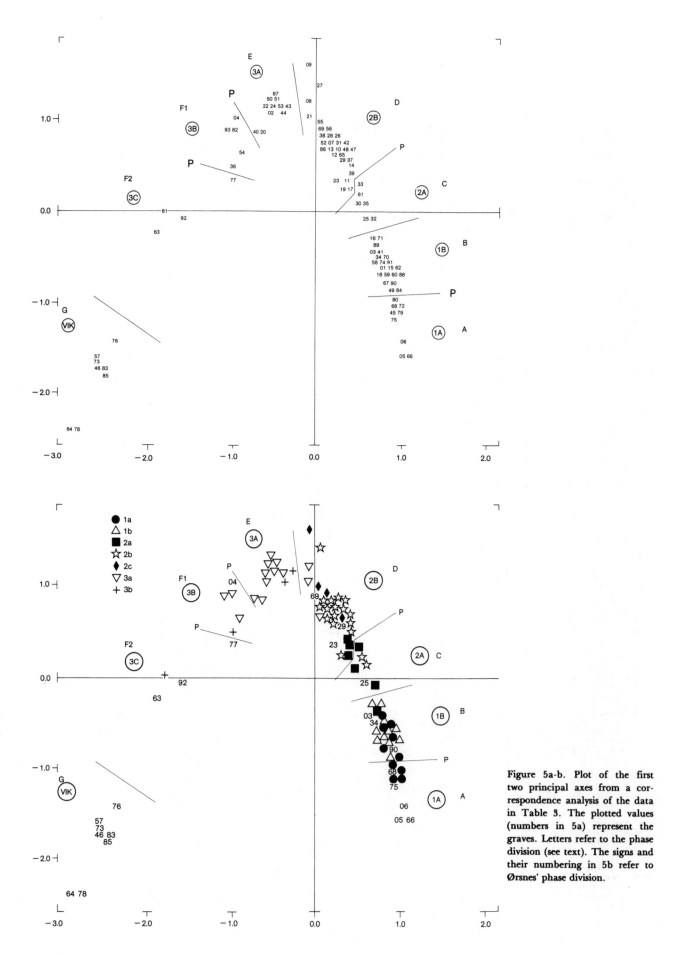

Figure 5a-b. Plot of the first two principal axes from a correspondence analysis of the data in Table 3. The plotted values (numbers in 5a) represent the graves. Letters refer to the phase division (see text). The signs and their numbering in 5b refer to Ørsnes' phase division.

44

each chronological phase, the types are placed in alphabetical order, and not in the order in which they are introduced. This way of presenting the matrix makes the clustering tendency more pronounced than it really is.

In order to reveal the degree of clustering versus the degree of seriation in the graves and at the same time to evaluate Vedel's (1886; 1897) and Ørsnes's (1966) chronological systems, I have carried out two correspondence analyses, one for the female graves of Bornholm, and one for the graves listed by Ørsnes in his two-way matrix.

To form a coherent picture of the chronological change through the use of a correspondence analysis or other seriation methods, one has to be careful with the inclusion of variables. Types that are not chronologically significant as well as types with too low a frequency should be avoided. Furthermore, only graves that show combinations of types can be used in the analysis. Thus in the classification one has to choose a level where there is close similarity to be found between the graves, but the level should not be so general that all become alike. In the present case, 93 graves have been accepted, and the chosen variables are 44 in number (Table 3).

In the graphical representation of the first two principal axes of the analysis of female graves from Bornholm (Figures 5 and 6) the points clearly follow a parabola, almost without any clustering. Indeed, if you want a chronological division you have to impose it. I have chosen to do this, but it should be considered only as a frame of reference.

If we reorder the data matrix so that the sequence of graves and types follows the order of the parabola from right to left, we find that the linear order of the matrix is very evident (Table 3).

The stages, which are defined with special reference to the groupings of the strings of beads (being the most frequent types), will be described in the following according to the order of the types in the reordered matrix.

Stage A (1A): This stage is characterised by square-headed bow brooches (E1), circular disc brooches (I1a), circular buckles (A2e), and small equal-armed fibulae (F). Fewer in number are pins with simple heads (P1) and beaked brooches (G1). This stage represents the transition from the Early to the Late Germanic Iron Age.

Stage B (1B): This stage is characterised by pins with simple heads (P1), beaked brooches (G1 and G2), circular disc brooches (I1b), bead suspensions (R1), and strings of beads (R3a). To these can be

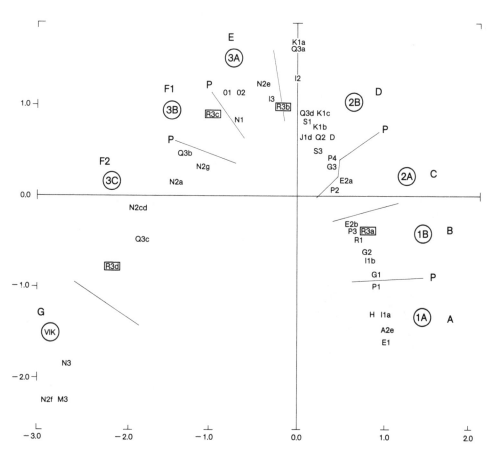

Figure 6. Plot of the first two principal axes from a correspondence analysis of the data in Table 3. The plotted values represent the ornament types. The major lettering refers to the phase division (see text). The minor lettering refers to the ornament types (see text).

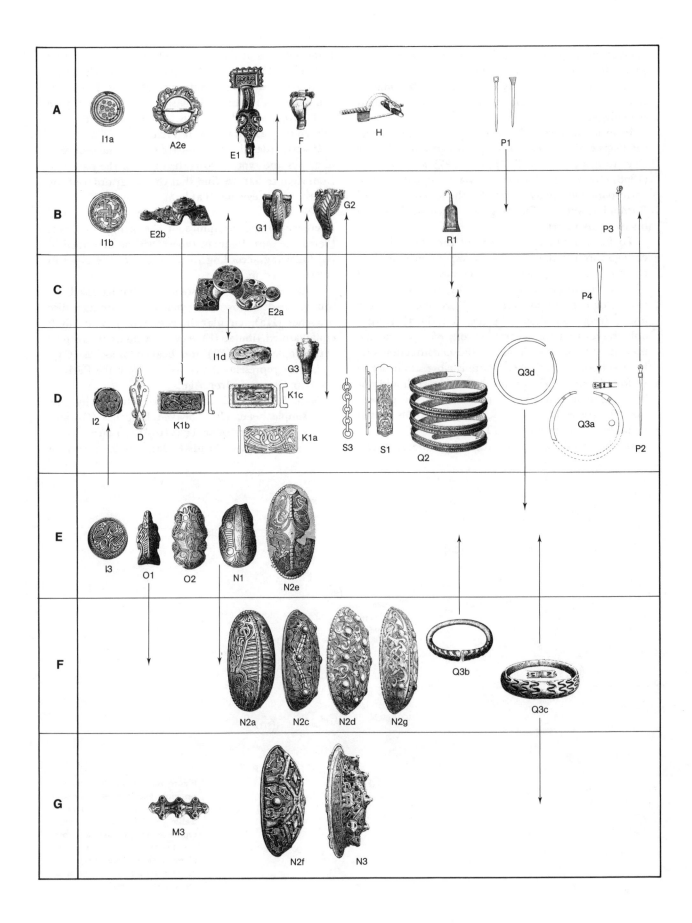

Figure 7. Table of the chronological relationship between the analysed ornament types.

added a few more sporadic types. The combination of G2/I1b/R1 and R3a is especially characteristic of this stage.

Stage C (1C): This stage is characterised by strings of beads (R3a) and simple pins (often made of iron) (P4). The combination of the types R3a and P4 is important.

Stage D (1D): This stage is characterised by pins with composite heads (P2), simple pins (P4), beaked brooches (G3), spiral bracelets (Q2), chains (S3), bird-shaped fibulae (D), bead spacers or discs to sew onto the clothes (S1), circular disc brooches (I2-3), rectangular disc brooches (K1b-c), simple arm-bands (Q3d), and strings of beads (R3b). Most characteristic is R3b in combination with D, S1, K1b-c and perhaps Q3d.

Stage E (2A): This stage is characterised by strings of beads (R3b), circular disc brooches (I3), animal-shaped bowl brooches (O2), and small tortoise brooches (N1 and N2e). The combination of R3b with I3, O1-2, N1 and N2e is especially characteristic of this stage.

Stage F (2 B-C): This stage can be divided into two. The characteristic features of F1 are strings of beads (R3c) in combination with animal-shaped bowl brooches (O1 and O2) or small tortoise brooches (N1). For F2 it is strings of beads (R3d) in combination with tortoise brooches of medium size (N2a, c-d) that are the characteristic forms. Arm-bands (Q3b and Q3c) are known from both.

Stage G (Viking): The arm-bands (Q3c) are still found, but most characteristic of this stage are large tortoise brooches (N3), equal-armed brooches (M3) and medium-sized tortoise brooches (N2f). Two tortoise brooches are often found in combination with an equal-armed brooch. This stage is of exclusively Viking date.

The stages can be illustrated as in Figure 7. Special attention should be paid to stage F, because it includes types of both traditional Late Germanic Iron Age and traditional Viking Age. This shows that a marked borderline between the Late Germanic Iron Age and the Viking Age cannot be maintained. There is clearly a gradual transition between the two periods. (Further information concerning the graves is published in K.H. Nielsen 1988.)

As can be seen from Table 3, the strings of beads show clear chronological significance. This answers one of the questions raised by the isolated analysis of the beads.

EVALUATION OF FORMER CHRONOLOGICAL SYSTEMS

The next issue was to check the results of Ørsnes's investigation, and we may here start by testing his published matrix representation (Ørsnes 1966:14-

15). This can be done by means of a correspondence analysis using his ornaments and graves. A few ornaments and graves have to be omitted, because of far too low frequencies. The remaining ornaments and graves are shown in the data matrix Table 4. The plot of the first two principal axes of the analysis is seen in Figures 8 and 9. Once more the result is a distinct parabola despite the fact that the graves come from all over Denmark and Scania.

Ørsnes divided his material into three main chronological stages. The graves that Ørsnes placed in each of his stages are shown in Figure 10. The chronological order is clear, although there are some problems with the transition from stage 1 to stage 2. In general we can thus rely on Ørsnes's main stages.

We can now turn to the sub-stages of Ørsnes's chronological system, and investigate how far these are reliable. Figure 11, where the sub-stages are marked with regard to the graves, does not show a clear-cut picture. The sub-stages of stages 1 and 3 are evidently problematic, whereas in stage 2 they seem more reliable. Ørsnes himself pointed out that his subdivision of stage 1 might have a social and not chronological cause. The results here bear this out since the graves from his two sub-stages (1a and 1b) run parallel to each other in the parabola. With respect to stage 3, the problem seems to be that I use a subdivision of N2 in the analysis, something that Ørsnes did not do. Thus we can still rely on Ørsnes's main stages, but not to the same degree on his sub-stages.

A comparison between Ørsnes's results and those achieved here from Bornholm shows that it is immediately possible to correlate the two chronological systems. Roughly, the stages A-B correspond to the later part of the Early Germanic Iron Age and Ørsnes's stage 1, C-D correspond to stage 2, E-F correspond to stage 3, and G corresponds to the Viking Age.

With respect to the sub-stages, there is not the same accordance. My division between stages A and B does *not* correspond to that of Ørsnes 1a and 1b. The partition of stage 2 into a-b-c partly corresponds to my stages C and D, in the sense that 2c is clearly later than 2a, but 2b overlaps both of them. Nevertheless, there are quite substantial deviations. In stage 3, the partition into a and b does not quite correspond with my stages E and F. Stages E and F1 agree fairly well with stage 3a, but both in stage E and stage F1 graves are found which Ørsnes relates to stage 3b.

The transition between the Early Germanic Iron Age and stage 1 (A-B of my chronological system) is gradual, whereas Ørsnes assumed a break between the two periods. The transition to the Viking Age can be clearly distinguished in my investigations, but this may be due to the very few finds included.

```
                              N R N Q R N Q O O N I R K Q I K K H Q J S D Q S P P G E P R R E G I G F P I A
                              2 3 2 3 3 1 3 1 2 2 3 3 3 1 3 2 1 1   3 1 1   2 3 2 4 3 2 3 3 1 2 2 1 1   1 1 2   3 3   2 2 2   1 1
                              c d a b c   c     e   b a a   c b   d d                     a   a b   b       a e   b a   c b a   b a
 70 Tranekær                  1 . 1 . . . . . . . . . . . . . . . . . . . . . . . . . . . . . . . . . . . .   *
 61 Lillevang-Melsted 2       2 1 . 2 . . . . . . . . . . . . . . . . . . . . . . . . . . . . . . . . . . .   *
 62 Lillevang-Melsted 4       . . . 1 1 . 1 1 . . . . . . . . . . . . . . . . . . . . . . . . . . . . . . .     *
 69 Ellegård                  . . . 2 1 . 1 . 2 . . . . . . . . . . . . . . . . . . . . . . . . . . . . . .     *
 28 Bækkegård 105             . . 1 . 1 2 . . . . 1 . . . . . . . . . . . . . . . . . . . . . . . . . . . .   *
 32 Bækkegård 132             . . . 1 . . . . . . 1 . . . . . . . . . . . . . . . . . . . . . . . . . . . .     *
 45 Lousgård 12               . . . 1 . 1 2 1 . . 1 . . . . . . . . . . . . . . . . . . . . . . . . . . . .     *
 18 Bækkegård 59              . . . . 1 1 1 . . . 1 . . . . . . . . . . . . . . . . . . . . . . . . . . . .     *
  2 St. Kannikegård 195       . . . . . 1 1 . . . 1 . . . . . . . . . . . . . . . . . . . . . . . . . . . .     *
 42 Lousgård 6                . . . . . 1 1 . . . 1 . . . . . . . . . . . . . . . . . . . . . . . . . . . .     *
 16 Bækkegård 44              . . . . 1 . . 2 . 1 1 . . . . . . . . . . . . . . . . . . . . . . . . . . . .     *
 41 Lousgård 3                . . . . . . . 2 . . 1 . . . . . . . . . . . . . . . . . . . . . . . . . . . .     *
 65 Nr. Sandegård 6           . . . . . . . 2 . . 1 . . . . . . . . . . . . . . . . . . . . . . . . . . . .     *
 19 Bækkegård 66              . . . . . 1 . . 1 . 1 . . . . . . . . . . . . . . . . . . . . . . . . . . . .     *
 44 Lousgård 11               . . . . . 1 . 1 2 . 1 . . . . . . . . . . . . . . . . . . . . . . . . . . . .     *
 36 Bækkegård 153             . . 1 . . . 2 1 1 . . . 1 . . . . . . . . . . . . . . . . . . . . . . . . .   *
 35 Bækkegård 143             . . . . . 1 2 1 . . . . . . . . . . . . . . . . . . . . . . . . . . . . . .     *
  4 Bækkegård 3               . . . . . 1 1 . 1 . 1 . . . . . . . . . . . . . . . . . . . . . . . . . . . .       *
 17 Bækkegård 50              . . . . . 1 1 . . . . 2 . . . . . . . . . . . . . . . . . . . . . . . . . . .       *
 64 Nr. Sandegård 4           . . . . . 2 . . 2 1 . . . . 1 . 1 1 1 . . . . . . 1 . . . . . . . . . . . . .       *
  5 Bækkegård 5               . . . . . . 1 2 1 . . . . . . . . . . . . . . . . . . . . . . . . . . . . . .         *
 21 Bækkegård 77              . . . . . . 1 1 1 2 . . . . . . . . 1 . . . . . . . . . . . . . . . . . . . .           *
 46 Lousgård 16               . . . . . 1 . . 1 . 1 . . . . . 1 . . . . . . . . . . . . . . . . . . . . . .           *
 20 Bækkegård 76              . . . . . 1 . 1 . . . . . 1 . . . 2 . . . . . . . . . . . . . . . . . . . . .               *
 30 Bækkegård 109             . . . . . 1 . . . . 1 . 1 1 . . . . 1 . . . . . . . . . . . . . . . . . . . .                 *
  3 Bækkegård 2               . . . . . 1 . . . 1 . . . . . . . 1 . . . . . . . . . . . . . . . . . . . . .               *
  9 Bækkegård 17              . . . . . 1 . . . 1 . . . . . . . 1 . . . . . . . . . . . . . . . . . . . . .                 *
 43 Lousgård 10               . . . . . 1 . . . . 1 . . 1 . 1 . . 1 . . . . . . . . . . . . . . . . . . . .                   *
 34 Bækkegård 141             . . . . . 1 . . . . 1 . . 2 . . 1 . . . . . . . . . . . . . . . . . . . . . .                   *
 22 Bækkegård 88              . . . . . 1 . . . . . . . 2 . 1 . . . . . . . . . . . . . . . . . . . . . . .                     *
 53 Lousgård 9                . . . . . 1 . . 1 1 . . . . 1 . . 1 2 . . . . . . . . . . . . . . . . . . . .           *
 15 Bækkegård 35              . . . . . 1 . . 1 1 . . . 1 . . 1 1 . . . . . . . . . . . . . . . . . . . . .           *
 47 Lousgård 18               . . . . . 1 . 1 1 . 1 . . 1 1 . . . . . . . . . . . . . . . . . . . . . . . .           *
 24 Bækkegård 93              . . . . . 1 . . 1 . . . . 1 1 . 1 . . . . . . . . . . . . . . . . . . . . . .               *
  6 Bækkegård 11              . . . . . 1 . . . . . . . 1 1 1 . 2 . . . . . . . . . . . . . . . . . . . . .               *
  8 Bækkegård 16              . . . . . 1 . . . . . . . 1 1 1 1 . . . . . . . . . . . . . . . . . . . . . .               *
 38 Bækkegård 157             . . . . . 1 . . . . 1 . . 2 2 1 1 . . 1 . . . . . . . . . . . . . . . . . . .               *
 39 Bækkegård 163             . . . . . . . . . 1 . . . 1 . . . 1 . . . . . . . . . . . . . . . . . . . . .               *
 29 Bækkegård 106             . . . . . . . . . . . . . 1 1 1 . . . . . . . . . . . . . . . . . . . . . . .               *
 72 Bodarp 9                  . . . . . . . . . . . . . 1 . . . 1 . . . . . . . . . . . . . . . . . . . . .               *
 10 Bækkegård 20              . . . . . . . . . . . . . 1 2 1 1 1 1 . 1 . . . . . . . . . . . . . . . . . .                 *
 31 Bækkegård 112             . . . . . . . . . . . . . 1 1 1 1 . 1 1 . 1 . . . . . . . . . . . . . . . . .                 *
  7 Bækkegård 14              . . . . . . . . . . . . 1 . . . 1 2 1 . 1 . . . . . . . . . . . . . . . . . .                   *
 26 Bækkegård 95              . . . . . . . . . . . . . 1 1 . 1 . . 1 . . . . . . . . . . . . . . . . . . .                     *
 73 Ørby Mark                 . . . . . . . . . . . . . . 2 . . . 1 . 1 1 . . . . . . . . . . . . . . . . .                     *
 13 Bækkegård 26              . . . . . . . . . 1 . . 2 . . . 1 . . 1 . 1 . . . . . . . . . . . . . . . . .                 *
 51 Lousgård 39               . . . . . . . . . . . . . . . . 1 . . . 1 1 . . . . . . . . . . . . . . . . .                   *
 23 Bækkegård 90              . . . . . . . . . . . . . . . . . . 1 . 1 1 . . . . . . . . . . . . . . . . .                     *
 27 Bækkegård 104             . . . . . . . . . . . . . . . . . 1 . 1 1 . . . . . . . . . . . . . . . . . .                     *
 71 Kyndby I                  . . . . . . . . . . . . 1 1 . . 1 1 1 2 . . . . . . . . . . . . . . . . . . .                     *
 25 Bækkegård 94              . . . . . . . . . . . . . . . . 2 . . 1 . 1 . . . . . . . . . . . . . . . . .                       *
 76 Jeppeshøje B              . . . . . . . . . . . . . . . . 2 . . . . 1 . . . . . . . . . . . . . . . . .                         *
 67 Nr. Sandegård 426         . . . . . . . . . . . . . . . . 1 . 1 1 2 1 . . . . . . . . . . . . . . . . .                           *
 56 Kobbeå 33                 . . . . . . . . . . . . . . . . 1 . . 1 . 1 . . . . . . . . . . . . . . . . .                           *
 12 Bækkegård 24              . . . . . . . . . . . . . . . . 1 . . 1 . . . 1 . . . . . . . . . . . . . . .                             *
 33 Bækkegård 139             . . . . . . . . . . . . . . . . 1 . . . 2 . . . . . . . . . . . . . . . . . .                             *
 55 Kobbeå 2                  . . . . . . . . . . . . . . . . . 1 . 1 1 . . 1 1 . . . . . . . . . . . . . .                             *
 58 Kobbeå 6                  . . . . . . . . . . . . . . . . 1 . . 1 . 2 . . 1 . . . . . . . . . . . . . .                             *
 68 Saltuna 10                . . . . . . . . . . . . . . . . 1 . . . . . . 1 1 . . . . . . . . . . . . . .                             *
 48 Lousgård 35               . . . . . . . . . . . . . . . . 1 . . 1 2 1 1 . . 2 . . . . . . . . . . . . .                               *
 75 Jeppeshøje A              . . . . . . . . . . 1 . . . . . . . . . . . . 2 2 . . . . . . . . . . . . . .                               *
  1 Gudmingegård              . . . . . . . . . . . . . . . . 1 . 2 . . . . . . . . . . . . . . . . . . . .                               *
 11 Bækkegård 23              . . . . . . . . . . . . . . . . 1 . 2 . . . . . . . . . . . . . . . . . . . .                                 *
 14 Bækkegård 30              . . . . . . . . . . . . . . . . 1 1 . . 1 . . . . . . . . . . . . . . . . . .                                 *
 50 Lousgård 36               . . . . . . . . . . . . . . . . 1 . 2 1 . 1 . . . . . . . . . . . . . . . . .                                 *
 52 Lousgård 40               . . . . . . . . . . . . . . . . 1 2 1 1 1 . . 1 . . . . . . . . . . . . . . .                                 *
 66 Nr. Sandegård 397         . . . . . . . . . . . . . . . . 1 2 . 3 . . . 2 . . . . . . . . . . . . . . .                                   *
 54 Melsted 15                . . . . . . . . . . . . . . . . 1 . . 1 2 . . . . . . . . . . . . . . . . . .                                 *
 74 Øster Tørslev 8           . . . . . . . . . . . . . . . . 1 . . . . . . . . 1 . . . . . . . . . . . . .                                 *
 40 Knarregård 1              . . . . . . . . . . . . . . . . . . 1 . 1 . 1 1 . . . . . . . . . . . . . . .                                   *
 49 Lousgård 37               . . . . . . . . . . . . . . . . . . 1 . . 1 . . . . . . . . . . . . . . . . .                                   *
 63 Lensgård                  . . . . . . . . . . . . . . . . . . 1 . 2 . . . . . . . . . . . . . . . . . .                                   *
 37 Bækkegård 155             . . . . . . . . . . . . . . . . . . 1 . . . 1 . . . . . . . . . . . . . . . .                                   *
 60 Melsted 9                 . . . . . . . . . . . . . . . . . . 1 . . 1 1 . . . . . . . . . . . . . . . .                                   *
 77 Jeppeshøje D              . . . . . . . . . . . . . . . . . . . 3 2 . . . . . . . . . . . . . . . . . .                                   *
 59 Lillevang B2              . . . . . . . . . . . . . . . . . . 2 . 1 . 1 . . . . . . . . . . . . . . . .                                   *
 57 Kobbeå 4                  . . . . . . . . . . . . . . . . . . 3 1 . . . . . . . . . . . . . . . . . . .                                   *
```

Table 4. Matrix showing counts of 39 types of ornaments in 77 female graves. Data after Ørsnes 1966. The right hand addition shows the datings according to Ørsnes.

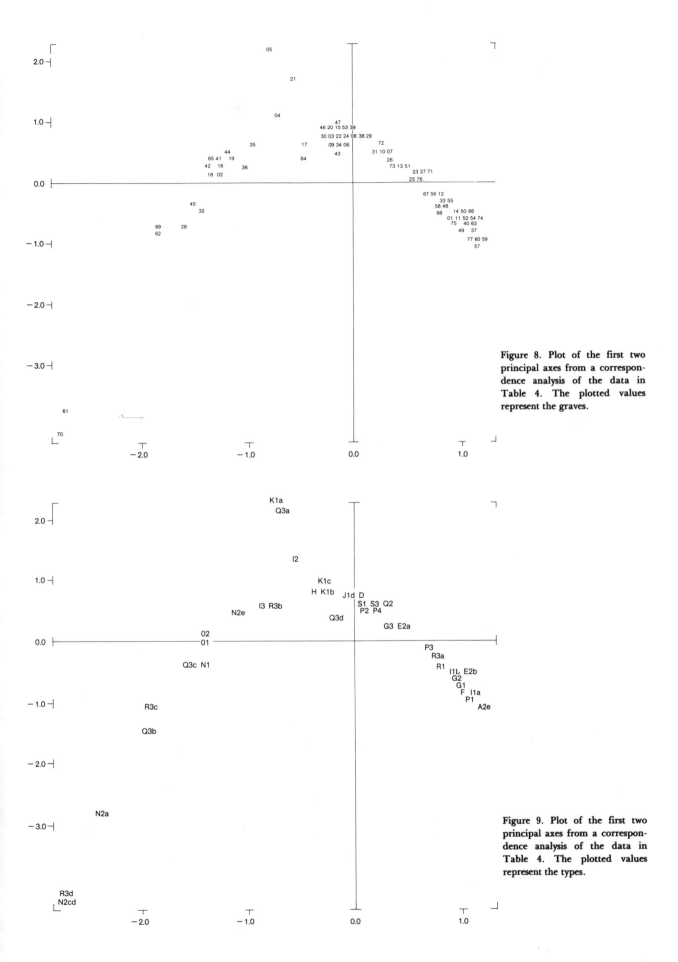

Figure 8. Plot of the first two principal axes from a correspondence analysis of the data in Table 4. The plotted values represent the graves.

Figure 9. Plot of the first two principal axes from a correspondence analysis of the data in Table 4. The plotted values represent the types.

49

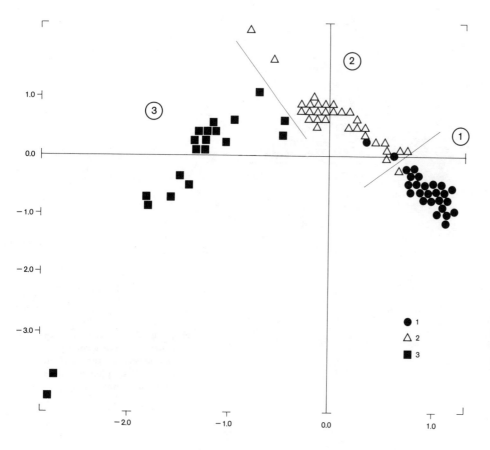

Figure 10. The same plot as in Figure 8 with the graves marked according to Ørsnes' main phase division.

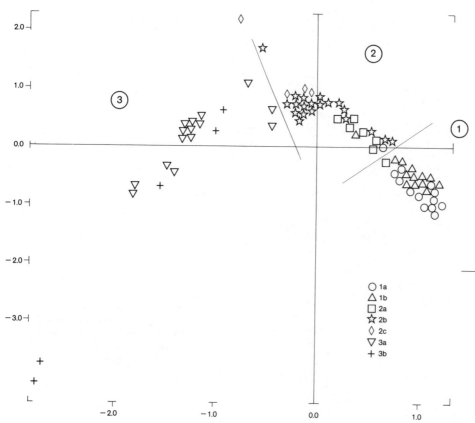

Figure 11. The same plot as in Figure 8 with the graves marked according to Ørsnes' sub-phase division.

The two chronological systems agree fairly well with each other. Ørsnes's system was made at a time when multivariate numerical analyses were not used in chronological investigations, and thus a greater margin of mistakes in the sorting of the type combinations has to be accepted.

The conclusion is that Ørsnes's partition into main stages can be trusted, but an alternative partition into sub-stages might prove more useful. Ørsnes's sub-stages do not seem to be purely chronological. Rather they may partly have a social or perhaps spatial background.

Vedel's dating of the graves was phrased in terms of styles: Germanic style, Irish style, and Carolingian style respectively. It turns out that his dating also agrees well with the results of the correspondence analysis. Germanic style corresponds to stages A, B, C, and the beginning of stage D, Irish style to the late part of stage D and stages E and F, and Carolingian style corresponds to stage G.

THE BRACTEATES

The previous analyses have all been performed on material in connection with which we had an a priori idea of the result. In the following I shall investigate the gold bracteates from Jutland using the combination of types. There is no agreement here as to what the result should be.

The bracteate finds are generally rather special in character. They contain only a very few items apart from the bracteates, and furthermore these are types not normally known from other groups of finds in Denmark. In Norway these types are found in graves, but a usable chronology cannot be produced from them.

In the following, I shall investigate those Jutish hoards that contain two or more bracteates, using a correspondence analysis (Table 5). In this way it should be possible to see whether the finds can be seriated at all (for further information see K.H. Nielsen 1984b).

The plot of the two first principal axes is shown in Figures 12 and 13. Both the units and the variables are divided along the 1st axis into two main clusters, both of which are further separated into two clusters.

As can be seen, the characteristic parabola-shaped layout produced by the correspondence analysis, in cases where the data can be properly seriated, is not present. On the contrary, a series of more or less distinct clusters is found that cannot be considered to represent a parabola layout.

Yet if we decide that the layout must represent some sort of chronological order, then there seem to be three completely different ways in which we may organise the data matrix according to the plot. They

are shown here in Tables 5a, 5b and 5c respectively. Even though they all have the appearance of good matrix seriations, only one of them can possibly be right. But which one, if any? According to the plot Figures 12 and 13, Table 5b ought to be the best and Table 5a the worst, but studying the tables directly would suggest that Table 5a is the best and Table 5c the worst.

The conclusion must be that even a nice-looking, apparently perfectly ordered matrix need not fulfil the criteria of continuity which form the base of the seriation principle. Further, only when the data are submitted to an analysis like the correspondence analysis do these shortcomings become evident. It is therefore imperative that ordinary matrix seriations with permutations of rows and columns be not used as (the only) seriation method.

CONCLUSION

In conclusion I should like to evaluate the results gained from the application of correspondence analysis to graves and hoards from the Germanic Iron Age.

One aim was to determine to what extent the method was applicable to the type of material presented here. Another was to investigate whether the analysis was suitable for seriations and clusterings, and at the same time to determine to what degree the results differed from the results of more traditional investigations.

The application of correspondence analysis has not actually influenced my opinion of the material, as I had already worked with it from a numerical point of view. The main problem was, however, that I could not survey a large and many-sided data material using manual methods. The correspondence analysis proved to give an easy and safe way of obtaining a result of which I had a suspicion beforehand. Moreover, an advantage of this method was that it showed the results far more clearly than expected, and also produced other pieces of information that could not have been obtained using manual methods. A manual (or semi-manual) permutation would invariably have given the impression of a stepwise change in the graves, whereas the plot from the correspondence analysis clearly shows that there is no stepwise or box-like development, just a very gradual alteration. The lesson is that the development of ornaments is not necessarily stepwise, unless external factors play an essential role. An even development is a quite normal occurrence, and we just cannot squeeze the development of material culture into boxes with separate names along the axis of time. What we can do, is either to place fixed points along the axis of time, or state that within a span of years a

a.

	24	23	22	19	18	17	21	20	14	11	15	16	13	12	10	09	06	08	07	25	05	04	03	02	01
U	1	.	3	.	.	.	.	.	.	.	.	.	.	.	.	.	.	2	.	.	.	.	.	.	.
T	.	1	2	.	.	.	.	.	.	.	.	.	.	.	.	.	.	.	.	.	.	.	.	.	.
R	.	.	.	1	1	.	.	.	.	.	.	.	.	.	.	.	.	.	.	.	.	.	.	.	.
Q	.	.	.	1	.	9	.	.	.	.	.	.	.	.	.	.	.	.	.	.	.	.	.	.	.
S	.	.	2	1	.	.	2	1	2	.	2	.	.	.	.	.	.	.	.	.	.	.	.	.	.
P	.	.	.	.	.	2	.	.	.	.	1	2	.	.	.	.	.	.	.	.	.	.	.	.	.
L	.	.	.	.	.	.	.	.	1	1	6	.	.	.	.	.	.	.	.	.	.	.	.	.	.
I	.	.	.	.	.	.	.	.	.	5	.	.	.	.	2	.	.	.	.	.	.	.	.	.	.
N	.	.	.	.	.	.	.	.	.	.	2	2	.	.	.	2	.	.	.	.	.	.	.	.	.
M	.	.	.	.	.	.	.	.	.	.	5	.	3	.	.	.	.	.	.	.	.	.	.	.	.
K	.	.	.	.	.	.	.	.	.	1	.	.	.	12	1	.	.	.	.	.	.	.	.	.	.
J	.	.	.	.	.	.	.	.	.	.	.	.	.	9	.	.	.	1	.	.	.	.	.	.	.
H	.	.	.	.	.	.	.	.	.	.	.	.	.	3	1	.	1	.	.	.	.	.	.	.	.
G	.	.	.	.	.	.	.	.	.	.	1	1	.	.	3	8	1	.	1	.	.	.	.	.	.
V	.	.	.	.	.	.	.	.	.	.	.	.	.	.	.	.	.	3	.	1	.	.	.	.	.
E	.	.	.	.	.	.	.	.	.	.	.	.	.	.	.	.	.	.	1	1	.	.	1	.	.
D	.	.	.	.	.	.	.	.	.	.	.	.	.	.	.	.	.	4	1	.	3	2	2	1	.
F	.	.	.	.	.	.	.	.	.	.	.	.	.	.	.	.	.	.	1	.	2	.	1	.	.
C	.	.	.	.	.	.	.	.	.	.	.	.	.	.	.	.	.	.	.	.	1	.	2	.	.
B	.	.	.	.	.	.	.	.	.	.	.	.	.	.	.	.	.	.	.	1	1	1	1	8	.
A	.	.	.	.	.	.	.	.	.	.	.	.	.	.	.	.	.	.	.	.	1	.	.	.	2

b.

	01	02	03	04	05	25	07	08	06	24	23	22	19	18	17	21	20	14	11	15	16	13	12	10	09
A	2	.	.	.	1	.	.	.	.	.	.	.	.	.	.	.	.	.	.	.	.	.	.	.	.
B	.	8	1	1	1	1	.	.	.	.	.	.	.	.	.	.	.	.	.	.	.	.	.	.	.
C	.	.	2	.	1	.	.	.	.	.	.	.	.	.	.	.	.	.	.	.	.	.	.	.	.
F	.	.	1	.	2	.	1	.	.	.	.	.	.	.	.	.	.	.	.	.	.	.	.	.	.
D	.	1	2	2	3	.	1	4	.	.	.	.	.	.	.	.	.	.	.	.	.	.	.	.	.
E	.	.	1	.	.	1	1	.	.	.	.	.	.	.	.	.	.	.	.	.	.	.	.	.	.
V	.	.	.	.	.	1	.	3	.	.	.	.	.	.	.	.	.	.	.	.	.	.	.	.	.
U	.	.	.	.	.	.	.	2	.	1	.	3	.	.	.	.	.	.	.	.	.	.	.	.	.
T	.	.	.	.	.	.	.	.	.	.	1	2	.	.	.	.	.	.	.	.	.	.	.	.	.
R	.	.	.	.	.	.	.	.	.	.	.	.	1	1	.	.	.	.	.	.	.	.	.	.	.
Q	.	.	.	.	.	.	.	.	.	.	.	.	1	.	9	.	.	.	.	.	.	.	.	.	.
S	.	.	.	.	.	.	.	.	.	.	.	2	1	.	.	2	1	2	.	2	.	.	.	.	.
P	.	.	.	.	.	.	.	.	.	.	.	.	.	.	2	.	.	.	.	1	2	.	.	.	.
L	.	.	.	.	.	.	.	.	.	.	.	.	.	.	.	.	.	1	1	6	.	.	.	.	.
I	.	.	.	.	.	.	.	.	.	.	.	.	.	.	.	.	.	.	5	.	.	.	.	2	.
N	.	.	.	.	.	.	.	.	.	.	.	.	.	.	.	.	.	.	.	2	2	.	.	.	2
M	.	.	.	.	.	.	.	.	.	.	.	.	.	.	.	.	.	.	.	5	.	3	.	.	.
K	.	.	.	.	.	.	.	.	.	.	.	.	.	.	.	.	.	.	1	.	.	.	12	1	.
J	.	.	.	.	.	.	.	1	.	.	.	.	.	.	.	.	.	.	.	.	.	.	9	.	.
H	.	.	.	.	.	.	.	.	1	.	.	.	.	.	.	.	.	.	.	.	.	.	3	1	.
G	.	.	.	.	.	.	1	.	1	.	.	.	.	.	.	.	.	.	.	1	1	.	.	3	8

c.

	20	21	17	18	19	22	23	24	01	02	03	04	05	25	07	08	06	09	10	12	13	16	15	11	14
P	.	.	2	.	.	.	.	.	.	.	.	.	.	.	.	.	.	.	.	.	.	2	1	.	.
S	1	2	.	.	1	2	.	.	.	.	.	.	.	.	.	.	.	.	.	.	.	.	2	.	2
Q	.	.	9	.	1	.	.	.	.	.	.	.	.	.	.	.	.	.	.	.	.	.	.	.	.
R	.	.	.	1	1	.	.	.	.	.	.	.	.	.	.	.	.	.	.	.	.	.	.	.	.
T	.	.	.	.	.	2	1	.	.	.	.	.	.	.	.	.	.	.	.	.	.	.	.	.	.
U	.	.	.	.	.	3	.	1	.	.	.	.	.	.	.	2	.	.	.	.	.	.	.	.	.
A	.	.	.	.	.	.	.	.	2	.	.	.	1	.	.	.	.	.	.	.	.	.	.	.	.
B	.	.	.	.	.	.	.	.	.	8	1	1	1	1	.	.	.	.	.	.	.	.	.	.	.
C	.	.	.	.	.	.	.	.	.	.	2	.	1	.	.	.	.	.	.	.	.	.	.	.	.
F	.	.	.	.	.	.	.	.	.	.	1	.	2	.	1	.	.	.	.	.	.	.	.	.	.
D	.	.	.	.	.	.	.	.	.	1	2	2	3	.	1	4	.	.	.	.	.	.	.	.	.
E	.	.	.	.	.	.	.	.	.	.	1	.	.	1	1	.	.	.	.	.	.	.	.	.	.
V	.	.	.	.	.	.	.	.	.	.	.	.	.	1	.	3	.	.	.	.	.	.	.	.	.
G	.	.	.	.	.	.	.	.	.	.	.	.	.	.	1	.	1	8	3	.	.	1	1	.	.
H	.	.	.	.	.	.	.	.	.	.	.	.	.	.	.	.	1	.	1	3	.	.	.	.	.
J	.	.	.	.	.	.	.	.	.	.	.	.	.	.	.	1	.	.	.	9	.	.	.	.	.
K	.	.	.	.	.	.	.	.	.	.	.	.	.	.	.	.	.	.	1	12	.	.	.	1	.
M	.	.	.	.	.	.	.	.	.	.	.	.	.	.	.	.	.	.	.	.	3	.	5	.	.
N	.	.	.	.	.	.	.	.	.	.	.	.	.	.	.	.	.	2	.	.	.	2	2	.	.
I	.	.	.	.	.	.	.	.	.	.	.	.	.	.	.	.	.	.	2	.	.	.	.	5	.
L	.	.	.	.	.	.	.	.	.	.	.	.	.	.	.	.	.	.	.	.	.	.	6	1	1

Table 5. Matrix of 25 types of bracteates in 21 hoards sorted according to three possible interpretations of Figures 12 and 13. References to the hoards and bracteate types are not given, since they are of no relevance in the actual context.

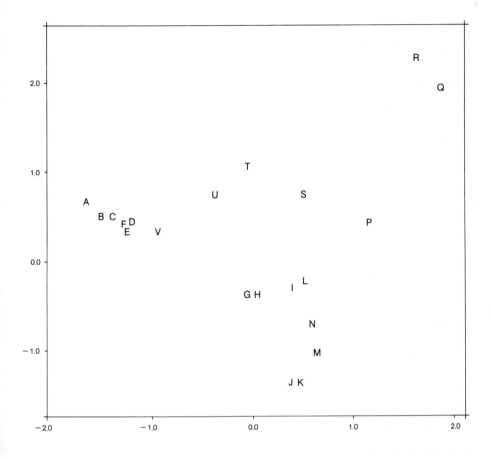

Figure 12. Plot of the first two principal axes from a correspondence analysis of the data in Table 5. The plotted values represent the hoards of bracteates.

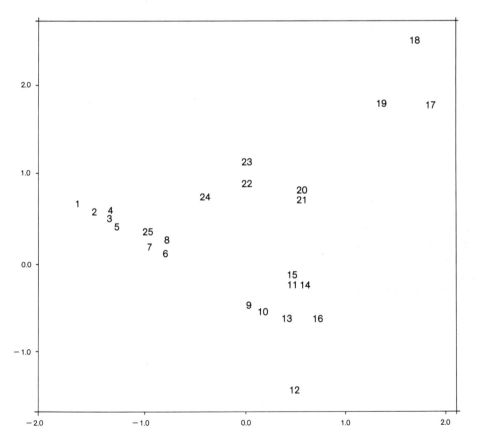

Figure 13. Plot of the first two principal axes from a correspondence analysis of the data in Table 5. The plotted values represent the types of bracteates.

certain amount of similarity in equipment is present. We can use boxes as a framework, but we should never forget that they are only a framework.

The application of correspondence analysis in this work shows that the change is continuous and that the box-like structure is something created by the lacuna of finds. This is something that not everyone has been willing to accept in advance. The accordance between the existing chronology and the seriation made here indeed shows that the correspondence analysis is very suitable for seriation.

Turning to the bead analyses, we find a clear case of clustering that partly corresponded with previously known results. The only groups not isolated until now were R3c and R3d. The plot of the first two principal axes shows a tendency to seriation, and this proves to be chronologically significant in connection with the seriation of the graves. The way the beads have been dealt with in the analysis is unusual, but may turn out to be useful when working with beads in many contexts. The problem is to choose a fair number of characteristics. To me the colours often seem to be a well chosen starting point for a bead typology, but they should not be the only elements used.

The results obtained from the correspondence analysis of the bracteates shows that simple matrix sorting with the aid of permutations is inadequate, and that matrix ordering should always be based on methods like correspondence analysis.

The three investigations presented here have demonstrated that correspondence analysis is very suitable for abundance data where clusterings, seriations, or combinations of both are expected. It means a great deal to have the possibility of reducing a large, multi-dimensional data material to a few clear dimensions. The method has thus brought new projects of data analysis within reach that otherwise would have been overwhelmingly complicated to carry out.

I hope that the applications of correspondence analysis presented here will stimulate others to use the method for clustering and chronological seriation. In this way, it should be possible to gain a greater clarity of chronology, and above all find a way to deal with the realities of those box systems that we call phases and periods. Concerning the bracteates, I also hope that the present results will form the basis of new investigations of the chronology.

Chronological and functional differences in Arabian Bronze Age pottery

A case study in correspondence analysis

By Flemming Højlund — University of Aarhus

In 1957 the Danish archaeological expedition to the Arabian Gulf was invited to undertake investigations in the Emirate of Kuwait. Between 1958 and 1963, four tells were excavated on the island of Failaka, with the generous support of the Kuwaiti government. Two of these tells, designated F3 and F6, proved to date to the Bronze Age (Bibby 1969:208; Kjærum 1980:45, 1986:77).

The role of Failaka during this period as a trading station between Mesopotamia and Dilmun (the ancient name for the East Arabian coastal area from Kuwait to Bahrain) is reflected in the pottery repertoire, which belongs to two different pottery traditions: an Arabian tradition called the Barbar tradition (named after the Barbar temple on Bahrain where this type of pottery was first identified) and a Mesopotamian tradition. The relative importance of these two traditions changed radically through the second millennium Bc (Højlund n.d.) in response to changing configurations in economy and politics in the area. Briefly stated, Failaka belongs to an independent Dilmun state at the beginning of the 2nd mill. and ends up as part of a Dilmun province of a Mesopotamian empire by the end of this millennium.

Tells F3 and F6 are situated close to the shore 300 m apart. They were occupied during approximately the same period, but in some periods there are clearly functional differences between them. Tell F3 is characterised by 'private houses', i.e. small-scale architectural units, which were probably living quarters for merchants and their families, with moderate facilities for production and storage. Tell F6, on the other hand, contains a large building, called the Palace. The size and complexity of this structure indicates a type of social organisation very different from the one found in the family-based units of F3. It is probable that some kind of large-scale organisation is manifest in the F6 evidence.

Based on a study of the pottery excavated in tells F3 and F6, the occupation has been divided into seven periods named period 1, 2A, 2B, 3A, 3B, 4A and 4B (Højlund 1987). This relative chronology has been correlated with the historical chronology of Mesopotamia by means of stamp- and cylinder-seals as well as pottery parallels (Kjærum 1983; Højlund 1983, 1986, 1987). The Bronze Age occupation on Failaka has thus been dated from approximately 2000–1900 up to the 13th century BC.

In connection with my work on the chronological system, samples of the pottery lots (i.e. assemblages of potsherds) were analysed through principal co-ordinate analysis and correspondence analysis (for these methods see Madsen this volume). In a number of cases these methods proved most helpful in the evaluation of the data structure. At present, where the pottery typology and chronology have been established (Højlund 1987), it may be of interest to study more closely the results obtained from the correspondence analyses of two partly different samples of pottery from tells F3 and F6. The total material analysed consisted of 114 selected pottery lots, characterised by (76) morphological types. The 114 lots cover all of the seven periods, and in Table 1 they are arranged according to the established chronology. Since pottery from period 3B and 4A differs in several respects, depending on whether it comes from F3 or F6, it has been listed separately for the two tells.

FIRST CORRESPONDENCE ANALYSIS

A sample of 87 lots that excludes the period 3B-4A lots from tell F6 was analysed through a correspondence analysis, using the original frequency counts as input. The plot (Figure 1) of the two first principal axes shows a nice parabolic layout of the units as should be the case when a good chronological seriation is expected. Furthermore, the order of the units fits rather well the expected order inferred from the chronology. However, an interesting deviation from

```
TYPES:  3 3 3 5 1 4 1 2 3 1 1 1 5 1 3 1 1 1 3 4 1 4 3 3 2 1 8 1 7 6 5 9 5 6 4 8 9 3 5 2 1 8 6 6 6 5 5 7 7 8 5 7 7 7 8 6 6 5 5 9 9 9 5 5 9 8 5 8 7 6 8 8 7 9 9 9 5 9
        8 8 8 4 A A 4 C 1 2 D B 4 3 5 1 E F 3   G 7 4 0 7 H   4   7 4 6 4 1 8 7 7 6 8 5 0 9 7 2 7 7 6 8 0 5 3 3 1 1 9 8 7 7 0 8 7 5 5 5 4 5 8 5 0 8 6 4 4 4 2 5 4
        A B C A           A   A                 B   B B   C A                       A   C   A D                 B A B                 A B     C D       C A       B     B C   A A

P   lot 1   4 2 1   6         1 1 . 3 2                           .               .               .                               .                                           .
E   lot 2   3 1 2 1           1 6       2                         .               .                       1     .                               .                               .
R   lot 3   1 1     1                   . 3     1                 .               .                             .                               .                               .
    lot 4   1         2   1   1 .                                 .               .                             .                               .                               .
1   lot 5   4       2 2 2 2 2 1 . 6   1                           .       1       .                             .                               .                               .
    lot 6           2 1 3 2   . 2 3           1                   .               .                             .                       2       .                               .

P   lot 7           2       . 2 1 2 1 1                           .               .                             .                               .                               .
E   lot 8       1   1       . 6 2 2   2                           .               .                             .                               .                               .
R   lot 9       2           1 2 2 1 2 1                           .               .                             .                               .                               .
    lot 10      1       1   1 7 1 1 3 2 1 1                       .               .                             .                               .                               .
2   lot 11          1   1   . 4 1 5     1                         .               .                             .                               .                               .
A   lot 12      4               2 5 2           1                 .               .                             .                               .                               .
    lot 13                      1 1                               .               .                             .                               .                               .
    lot 14    1             1 . 2                                 .               .                             .                               .                               .
    lot 15                  2 4 3 1       1           1           .               .                             .                               .                               .
    lot 16              1       . 1 1 2   1 1         1   . 1     .               .                             .                               .                               .
    lot 17                  1 . 5 2 4     1                       .       1       .                             .                               .                               .

P   lot 18          2       . 2               . 1                 .           1   .                             .                               .                               .
E   lot 19                  1           1   1                     .               .                             .                               .                               .
R   lot 20    1 2   4 2 3 9 2 1   1 1   1 2 1 2 4 1 1 1   1   1   .               .                             .                               .                               .
    lot 21    1       2 1 . 8 5       6       1 4     1 1 2 2 1   .       1       .                       2     .                               .                               .
2   lot 22              . 3     2     3 1     3           1       .               .           1                 .                               .                               .
B   lot 23    2 2 1 . 4           7           5 4 3   1 1         .               .                             .                               .                               .
    lot 24          1 . 3 1 2         3 2 1 1 2 8                 .               .                             .                               .                               .
    lot 25    1       . 1                     1 . 1       1       .               .                             .                               .                               .
    lot 26          2 . 1       3         3 2     2 5 1           .               .                             .                               .                               .
    lot 27    1       . 1   1           2     1           1       .               .           1                 .                               .                               .
    lot 28    1 2 1 . 2         2 1     5 5           4           .               .                             .                       2       .                               .

P   lot 29          2       . 1             1 2   .     1   1     .               .                             .                               .                               .
E   lot 30  3       2       . 1             4 1   1     1         .               .                             .                               1 .                             .
R   lot 31              . 1                 1 1   2       1 1     .               .                             .                               .                               .
    lot 32              . 1   1   1 1 1 3     1 2         3 1     .               .       1 . .                 .                               .                               .
3   lot 33              . 1       1 1 3   2 1   3             .   .               .                             .                               1 .                             .
A   lot 34              . 1       . 1 1   1   2   1               .               .                             .                               .                               .
    lot 35              . 1   1   . 1     1   2       2 1         .               .                             .                               .                               .
    lot 36              . 1       . 1     1   2   . 1   5         .               .                             .                               .                               .
    lot 37              . 1             . 1   2   1 1 1 2         .               .                             .                               .                               .
    lot 38              . 2       1       1 7 2 8 2     3         .               .                             .                               1 .                             .
    lot 39              .                 . 2   7                 .               .                             .                               1 .                             1
    lot 40              .                 1 2   6     2 1         .               .               2             .                               1 .                             .
    lot 41              .           1     1 . 1 1 2     1         .               .                             .               1 1             1 1 .                           .
    lot 42              .                 . 1 1 2       3 1       .       1       .           . 2               .                               1 .                             .

P   lot 43          2 . 2       1         7 5 1     1             .               .       2   1     1   2         .                             2 .                             .
E   lot 44          . 1                   3 1               1     .               1   1               1           .                             1 .                             .
R   lot 45          1 .         1         . 6 1                   .               .     2 1 1                     .                             2 .                             .
    lot 46              .         1       . 1                 2   .           2           3 1                     .               1             2 .                             .
3   lot 47              .         1       . 3                     .               1 2 2 1                 1 . .   .                               .                             .
B   lot 48              .         2       . 1         1   2 1 1   .     1 1       1     1 1 4       . 1           .                               1 .                             .
    lot 49              .           3   1       2   2 2 1 1   . 1 1     3 3 3 1   1 1 2 1 5   2 1       1         .                             1 .                             .
F   lot 50              .           3   1     2         . 1   2 5 2 1 1 . 3 1 2 2 2 3 1                           .               1             2 .                             .
3   lot 51              .           1         1       . 1 2 . 5 2 1   5 1                     .                   .               1 .             .                             .
    lot 52              .                   . 1         1 2 . 5 2 1 1   5   .                                     .                             1 .                             .
    lot 53              .                     1 2     . 5 1 3 2 1                     1                           .                             1 .                             .
    lot 54          1 .                     1 2     . 1     1   1 1 2 1 1                                         .               1 .           3 .                             1
    lot 55              .                     . 2     1 2 . 2               1 1 1 2 . .                           .                             1 1 . .                         .

P   lot 56      2 1 .     1   1 1 1 2 2     1 1   . 2     . 2 1           .               .                       .                             .                               .
E   lot 57          1 .                       .             1           .               .                       .                             .                               .
R   lot 58              .                       . 3 1 0   5   1 .       .               .                       .                             1 .                             .
    lot 59              .                       . 1 4     3 1 9 7 4 2   .               .                       .                             1 .                             .
3   lot 60              .                       . 4 2 1 2 7 3 3     .   .               .                       .               1   5   1 . .   .                             .
B   lot 61          1   .                       . 2 3 6 6     4 . .     .           3 . .                       .               3             .                               .
    lot 62              .                       . 2   1 1   8 3 2 2   . .               .               2 1 . . .                             .                               .
F   lot 63              .                       . 1     6 1           . .               .               2 .     .                             .                               .
6   lot 64              .           1   . 2     2   . 2 1 1 5 1 1       . .               .               2   3   .               1 1 6         1 .                           .

P   lot 65              .                       . 1           1 2 1   2 .       . 2     . 2 1 2 2     .                                       .                               .
E   lot 66              .                       . 1               1   . 3   2 1 .       2 . 1         .                                       .                               .
R   lot 67      2 . 1   .                       . 1         1   2 1 4 1 . 1   . 2 1 4 2 1 . 1         .                                       .                               .
    lot 68          . 2 .                       . 1                 1 2 2 2   1 2 8 2 . 1   4 2 1     .               1                       .                               .
4   lot 69          . 1 .                       . 1                 . 2 1 1 2 8   1 2     1   1 . 1   .                                       .                               .
A   lot 70              .                       . 2 .           1 2   1 1   1 1 1 5 1 4 . 1   3 1     .                                       .                               .
    lot 71              .           1           .     . 1     . 2     1 1 5   1 . 1 1 5     2 1       .                               1       .                               .
F   lot 72              .         1             .       1 . 2   1 1 2 2 5   1 . 1 1 4 5 7   1   1 1 1 .                                       .                               1
3   lot 73              .                       . 1         1 2 . 1   1 1 2 1 .   . 3       1   1     .                                       .                               .
    lot 74              .                       .                 1 1 3 . 5           1 2 2 2 1 . 2   .                                       .                               .
    lot 75      1       .         1             . 1             2 1 . 3 4 5         1       1   2 2 2 1 .                                     .                               .
    lot 76              .                       .     1         2 . 1 . 3 4 4 4   1 2 1 . 1     1 2 2 2 1 1 .                                 .                               1
    lot 77              .           1           . 1       1 3 . 1 1 1 3 8 8     . 2 1         2                                               .                               1
    lot 78              .                       .           2 1 . 2 2 1 3 1 . 2   2                                                           .                               .
    lot 79              . 1                     .             . 1 3 1 1 1 8   1 1 1 2                                                         .                               .
F   lot 82              .                       .             2     1 1   2     1 . 2                                                         .                               .
E   lot 83              .                       .         1   4     1   1 . 2 . 1 2 1                                                         .                               .
R   lot 84              .                       . 1 3 . 1                                                                                     .                               .
    lot 85              .                       .         1   1 .   2 4 1 1 6 1 2   4 1                                                       .                               .
4   lot 86              .                       .           1     8   7 5 1 1 1 4                                                             .                               .
A   lot 87              .                       .         1       1 1 5 5     1 . 1                                                           .                               .
    lot 88              .                       . 1           3 4 1 2 1     3                                                                 .                               .
F   lot 89              .                       .                 1 . 6 2     6                                                               .                               .
6   lot 90              .                       .             2 . 8 2                                                                         .                               .
    lot 91              .                       . 2 1 1 1                                                                                     .                               .
    lot 92              .                       1 1 3 5 1 1       9                                                                           .                               .
    lot 93              .                     2   1   . 1 6 1 1 6 7 2 1 1 0 1                                                                 .                               .
    lot 94              .                     2         1 8 3 3 1 8     1 2 9                                                                 1 .                             .
    lot 95              .                   1 . 2       6 1 1 2 6     1 4 1                                                                   .                               .
    lot 96              .                     1         8 2 6 1 2 5     6                                                                     .                               .
    lot 97              .                     1         3 1 1 4       1 2                                                                     .                               .
    lot 98              .                     2       1 0   4 1 2 2 2 1 1 3 1                                                                 .                               .
    lot 99              .                         1 1 2     5 4 2       3 5                                                                   .                               .

P   lot 100             .           1   .       1                           2                   2           2                                 .                               .
E   lot 101             .                   1   .         1     1 1 . 1       2       . 1       1                                             .                               .
R   lot 102             .                       .                 1           2       . 1 1                                                   .                               .
    lot 103             .                       .           1   . 1 2     1 2       1 1                                                       .                               .
4   lot 104             .                       .   1     2 1       1 1   . 1 1     1                                                         .                               .
B   lot 105             . 1                     .   1     1         1 1   2 1 . 2       1 2               1 2                                   .                             .
    lot 106   1   . 1                           .         2 1       1 1 2 1 . 1 1 5                                                           .                               .
    lot 107             .                       .     1   3 2 1 . . 1 1   . 1 1 . 1 3 1 3                                                     .                               .
    lot 108             .                       .         1       2 1     1 2 . 1 . 1 3 1 2 2                                                 .                               .
    lot 109             .                       .         1       2   . . 2 1 . 1 . 2 . 1 . 2                                                 .                               .
    lot 110             .                       .           1   1 1 . 1   2 1 . 2   1 2 2                                                     .                               .
    lot 111             .                       .       3 1     1 . 2 . 1   1 1 . 2   1 2 2                                                   .                               .
    lot 112             .                   1 .             2 1         1 1 . 2   2 . 1                                                       .                               .
    lot 113       1 .                           .         1                           1 . 3 4 5 7                                             .                               .
```

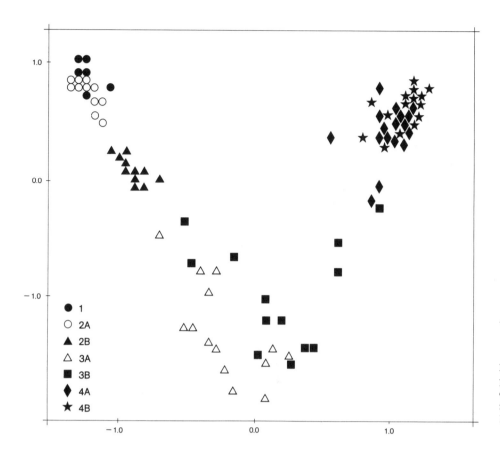

Figure 1. Plot of the two first principal axes from a correspondence analysis of 87 lots extracted from Table 1 so as to exclude the Period 3B–4A lots from tell F6.

this pattern can be pointed out. Some period 3B lots do not follow after the period 3A lots, but rather fall parallel to them.

In order to explain this anomaly we must return to the presence of the two pottery traditions on Failaka, mentioned above. Periods 1–2B have very little Mesopotamian pottery relative to Barbar pottery, while the opposite is the case for period 4A–B (Table 2). In period 3A–B there is more of a balance between the two traditions. This relationship is neatly illustrated in Figure 1, where the comparatively unmixed periods 1–2B and period 4A–B lots cluster tightly in two opposing corners, while the period 3A–B lots that contain both of the two traditions are more freely distributed in between.

Figure 2 shows the period 3A–B lots in the same relative positions as in Figure 1, with the percentage of Mesopotamian types in each lot indicated. The 13 lots lying to the negative side on the first axis, including 3 lots dating to period 3B, have a mean value of 25% Mesopotamian pottery. Conversely, the 14 lots lying to the positive side on the first axis have a mean value of 76%. It seems obvious that the distribution of the period 3A–B lots in Figure 1 is not entirely determined by the time factor. Primarily, it is a ques-

	B	M	Total
Period 1	93%	7%	95
Period 2A	99%	1%	132
Period 2B	98%	2%	256
Period 3A	50%	50%	174
Period 3B	40%	60%	237
Period 4A	10%	90%	352
Period 4B	11%	89%	171

Table 2. The relative frequencies of Barbar (B) and Mesopotamian (M) types in the pottery material from Failaka.

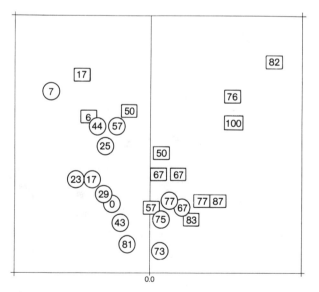

Figure 2. Excerpt from Figure 1 of the period 3A–B lots, with the percentage of Mesopotamian types in each lot indicated.

← Table 1. Data matrix showing count of 76 morphological types in 114 selected pottery lots. The matrix is sorted according to the established chronology.

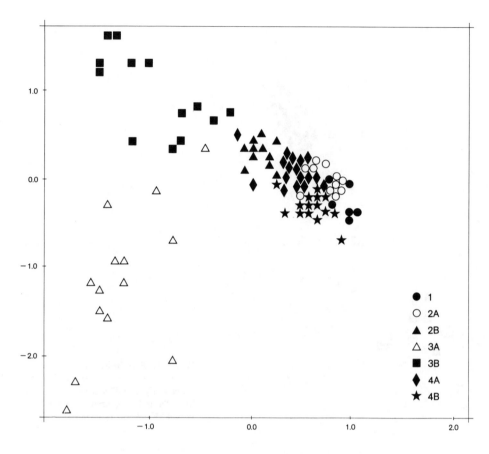

Figure 3. Plot of the second and third principal axes from the same correspondence analysis as in Figure 1.

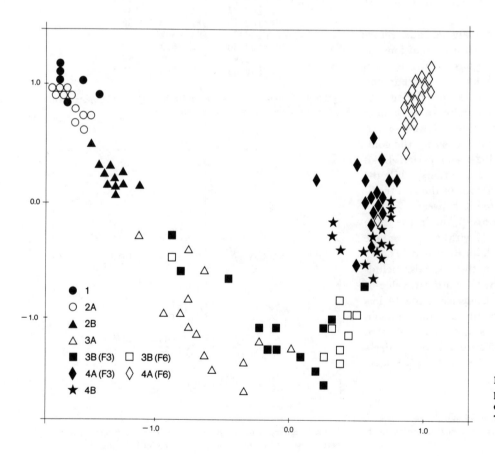

Figure 4. Plot of the two first principal axes from a correspondence analysis of all the lots in Table 1.

tion of the degree of mixture between the Barbar tradition and the Mesopotamian tradition, and this is not merely a time phenomenon. It may be related to functional and social factors as well.

It is interesting to note that the time difference between the lots from period 3A and 3B is clearly expressed along the third axis in the correspondence analysis (Figure 3).

SECOND CORRESPONDENCE ANALYSIS

All 114 lots in Table 1, including the period 3B-4A lots from the Palace, were subsequently subjected to a correspondence analysis. Again we find a nice parabolic layout (Figure 4), as we should expect in connection with a perfect time seriation. But a closer examination of the plot immediately reveals that the chronological value of parts of this seriation is limited indeed. The distortion is such that the period 4B lots are now placed between the period 3B and 4A lots.

The nice parabola seriation we find in Figure 4 is again partly determined by the relations between Barbar types and Mesopotamian types. It turns out that the period 4A pottery from the Palace consists almost exclusively (99%) of Mesopotamian types (Table 3), and, in addition, it is a very homogeneous assemblage. Invariably, the computer singles out this

	B	M	Total
Period 3B (F6)	9%	91%	212
Period 4A (F6)	1%	99%	471

Table 3. The relative frequencies of Barbar (B) and Mesopotamian (M) types in the period 3B and 4A material from Tell F6.

assemblage as the one that is most different from the early Barbar-dominated assemblages and thus separates these two poles as much as possible on the first axis.

A contributing cause to the distortion is the fact that 11% of the period 4B sample consists of Barbar types, which in this case are probably intrusive. The period 4B buildings lie directly above earlier buildings dating to period 2, and later digging for building-stone has brought early material up into the period 4B levels. The Barbar types found in the 4B lots here fit well into the period 2 assemblage, whereas the Barbar types in the period 4A sample from tell F3 include what could be characterised as quite degenerate shapes, and probably represent the latest phase of the Barbar pottery tradition.

Again, as was the case in the first analysis, the third axis (Figure 5) gives a fine separation of the period 4B lots, which are obviously not correctly placed with respect to time in Figure 4.

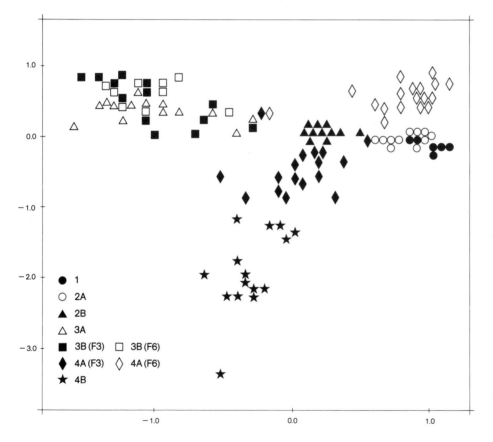

Figure 5. Plot of the second and third principal axes from the same correspondence analyses as in Figure 4.

59

CONCLUSION

Correspondence analyses of two partly different samples of Bronze Age pottery from Failaka, Kuwait, produced in both cases parabolic plots of the units on the first two axes. These parabolic layouts are of the type one would expect in cases of perfect time seriation (Madsen, this volume). Yet it is obvious that time is not the only factor involved in the neat seriation result.

The seriation is also based on the relationship between two pottery traditions. Where functional or social factors determine this relationship, as is obviously the case with the period 4A assemblages from the Palace, we are bound to receive a partly false time series.

In this respect, the seriations carried out here on the pottery material from Failaka are most thought-provoking, and, indeed, strike a warning note: not every nice looking seriation should be accepted as a time seriation.

Acknowledgement

I am indebted to Torsten Madsen for introducing me to multivariate statistics and for his comments on this article.

The archaeological survey of North Norway

An evaluation using correspondence analysis

By Inger Marie Holm-Olsen — Tromsø Museum

Within the next few years a systematic archaeological survey of Norway north of the Arctic Circle will be completed. Immediately following the completion of the first survey round, which started in 1964, a revision of the survey will begin. Thus, an evaluation of the first 20 years of survey work is called for, to assess the quality of the resulting Monuments Register as an archaeological database, and to guide the revision of the survey towards the most relevant problem areas. The aim of this paper is to make a first attempt at an evaluation of the total Monuments Register as a basis for gaining a general understanding of settlement history in North Norway. Secondly, I wish to explore the potential of correspondence analysis as a method towards this end.

The survey of North Norway is part of a nation-wide project that started in 1963 to produce an Economic Map of Norway (Skjelsvik 1978). The aim of this map is to create a tool for local planning. As all ancient monuments older than A.D. 1536, and all Sami monuments more than 100 years old are protected by the Ancient Monuments Act of 1978 (replacing earlier versions of the Act, the first dating back to 1905), these monuments constitute a restriction on land use and may be included in the content of the economic map. The archaeological survey is directed, and the field work carried out, by the five regional archaeological museums of Norway: in Oslo, Stavanger, Bergen, Trondheim and Tromsø.

Though the purpose of the Economic Map survey is to produce a complete inventory of sites covered by the Ancient Monuments Act, this aim has, of course, not been fulfilled. This is due to a variety of factors. Of the most fundamental importance is the fact that the archaeological site concept is continuously widening. There are types of sites which are today routinely recorded by surveyors, but which were not yet recognised by the archaeological community when this survey started twenty years ago. Another important factor is the concentration of the survey on sites with visible surface structures. The use of test pits has been almost non-existent in the first survey round now being completed. Thirdly, the survey has, so far, tended to concentrate on built-up areas where threats to the ancient monuments from modern development are the strongest. These inherent problems of the Monuments Register should be kept in mind through the following analysis.

The analysis to be presented here has been designed to explore the distributional patterning of a number of different types of sites, from the Stone Age to the post-Mediaeval period. The most obvious choice of method to meet this end would be the use of maps. The best example of this is Hyenstrand's extensive analysis of the Swedish Ancient Monuments Register (Hyenstrand 1979a, 1979b). Correspondence analysis, as applied in this paper, does not replace the use of distribution maps. Rather, it may be viewed as a complementary method, well suited to give a general overview of the distributional tendencies within the total data set. These tendencies may then be further analysed using either statistical techniques or other methods.

Correspondence analysis (CA) works by comparing the profiles of units (in this case municipalities) and of variables (in this case types of sites). That is, what is compared is the relative frequency of types of sites within and between municipalities (Bølviken et al. 1982). The resulting correspondence plot may be read as a condensed representation of the main tendencies of a series of distribution maps. As the aim of this paper is to make a first assessment of the North Norwegian Ancient Monuments Register as a basis for constructing a general history of settlement for this area, CA would appear to be an appropriate method. If the analysis results in a coherent and interpretable picture of the settlement pattern, then the inherent problems within the set of survey data are not so severe as to make the Monuments Register unsuitable as a database for archaeological analysis. At the same time lacunae and inconsistencies within the data set may be revealed.

The chronological framework adopted in this paper is:

8000 – 4000 B.C.	Mesolithic
4000 – 500 B.C.	Late Stone Age
500 B.C. – A.D. 1050	Iron Age
A.D. 1050 – 1536	Mediaeval
A.D. 1536 –	Post-Mediaeval

Though the absolute dates may be open to debate, this is of minor importance to the present analysis. In accordance with the traditional way of presenting the prehistory of North Norway, the Bronze Age has not been distinguished as a separate period, and such a distinction would not be possible on the basis of the Monuments Register, anyway. Neither is it possible, in most cases, to distinguish between monuments from the Early and the Late Iron Age.

The data set presented in Table 1 consists of the absolute frequencies, according to the Ancient Monuments Register, of 10 types of sites within 46 North Norwegian municipalities (Figure 1). The sites chosen as variables are those that most directly reflect settlement. From the Stone Age both house sites, open-air sites, and stray finds have been included. Though house sites from the Early Stone

Variables Units	A	B	C	D	E	F	G	H	I	J
1 Kvæfjord	0	2	2	1	2	107	2	32	65	21
2 Skånland	0	4	0	0	0	11	1	15	2	5
3 Bjarkøy	0	0	0	1	4	109	0	6	0	4
4 Harstad	2	0	0	2	7	303	2	37	45	57
5 Ibestad	0	0	0	1	0	21	2	10	23	22
6 Gratangen	0	0	0	0	0	3	0	10	29	18
7 Salangen	0	2	6	0	1	11	0	7	2	1
8 Dyrøy	0	4	5	0	0	21	1	6	1	14
9 Bardu	0	0	1	0	0	0	0	0	0	19
10 Målselv	0	0	2	0	0	3	0	2	10	0
11 Sørreisa	0	1	12	0	0	0	0	0	0	0
12 Torsken	107	4	10	22	6	36	6	13	12	25
13 Berg	24	5	6	14	3	20	2	8	9	11
14 Lenvik	0	4	20	0	0	27	3	2	61	22
15 Balsfjord	0	0	4	0	0	1	1	0	12	15
16 Tromsø	19	16	46	18	4	139	9	13	70	253
17 Lyngen	16	0	30	0	0	16	0	2	137	42
18 Storfjord	0	0	3	0	0	0	3	0	47	19
19 Kåfjord	0	0	3	0	0	0	1	0	57	19
20 Skjervøy	238	5	5	0	3	8	33	2	61	143
21 Nordreisa	73	2	0	0	0	0	4	5	148	92
22 Kvænangen	510	8	20	1	0	0	8	6	62	189
23 Steigen	0	4	10	2	10	264	2	23	1	9
24 Hamarøy	0	0	4	0	5	108	2	8	0	2
25 Tysfjord	0	0	2	0	0	13	0	2	14	0
26 Lødingen	0	3	2	2	3	172	10	10	10	23
27 Tjeldsund	0	7	5	0	1	101	4	12	3	10
28 Evenes	0	1	1	0	0	2	0	3	10	1
29 Ballangen	0	9	10	0	0	2	0	2	17	7
30 Narvik/Ankenes	0	12	3	0	0	10	0	6	45	5
31 Vestvågøy	24	5	5	13	45	469	34	32	5	38
32 Vågan	0	4	12	0	6	54	0	7	3	4
33 Hadsel	0	3	3	10	15	244	7	35	13	12
34 Bø	4	0	11	0	6	367	5	12	0	26
35 Sortland	4	1	37	0	0	154	8	16	7	17
36 Kautokeino	8	21	0	0	0	0	0	0	5	1
37 Alta	102	18	28	0	0	3	12	3	107	227
38 Loppa	114	0	1	2	1	6	4	3	95	96
39 Hasvik	127	0	5	0	0	0	0	5	69	18
40 Sørrøysund	32	0	2	0	0	0	0	0	10	44
41 Porsanger	222	4	2	0	0	8	0	0	85	83
42 Karasjok	2	1	0	0	0	0	0	0	6	14
43 Lebesby	267	0	0	1	0	17	2	0	44	91
44 Gamvik	187	4	0	0	0	23	7	0	42	47
45 Tana	46	0	7	0	0	0	0	0	75	133
46 Nesseby	327	28	3	0	0	3	1	0	118	60

A: Stone Age house
B: Stone Age open-air site
C: Stone Age stray find
D: Iron Age house
E: Iron Age boat house
F: Iron Age burial mound/cairn
G: Med./Post Med. boat house
H: Med./Post Med. farm mound
I: Med./Post Med. round 'gamme'
J: Med./Post Med. rect. 'gamme'

Table 1. Counts of 10 different site types within 46 North Norwegian municipalities.

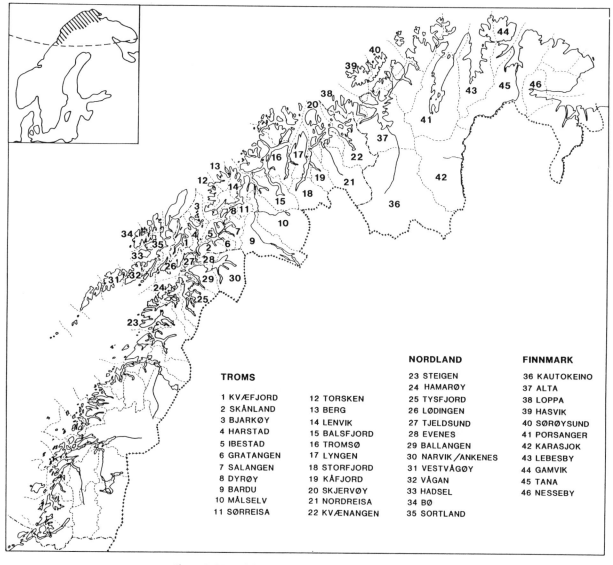

TROMS

1 KVÆFJORD	12 TORSKEN
2 SKÅNLAND	13 BERG
3 BJARKØY	14 LENVIK
4 HARSTAD	15 BALSFJORD
5 IBESTAD	16 TROMSØ
6 GRATANGEN	17 LYNGEN
7 SALANGEN	18 STORFJORD
8 DYRØY	19 KÅFJORD
9 BARDU	20 SKJERVØY
10 MÅLSELV	21 NORDREISA
11 SØRREISA	22 KVÆNANGEN

NORDLAND

23 STEIGEN
24 HAMARØY
25 TYSFJORD
26 LØDINGEN
27 TJELDSUND
28 EVENES
29 BALLANGEN
30 NARVIK / ANKENES
31 VESTVÅGØY
32 VÅGAN
33 HADSEL
34 BØ
35 SORTLAND

FINNMARK

36 KAUTOKEINO
37 ALTA
38 LOPPA
39 HASVIK
40 SØRØYSUND
41 PORSANGER
42 KARASJOK
43 LEBESBY
44 GAMVIK
45 TANA
46 NESSEBY

Figure 1. Map of the 46 municipalities used as analytical units.

Age have recently been found in North Norway (Schanche 1985), all houses included in this analysis are probably from the Late Stone Age. The open-air sites and stray finds are categories that comprise both Early and Late Stone Age material, but with a clear bias towards the Late Stone Age.

The Iron Age monuments included are long-houses, boat houses and burial mounds. Together these types of monuments constitute the main features of the typical Iron Age farm. In North Norway this type of farm is traditionally considered to be 'Norwegian', as opposed to 'Sami'. Knowledge of monuments of the Sami Iron Age is still sparse, and largely confined to the Varanger area in Finnmark (Storli 1986). They are poorly represented in the Monuments Register, and are, therefore, not included in this analysis.

The farm mounds of North Norway are accumulations of cultural layers resulting from continuous settlement activity through several hundred years. C-14 dates have shown that the earliest farm mounds may date back to about 100 B.C., whereas the latest were founded as late as A.D. 1600 (Bertelsen 1979; Holm-Olsen 1981:89-91, 1985).

The last group of monuments included are boat houses and house sites of the *gamme* type. A *gamme* consists of an inner wooden framework covered by an insulating layer of sod. It is this sod layer that is now visible on the surface as a low bank. C-14 dates have proved that some of these houses date back to the Mediaeval period (Søbstad 1981:102-104). *Gammer* have, however, been used as dwellings up to the present in parts of North Norway. No typology exists to make possible a chronological classification of *gamme* sites without prior excavation.

The units of this analysis are made up by the contemporary municipalities. Units 1-22 of Table 1 belong to the county of Troms, units 23-35

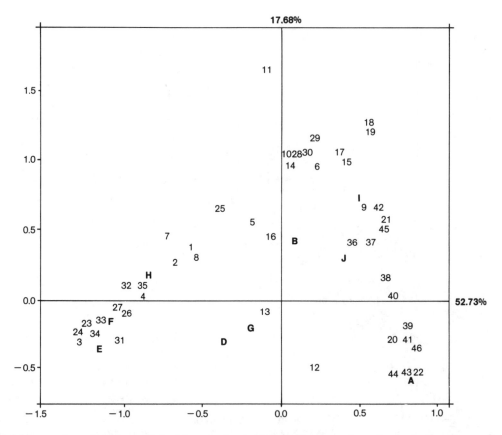

Figure 2. Plot of the two first principal axes of the CA on the data in Table 1. Numbers refer to the numbering of the municipalities used in Table 1 and Figure 1. Letters refer to the numbers of site types used in Table 1.

to Nordland and units 36–46 to Finnmark. From Troms, all surveyed municipalities are included. From Nordland, the 13 northernmost surveyed municipalities are included, i.e. those closest to the Troms border. The 11 Finnmark municipalities are spread out all over that county, and are somewhat arbitrarily chosen, depending on which parts of the Monuments Register were most readily available at the time of the analysis.

Table 2 and the margins of Table 3 document how the correspondence analysis works on the data in Table 1, and provide a guide to the interpretation of the plot in Figure 2. As a correspondence analysis is sensitive to outliers, it is important to ascertain whether the emerging pattern is the result of the impact of only a small number of units or variables. The sums and inertia percentages for the units (Table 3) show that these have a uniform impact. The variables present a much more unbalanced picture. A, F, I and J, representing Late Stone Age houses, Iron Age burial mounds and Mediaeval/Post-Mediaeval *gammer*, are much more numerous than the rest of the variables (Table 3). As can be seen from the inertia percentages, the first three of these variables dominate the pattern created by the CA, whereas variable J, rectangular *gammer*, has less influence on the resulting plot.

Figure 2 presents the two first CA axes plotted against each other. The first axis accounts for 52.73% of the total variation and the second for 17.68%. Taken together the two first axes account for 70.41% of the total variation in the material presented in Table 1 (Table 2).

Starting the interpretation of the plot with the four most influential variables, the first axis clearly distinguishes between municipalities characterised by Iron Age burial mounds as opposed to municipalities characterised by *gammer* and Stone Age houses. Associated with Iron Age burials are Iron Age boat houses and farm mounds. The second axis distinguishes between Iron Age burials and Stone Age houses as opposed to *gammer*. On this axis, Stone Age stray finds and open-air sites appear to be associated with *gammer*.

The distinctly concave shape of the distribution of units and variables in the plot of the first two axes in Figure 2 indicates that the result of the correspondence analysis may be interpreted as a seriation (Bølviken et al. 1982). The new matrix, as reordered by the correspondence analysis according to the ordering of units and variables on the first axis, is presented in Table 3.

So far, the analysis of the Monuments Register data has proved that this material is clearly struc-

```
Axis    :   1      2      3      4      5      6
Expl.%  : 52.7   17.7    8.1    7.3    5.4    4.2
```

Table 2. Explanation percentages for the first six principal axes.

Variables Units	F	E	H	D	G	C	B	J	I	A	SUM	INT.%
3 Bjarkøy	109	4	6	1	0	0	0	4	0	0	124	1.89
24 Hamarøy	108	5	8	0	2	4	0	2	0	0	129	1.82
23 Steigen	264	10	23	2	2	10	4	9	1	0	325	4.17
34 Bø	367	6	12	0	5	11	0	26	0	4	431	5.70
33 Hadsel	244	15	35	10	7	3	3	12	13	0	342	3.84
31 Vestvågøy	469	45	32	13	34	5	5	38	5	24	670	7.48
27 Tjeldsund	101	1	12	0	4	5	7	10	3	0	143	1.38
26 Lødingen	172	3	10	2	10	2	3	23	10	0	235	2.16
32 Vågan	54	6	7	0	0	12	4	4	3	0	90	1.06
35 Sortland	154	0	16	0	8	37	1	17	7	4	244	2.59
4 Harstad	303	7	37	2	2	0	9	57	45	2	464	3.24
7 Salangen	11	1	7	0	0	6	2	1	2	0	30	0.62
2 Skånland	11	0	15	0	1	0	4	5	2	0	38	1.36
1 Kvæfjord	107	2	32	1	2	2	2	21	65	0	234	1.52
8 Dyrøy	21	0	6	0	1	5	4	14	1	0	52	0.40
25 Tysfjord	13	0	2	0	0	2	0	0	14	0	31	0.28
5 Ibestad	21	0	10	1	2	0	0	22	23	0	79	0.44
11 Sørreisa	0	0	0	0	0	12	1	0	0	0	13	2.60
13 Berg	20	3	8	14	2	6	5	11	9	24	102	1.71
16 Tromsø	139	4	13	18	9	46	16	253	70	19	587	2.89
10 Målselv	3	0	2	0	2	2	0	0	10	0	17	0.28
14 Lenvik	27	0	2	0	3	20	4	22	61	0	139	1.29
28 Evenes	2	0	3	0	0	1	1	1	10	0	18	0.29
30 Narvik/Ankenes	10	0	6	0	0	3	12	5	45	0	81	1.52
29 Ballangen	2	0	2	0	0	10	9	7	17	0	47	1.24
12 Torsken	36	6	13	22	6	10	4	25	12	107	241	2.19
6 Gratangen	3	0	10	0	0	0	0	13	29	0	60	0.82
17 Lyngen	16	0	2	0	0	36	0	42	137	16	249	3.35
15 Balsfjord	1	0	0	0	1	4	0	15	12	0	33	0.37
36 Kautokeino	0	0	0	0	0	0	21	1	5	8	35	5.14
9 Bardu	0	0	0	0	0	1	0	19	0	0	20	0.60
19 Kåfjord	0	0	0	0	1	3	0	19	57	0	80	1.59
18 Storfjord	0	0	0	0	0	3	0	19	47	0	69	1.28
37 Alta	3	0	3	0	12	28	18	227	107	102	500	2.88
42 Karasjok	0	0	0	0	0	0	1	14	6	2	23	0.27
45 Tana	0	0	0	0	0	7	0	133	75	46	261	2.09
21 Nordreisa	0	0	5	0	4	0	2	92	148	73	324	2.42
38 Loppa	6	1	3	2	4	1	0	96	95	114	322	1.38
20 Skjervøy	8	3	2	0	33	5	5	143	61	238	498	2.92
44 Gamvik	23	0	0	0	7	0	4	47	42	187	310	1.97
40 Sørrøysund	0	0	0	0	0	2	0	44	10	32	88	0.66
43 Lebesby	17	0	0	1	2	0	0	91	44	267	422	3.26
41 Porsanger	8	0	0	0	0	2	4	83	85	222	404	2.41
39 Hasvik	0	0	5	0	0	5	0	18	69	127	224	1.75
22 Kvænangen	0	0	6	1	8	20	8	189	62	510	804	6.52
46 Nesseby	3	0	0	0	1	3	28	60	118	327	540	4.39
SUM	2856	122	355	90	173	334	191	1959	1637	2455	10172	
INT.%	30.15	2.52	4.62	3.86	1.49	6.85	7.44	8.62	12.32	22.13		

A: Stone Age house
B: Stone Age open-air site
C: Stone Age stray find

D: Iron Age house
E: Iron Age boat house
F: Iron Age burial mound/cairn

G: Med./Post Med. boat house
H: Med./Post Med. farm mound
I: Med./Post Med. round ´gamme´
J: Med./Post Med. rect. ´gamme´

Table 3. Count of 10 different site types within 46 North Norwegian municipalities, sorted according to the seriation suggested by correspondence analysis. Sums and inertia percentages from the CA are given along the margins.

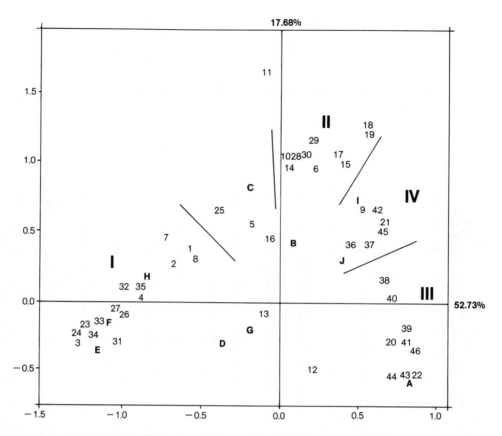

Figure 3. Plot identical to that in Figure 2, but interpreted in terms of clusters.

tured. It remains to be seen whether this structure is meaningful in terms of settlement history. The position of the variables in the reordered matrix (Table 3) indicates that the seriation performed by the CA is not a chronological one. The ordering of the units within this table rather points towards a geographical ordering: units 1-15 belong to the coast of Nordland and South Troms, units 16-29 to the fjord parts of Nordland and Troms (including a few coastal Troms municipalities), and units 30-46 to North Troms and Finnmark. Within these three groups, however, the ordering of the units does not appear to follow any strict geographical pattern.

Alternatively, the distribution of the units within the plot may be interpreted as consisting of three, or possibly four, clusters. These clusters may be delineated as suggested in Figure 3. The position of the variables within the same plot helps to interpret the clusters archaeologically. Starting again with the four most frequent types of sites, variables A, F, I and J, each of these variables can be seen to coincide with one of the four clusters. Thus, the municipalities within cluster I are characterised by a high frequency of Iron Age burial mounds. Cluster II is characterised by round house plans of the *gamme* type, cluster III by Late Stone Age houses and cluster IV by rectangular *gammer*. Of the less influential variables, farm mounds and Iron Age boat houses are clearly associated with Iron Age burial mounds, and Stone

Age stray finds and open-air sites with *gamme* sites. Iron Age houses and Post-Medieaval boat houses are not well explained by the first two axes, and neither are units 5, 12, 13, 16, and 25.

The interpretation of the CA plot as a seriation may be the most satisfactory in terms of cultural history, indicating a gradual decrease-increase in the frequency of different types of sites. The geographical structure emerging from the CA is, however, more immediately readable when viewed as a group of clusters and transferred to a map. On the map Figure 4, the units within each of the four clusters of Figure 3 are plotted. This map confirms that the structure emerging from the CA is clearly a geographical one. The units in cluster I are found along the coast of Nordland and the southern part of Troms. Cluster II contains the fjord municipalities of Nordland and Troms. Cluster III contains the two northernmost municipalities of Troms and those on the coast of Finnmark. The units of cluster IV are found in the interior of Finnmark and, in one instance, in Troms.

Units 5, 12, 13, 16, and 25 do not fit into this proposed pattern of clusters. In the plot they occupy a middle position, and this is also the case in geographical terms. On the map Figure 4 they are called cluster V and can be seen to be situated along part of the coast of Nordland and Troms, surrounded by clusters I, II, and III.

How, then, does the chorological and chronological picture emerging from the correspondence analysis contribute to our understanding of settlement history in North Norway? When Tromsø Museum was founded, in 1872, little was known about the prehistory of this area. So the first curators of the Archaeological Department started a systematic survey covering all municipalities north of the Arctic Circle, with the exception of the inner fjord areas. This survey was completed in 1892 (Nicolaissen 1893:11–13). Though other sites are mentioned occasionally, the survey concentrated almost entirely on Iron Age burial mounds, in accordance with the general trend of Norwegian archaeology in the 19th century. The main conclusion drawn from this first survey was that the Norwegian (as opposed to Sami) Iron Age monuments were to be found along the outer coast of Nordland and Troms, up to the Tromsø area (Th. Winther 1877:135–136; Brøgger

1931:7–9). Within the county of Troms, stray finds of slate artifacts from the Late Stone Age were, however, more numerous along the inner coast and in the fjord areas (Th. Winther 1877:134).

In more recent reviews of North Norwegian prehistory, the old picture of the distribution of Iron Age monuments has not been challenged (Sjøvold 1962, 1974). From the Stone Age, however, vast amounts of new material have been found which have considerably altered our knowledge of this period since the first survey in the 19th century (Simonsen 1974, 1975b, 1979). Mediaeval and Post-Mediaeval sites have only recently been included in the archaeologists' sphere of interest. For these periods the Economic Map survey offers a first approximation of the distribution of sites and monuments.

Within the CA plot (Figure 2), the most striking

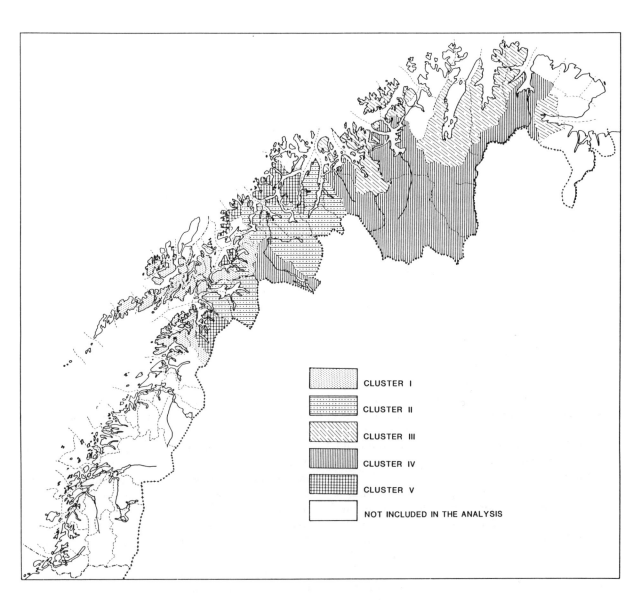

Figure 4. The geographical distribution of the clusters in Figure 3.

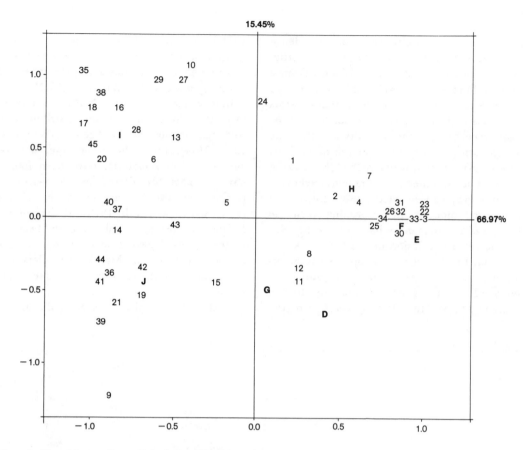

Figure 5. Plot of the two first principal axes of the CA on the data in Table 1 with the three Stone Age variables removed.

feature concerning the Stone Age variables is the distance between Stone Age houses and Stone Age open-air sites and stray finds. The coastal municipalities of Finnmark and the two northernmost municipalities of Troms cluster tightly around the variable 'Stone Age house'. Though, as can be seen from Table 1, Stone Age houses have been found further south, the decrease in frequency is marked. One explanation for this decrease may be the fact that it coincides quite closely with the traditional northern limit of regular grain cultivation: plowing may long since have destroyed the Stone Age houses south of this border zone, and at the same time have brought to light the artifacts now recorded as open-air sites and stray finds. However, Simonsen has suggested the existence of several distinct Late Stone age groups along the coast of North Norway (Simonsen 1975b), and building of substantial houses may not have been universal among them.

The association of Stone Age stray finds, and, to a lesser degree, open-air sites, with the fjord parts of Nordland and Troms (cluster II on Figure 3) is in accordance with the view of Troms presented by Winther (Th. Winther 1877:134) and later also by Simonsen (Simonsen 1956:6-10). However, with the lack of use of test pits, open-air sites and stray finds recorded by the survey consist to a large degree of

documentation of earlier known finds, and so do not present new and independent evidence.

The existing general impression of the Iron Age settlement has not been altered by the Economic Map survey. Cluster I in Figure 3, characterised by a high frequency of Iron Age burial mounds, consists of municipalities located along the outer coast of Nordland and Troms as may be seen from the map Figure 4. The Iron Age houses included in the recent survey do not, however, quite conform to this picture. Table 1 and Figure 2 indicate that few houses have been located, and that they show a marked concentration in a small number of municipalities.

The low frequency of Iron Age house sites may be discussed in connection with the distribution of farm mounds. Figure 2 indicates that there is a close association between high frequencies of Iron Age burial mounds and of farm mounds. Thus it seems probable that the farm mounds represent a continuation of the Iron Age settlement. And radiocarbon dates from the bottom of several farm mounds have proved that they were already settled during the Iron Age (Bertelsen 1979). The apparent lack of Iron Age house sites may thus, tentatively, be explained by the fact that at those localities where settlement continued into the Mediaeval period, the houses of the Iron Age farms are to be found at the bottom of the farm mounds.

However, it is clear that settlements resulting in farm mounds being accumulated were established over a long period of time, probably ending around A.D. 1600 (Holm-Olsen 1981, 1985). The data in Table 1, and the position of farm mounds within the arc pattern in Figure 2, suggest that the geographical distribution of farm mounds extends beyond that of Iron Age burial mounds.

The last two types of sites to be discussed here are the round and the rectangular *gammer*. The most obvious feature emerging from the CA plots is the clear geographical distinction between Iron Age barrows, farm mounds and round *gammer*. This agrees well with the historically known pattern of settlement, where the outer coast of Nordland and Troms is predominantly Norwegian and the fjord areas are predominantly Sami.

The plots do, however, also indicate a distinction between a higher frequency of round *gammer* in Nordland/Troms and a higher frequency of rectangular *gammer* in Finnmark. As rectangular *gammer* in the plot are associated with Stone Age houses, which have a much stronger influence on the shape of the plot, a second analysis was run on the data of table 1, but with all three Stone Age variables removed (Figure 5). The new plot confirms the distributional distinction between round and rectangular *gammer*. Otherwise, there are only minor differences between Figure 5 and Figure 2, other than that the direction of the first axis has been reversed, and that has no influence on the interpretation of the plot.

The choice of units, present day municipalities, places this analysis on a very general level, and obscures all local variation. On this general level, however, the analysis has brought into focus one characteristic feature of our present understanding of North Norwegian settlement history: its discontinuous character. Though the clusters produced by the CA are geographical ones, they also differ in chronological content. As it is not probable that this is due to discontinuous settlement within the various geographical areas, it illustrates that there are still important lacunae in the database. This is especially true regarding the transition periods: between Stone Age and Iron Age, and between Iron Age and the Mediaeval period.

Pit-houses in Arctic Norway

An investigation of their typology using multiple correspondence analysis

By Ericka Engelstad — University of Tromsø

The archaeology of the Late Stone Age of Arctic Norway is characterised by the excavations of house remains, found primarily along the coast. Few open-air sites have been examined, and these are primarily along interior rivers and lakes. Thus, excavation of house remains was, and still is, our major source of data on the Late Stone Age. The artefactual material associated with houses forms the basis of a four-part phase/period division of the Varangerfjord area, a sequence which is sometimes applied to the whole of north Norway. The osteological material from middens directly associated with Late Stone Age houses forms the basis of our interpretations of seasonality of settlement and resource utilisation. The variation in the houses themselves forms the basis for interpretations of socio-economic, kinship, and settlement patterns. Recently, the chronological sequence (K. Helskog 1974, 1978a, 1980; E. Helskog 1983), the interpretations of the osteological material (Engelstad 1984; Renouf 1981, 1984), and the size and composition of settlements (K. Helskog 1984; Helskog & Schweder n.d.) have been, at least partially, re-examined (Engelstad 1985).

It is now time to take a closer look at the source of data for many of these interpretations - the houses themselves. The house remains were first classified into types in the 1960s on the basis of extensive surveys and excavations in the Varangerfjord area. Since that time there has been not only a steady increase in the number of houses recorded (due to extensive surveys in connection with economic mapping of all townships), but also a steady increase in the number of prehistoric houses excavated (due primarily to salvage archaeology in the entire area and a large research project on the island of Sørøya). Despite some variation of features and numerous 'atypical' houses the majority of newly recorded houses are placed in the existing typology. However, the number of anomalous cases is becoming large and the house typology is clearly in need of re-examination. This, then, is the aim of the present paper.

PIT-HOUSE TYPOLOGY

Three major types of pit-houses are recognised in Arctic Norway. These three types are named after the original type sites - Karlebotn, Gressbakken, and Mortensnes - all of which are on the inner part of Varangerfjord. Historically, the house remains at both Karlebotn and Gressbakken were the first Stone Age houses recognised archaeologically in northern Norway (Nummedal 1937, 1938; Gjessing 1942), although the house types were first described later (Simonsen 1976). The Mortensnes house type was first described in the early 1960s (Odner 1963), although the existence of these houses was known earlier. Both Karlebotn and Gressbakken type houses are from the Late Stone Age (4000 BC to ca. 300 BC). The Karlebotn type house is believed to be the earliest, although it also appears to have been used throughout the entire Late Stone Age. The Gressbakken type house is from the latter part of the Late Stone Age, with a few dated examples in Varangerfjord from ca. 3000 BC, but with the majority of dated houses from approximately 2500-1800 BC (K. Helskog 1974, 1984). The Mortensnes type house is believed to be later than both of these and is associated with the Sami Iron Age, approximately 1- 1700 AD (Kleppe 1974; Johansen & Odner 1968; Olsen 1984). But it is recognised that some could date to the latter part of the Late Stone Age (K. Helskog 1978a, 1978b; Simonsen 1979:379), and the Mortensnes type house will therefore be initially included in this analysis. The following 'type' descriptions are based on Simonsen (1976, 1979), unless otherwise stated.

The earliest well-known house type is the Karlebotn house, which is best seen at the type site Gropbakkeengen at Karlebotn in the inner part of Varangerfjord (Figure 1). Karlebotn houses are small (10-25 m^2 floor area), shallow depressions which can be round or rectangular in form, contain a single, stone-lined hearth in the middle of the floor area,

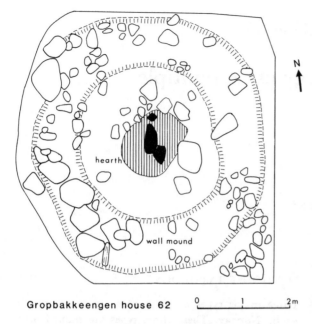

Gropbakkeengen house 62 0 1 2m

Figure 1. Plan drawing of a Karlebotn type house, house 62 from the Gropbakkeengen locality (after Simonsen 1961:113).

and have an entrance passage which is on the side of the house away from the sea, i.e. at the back. These are easily recognised today by the presence of low turf walls and are found at numerous localities along the entire coast of Finnmark. This house type is often considered to be typical of the Varangerfjord Period III. K. Helskog (1980:59) dates the Gropbakkeengen site by radiocarbon to ca. 3700-3200 BC, and Period III to ca. 2600-1800 BC. (For a description and discussion of the dating of these periods see E. Helskog 1983:49-52; Engelstad 1985.) Thus, this house type first appears relatively early in the Late Stone Age. However, it should be remembered that although it is considered 'typical' of Period III in Varangerfjord, excavated Karlebotn houses can be dated to all parts of the Late Stone Age.

Associated with the latter part of the Late Stone Age is the Gressbakken type house, first recognised in Varangerfjord at the Gressbakken Nedre sites (Figure 2), where the interiors of several houses were more or less totally excavated. Gressbakken houses are large (40 m^2 and sometimes as large as 70 m^2 floor area), oval, semi-subterranean houses with thick turf walls, and a semi-subterranean entrance passage through the wall on the long side of the house towards the sea. There are at least two stone-lined hearths along the longitudinal mid-axis of the floor area. Numerous Gressbakken type houses are reported from surveys along the coast and islands of Finnmark, Troms, and northern Nordland. This house type is said to be typical of the Varangerfjord Period IV. The houses at the Gressbakken Nedre sites range in radiocarbon dates from ca. 2600 BC to 2000 BC (K. Helskog 1980), and

Period IV is dated by K. Helskog (1980) to 2100-1200 BC.

The Mortensnes type house was first recognised at the Mortensnes site on the north side of the Varangerfjord (Johansen & Odner 1968; Simonsen 1963) and was originally associated solely with the Sami Iron Age. However, two excavated houses at Mortensnes have a Late Stone Age lithic assemblage as well as some iron tools, and were radiocarbon-dated to ca. 200 BC (Johansen & Odner 1968; K. Helskog 1978a, 1978b) (Figure 3.). This is the least understood of the three major house types, partially because so few have been excavated, but also because the 'type' has been described differently by some archaeologists. The major excavator of the Mortensnes localities, E. J. Kleppe, describes this house type as an oval to almost rectangular, very deep depression with thick turf walls. The length of the house is oriented parallel with the terrace on which it is situated, and is thus parallel with the contemporary shore line. The interior floor area is ca. 20 to 30 m^2 with a single, long, almost rectangular stone-lined hearth slightly asymmetrical to the middle of the floor area. There is no sign of an entrance (Kleppe 1974:125). Unfortunately, Simonsen's more recent descriptions have deviated considerably from the original one. His description is as follows:

A large house of more sharply rectangular form than any of those from the Stone Age, and with two hearths. It looks like a further development of the transitional type, i.e. the Karlebotn type with two hearths, but in contrast to all other houses, we know, from the Stone Age, these often lie with the gable towards the sea (Simonsen 1979:359-361, my translation).

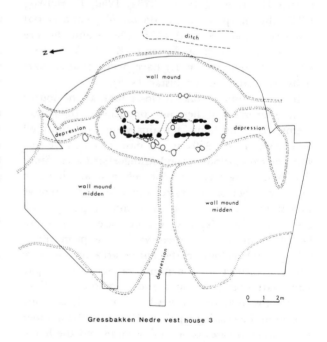

Gressbakken Nedre vest house 3

Figure 2. Plan drawing of a Gressbakken type house, house 3 from the Gressbakken Nedre Vest locality (After Simonsen 1961:290).

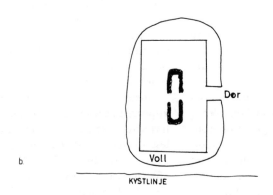

b.

Figure 3. Plan drawing of a) a Mortensnes type house, house 26 from the Mortensnes locality (after Johansen & Odner 1968:64; Kleppe 1974:figs. 26 and 27), and b) Simonsen's schematic plan of a Mortensnes house (Simonsen 1979:380, fig. 209).

In addition, in the same publication a schematic plan of this type shows a door passage in one long wall (Simonsen 1975b:360). This is clearly totally contrary to the original descriptions and does not seem to be based on any real evidence from the area. Although there are obvious discrepancies in how this house type is described, there have been no new excavations of this particular type. Mortensnes houses are reported only from Finnmark and primarily from Varangerfjord, where Mortensnes, with approximately 100 houses, is the largest known locality. There are, in fact, only four Mortensnes houses which have been excavated. These are: one from Høybukt, one from Angsnes, and two from Mortensnes (Simonsen 1963:227, 270-273; Johansen & Odner 1968:57-85).

In addition to the three major types, there are some excavated houses from other localities which vary from the major types or which appear to have a different mixture of morphological characteristics. For example, the so-called Sæleneshøgda house 'type' is described as an early version of the Karlebotn house, but is represented by only three houses from a single locality (Simonsen 1976:23). A mixture of features characteristic of both Karlebotn and Gressbakken type houses is reported for excavated houses at Nyelv in Varangerfjord (Simonsen 1961:437), Iversfjord (E. Helskog 1983:84-86), and several localities on the island of Sørøya in western Finnmark (Simonsen 1968). Such houses have recently been described by Simonsen (1979:376-377) as transitional types between an earlier Karlebotn type and a later Gressbakken type. However, radiocarbon dating does not entirely support this unilineal chronological development from one house type to another. In fact, the mixture of structural features goes both ways, with large and deep Gressbakken type houses having only a single hearth or no hearth at all (see for example E. Helskog 1983 and Simonsen 1961:461).

The majority (perhaps all) of Late Stone Age pit-houses probably functioned as dwellings. However, some houses with non-residential functions are reported to be associated with some of the house clusters in the Varangerfjord area and are referred to by Simonsen (1976), as workshops or men's houses. Unfortunately, only one of these so-called men's houses has been excavated at the Gropbakkeengen site. Two men's houses or workshops/meeting-houses for men are reported from the Gressbakken Nedre Vest site (Simonsen 1975a). Although numerous finds of flakes from the production of lithic tools are reported, the interiors of these houses were not excavated, and the interpretation is impossible to substantiate. Thus, the evidence for their non-residential function is highly equivocal. Houses with an unusual feature or inventory, apparently inhabited by specialists, and functioning at least partly as workshops (for pottery or slate point production) are reported from two sites on the island of Sørøya (Simonsen 1975a). However, these houses have been as yet only cursorily reported in the literature, although a full publication is in preparation (Simonsen, personal communication).

Since most pit-houses probably functioned as dwellings they have been associated with particular types of family structure; and changes in the houses through time have been interpreted as representing changes in family structure (Simonsen 1972:164). The Karlebotn house, because of its single hearth and interior space of 12-20 m^2 (Simonsen 1979:371), has been associated by Simonsen with a nuclear family of five persons on the basis of unspecified ethnographic parallels (Simonsen 1976, 1979:371). The Gressbakken house because of its double hearths and larger floor area (40-70 m^2), is in contrast referred to as a multifamily or extended family house (Simonsen 1972, 1975b, 1976, 1979:371).

As stated earlier, Gressbakken type houses are generally late (2500-1800 BC) in the Late Stone Age. Because of the chronological placement of Gressbakken type houses, the data show a change from single to double hearths and from small to large houses, and it is often postulated that family structure also changed. Thus »one has gone over from living in small units, probably nuclear families, to joining together into larger units, either extended families or work cooperatives« (Simonsen 1979:375).

Most recently, Simonsen has stated that the extended family house, i.e. a house with two or more hearths, was introduced from Finland already in Period II but does not 'join' with the semi-subterranean construction form of the Gressbakken house until the beginning of Period IV, when the subterranean aspect of house construction comes to Varangerfjord from the east (Simonsen 1979:376). As evidence for this, Simonsen refers to finds, from Åland and southern Sweden, of hearths possibly associated with houses (Meinander 1962:11-16). There are apparently no such finds between this area and Varanger. Where the traits have come from further east is not disclosed by Simonsen. Nor does he discuss the reasons for this change in family and house structure, why it should be accepted by the existing population, or its implications for changes in socio-economic structure.

In conclusion it is clear that what in the early 1950s appeared as three chronologically distinct house types has after many new surveys and excavations become less distinct, both chronologically and morphologically (Andreassen 1985:193-197; Helskog 1983:84-86) (Figure 4). As 'types' both the Karlebotn and Gressbakken houses are still generally 'understood' and recognised both in the field and in the literature, but a detailed understanding of their contents is now a thing of the past. New data have revealed a greater variation in the combination of structural at-

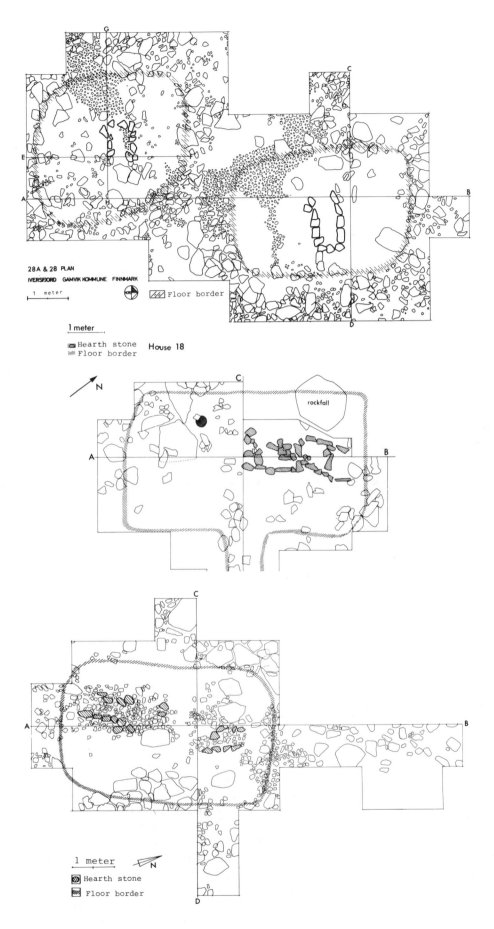

28A & 28 PLAN
IVERSFJORD GAMVIK KOMMUNE FINNMARK
1 meter
Floor border

1 meter
Hearth stone   House 18
Floor border

N
rockfall

1 meter   N
Hearth stone
Floor border

Figure 4. Plan drawing of houses from the Iversfjord locality showing some of the variation of morphological characteristics of Late Stone Age houses (after Helskog 1983).

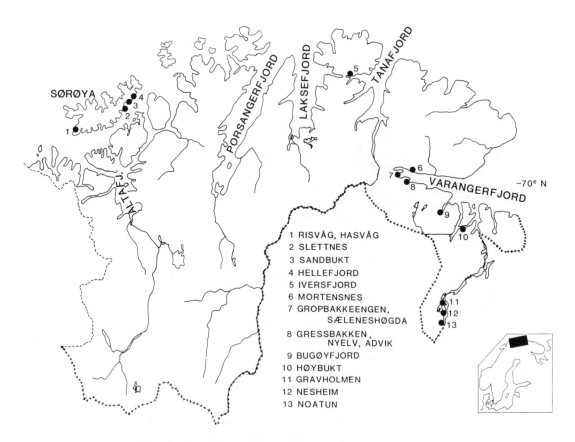

Figure 5. Map of Finnmark showing the localities discussed in the text.

tributes both for excavated and unexcavated houses. It is, therefore, necessary to re-examine the composition of Late Stone Age house types as to their combination of morphological attributes in order to see whether the current typology is still valid and, indeed, whether it is still useful. And it is also important to investigate whether a typology based on the attributes of unexcavated houses can be related to a typology based on a particular set of attributes which come to light only after excavation. And, since a particular combination of structural features has been associated previously with changes in family structure, it is important to examine these house types in relation to their sociocultural meaning for interpretations of family, or rather household, structure.

MULTIPLE CORRESPONDENCE ANALYSIS OF HOUSE TYPES

Major excavations of house remains have been carried out in Varangerfjord, in Iversfjord, and on Sørøya (Figure 5). For the present analysis, information on Stone Age houses was taken from the published reports on the excavations in Varangerfjord (Simonsen 1961, 1963) and Iversfjord (E. Helskog 1983). Houses at several Stone Age localities on Sørøya have been excavated, but

these have until now been reported only summarily (Simonsen 1968, 1973) and, therefore, the unpublished excavation reports were used for the Sørøya sites considered here. In all cases, both the text descriptions and the line drawings have been used for the measurements on which the variables are based. Since some of the variables, such as number of hearths etc., can be seen only after excavation, only those houses which had a totally excavated interior were utilized in the analysis. A total of 84 houses were utilized: 15 from Iversfjord, 44 from eleven sites in the Varangerfjord-Pasvik Valley area and 25 from eight sites on Sørøya. The sites and houses used in the analyses are presented along the row margins in Table 1 and 3.

As stated earlier, none of the house types was strictly defined, but rather descriptions of houses from the original type sites were used as a general type classification. It is possible from these descriptions to pick out certain structural features whose presence, absence, or variation is always considered when describing a house. Central to all houses is that they were all to some degree dug into the ground surface and even today the vast majority can be distinguished as depressions or 'pits' in the ground. The other characteristics which have been used in house descriptions are the form, size, and depth of the house depression, the presence or absence of depres-

76

sions or other features in the walls which can be interpreted as entrances, the number of hearths, and the orientation of the house in relation to the shore line. In addition, Gressbakken houses are often said to be dug into a slope, so that the character of the terrain on which a house is built can also be considered as a 'structural' feature. These seven variables will be considered in the present analysis and will be discussed in greater detail below (refer also to the bottom parts of Table 1 and 3).

Variable 1 refers to hearths: their presence, absence, or number. The number of stone-lined hearths in a house varies from 0 to 3. No excavated houses have been reported as having more than three hearths. Although some houses have no hearth, they may have a concentration of charcoal, possibly associated with some scattered stones, which have been interpreted as the remains of a possible hearth. It should be remembered that hearths can and do vary considerably in size, shape, and placement within a house interior. This variation, which has implications for their use, function, and associated social unit, is beyond the scope of the present paper and will not be considered here.

Variable 2 refers to the depth of the pit house depression. It is a measurement of the depth as it appears today after excavation, from the top of the wall remains to the interior floor level. It is believed that this is a reflection of the original depth of the house. Thus it has been divided into only two coarse categories: deep and shallow. The border between these two is placed at 35 cm, on the basis of the analysis of Late Stone Age houses at the Iversfjord locality (E. Helskog 1983).

Variable 3 is house size. This is a measurement of the interior floor area of the excavated house and reflects the size of the original floor space. House size is occasionally measured from the middle or highest point on the wall mound or even from the outside of the wall mound. But since these measurements are more a reflection of turf wall decomposition than of living space, they are not considered here. This variable is divided into three values: small (1 to 20 m^2), medium (20 to 30 m^2) and large (greater than 30 m^2) on the basis of the analysis of house size at Iversfjord (E. Helskog 1983:84–86), Simonsen's size limits for Karlebotn and Gressbakken houses, and K. Helskog's (1984: 63–64) discussion of house size in the Varangerfjord area.

Variable 4 is house form. This measurement refers to the form of the excavated interior floor area. The form of the unexcavated house depression generally reflects the form of the excavated interior. However, there are occasions when this is not true, as is most often the case for oval depressions where the floor space turns out to be more rectangular after excavation. This variable is divided into four geometric shapes: round, oval, rectangular, and square.

Variable 5 is the orientation of the house in relation to the contemporaneous shore-line. Orientation (of the Mortensnes houses, for example) has been given chronological significance by Simonsen. Houses are oriented with their length parallel to the shore or with their gable towards the shore. Of course, neither round nor square houses will have a particular orientation.

Variable 6 is the slope of the terrain. Sloping terrain has often been associated with Gressbakken type houses, which can be dug into a slope and at times appear to have great depth simply because of this. However, these houses can also be found on flat terrain, and this variable, although not directly an aspect of house structure, was included to see whether there is any association between terrain and house type.

Variable 7 is the presence, absence, and placement of entrances in the turf walls. Houses can have elongated, ditch-like depressions in any or all of their turf walls. These are related to house construction and/or decomposition, and are most generally interpreted as entrance passages. Placement of the entrance passage has been used as a defining characteristic for the house types investigated. This last variable will be investigated in two different ways in the multiple correspondence analyses. Firstly, passages will be strictly defined as depressions in turf walls. Secondly, all disturbances or irregularities in turf walls, such as lack of stone, fine gravel spread, flat 'threshold' stone, etc., which have been interpreted as entrance passages, will be included in the analysis. For the sake of the present analysis, the 'front' of a house is the seaward side. This variable has initially seven values: no entrance, entrance in front, entrance in front and on one side, entrance in front and on two sides, entrance in back, entrance on all four sides, and entrance on one side only.

As can be seen from the above description, the variables are mixed, with both ordinal and nominal scale variables represented. Mixtures of ordinal and nominal scale variables are especially difficult to handle in multivariable data analysis. Most often there exists no optimal way of performing the analysis. This is especially true when the number of variables (or categories) is 'high' when compared to the number of units. Multiple correspondence analysis is suited to this type of situation and seems to do well in practice. (Bølviken n.d.; Bølviken & Schweder 1983:106–120; Greenacre 1984:126–168). MCA is essentially the use of correspondence analysis on three or more categorical variables or an indicator matrix consisting of units characterised by categories of variables. And, although the variables can vary in size and type, only bivariate relationships are used in the analysis. The present analysis is an effort to find the underlying structure of similarities and differences in Stone Age houses, based on the analysis

Table header:

Variables	Var 1	Var 2	Var 3	Var 4	Var 5	Var 6	Var 7	Group	Var 7
Sites	A B C D E	F G	H I J	K L M N	P Q R	S T	U V W X Y Z A1 B1		U V W X Y Z A1 B1

```
                  Var 1     Var 2  Var 3   Var 4    Var 5  Var 6    Var 7      Group    Var 7
Sites                                                                          A B               A B
                 A B C D E   F G   H I J   K L M N   P Q R  S T   U V W X Y Z 1 1         U V W X Y Z 1 1
Iversfjord
   15       1    . . 1 . .   1 .   . 1 .   . . 1 .   . 1 .  1 .   . . . . . . . 1    C     . . . . . . . 1
   15A      2    . 1 . . .   1 .   1 . .   . . 1 .   . 1 .  1 .   . . . . . . . 1    C     . . . . . . . 1
   59       3    . . 1 . .   1 .   1 . .   . . 1 .   . 1 .  1 .   . . . . . . . 1    C     . . . . . . . 1
   17       4    1 . . . .   . 1   1 . .   . . 1 .   . 1 .  1 .   . 1 . . . . . .    C     . 1 . . . . . .
   18       5    . . 1 . .   . 1   1 . .   . . 1 .   . 1 .  1 .   . . 1 . . . . .    C     . . 1 . . . . .
   19       6    1 . . . .   . 1   . 1 .   . . 1 .   . 1 .  1 .   . . 1 . . . . .    C     . . 1 . . . . .
   20       7    . . . . 1   . 1   . 1 .   . . 1 .   . 1 .  1 .   . . 1 . . . . .    C     . 1 . . . . . .
   22       8    . . . 1 .   1 .   . 1 .   . . 1 .   . 1 .  1 .   . . . . . . . 1    -     . . . . . . . 1
   23       9    . . . 1 .   1 .   . 1 .   . . 1 .   . 1 .  1 .   . . . . . . . 1    C     . . . . . . . 1
   24      10    . 1 . . .   1 .   1 . .   . . 1 .   . 1 .  1 .   . . . . . . . 1    C     . . . . . . . 1
   26      11    . 1 . . .   1 .   1 . .   . . 1 .   . 1 .  1 .   . . . . . . . 1    C     . . . . . . . 1
   27      12    . 1 . . .   1 .   1 . .   . . . 1   . 1 .  1 .   . . . . . . . 1    -     . . . . . . . 1
   28A     13    . 1 . . .   1 .   1 . .   . . 1 .   . 1 .  1 .   . . . . . . . 1    C     . . . . . . . 1
   28      14    . 1 . . .   . 1   1 . .   . . . 1   . 1 .  1 .   . . . . . . . 1    C     . 1 . . . . . .
   32      15    . 1 . . .   1 .   1 . .   . . 1 .   . 1 .  1 .   . . . . . . . 1    C     . . . . . . . 1
Gropbakkeengen
   62      16    . . . . 1   . 1   1 . .   . . 1 .   1 . .  1 .   . . . . . . . 1    A     . . . . . . . 1
   69      17    . . . . 1   . 1   . 1 .   . . 1 .   1 . .  1 .   . . . . . . . 1    C     . . . . . . . 1
   59      18    . . . . 1   . 1   . 1 .   . . 1 .   1 . .  1 .   . . . . . . . 1    C     . . . . . . . 1
   56      19    . . . . 1   . 1   . . 1   . . 1 .   1 . .  1 .   . . . . . . . 1    C     . . . . . . . 1
   53      20    . . . . 1   1 .   1 . .   . . 1 .   1 . .  1 .   . . . . . . . 1    A     . . . . . . . 1
   52      21    . . . . 1   1 .   . . 1   . . 1 .   1 . .  1 .   . . . . . . . 1    A     . . . . . . . 1
   51      22    . . 1 . .   1 .   . . 1   . . 1 .   1 . .  1 .   . . . . . . . 1    C     . . . . 1 . . .
   26      23    . . . . 1   1 .   1 . .   . . 1 .   1 . .  1 .   . . . . . . . 1    A     . . 1 . . . . .
   12      24    1 . . . .   1 .   1 . .   . . 1 .   1 . .  1 .   . . . . . . . 1    C     . . . . . . . 1
   11      25    . . . . 1   . 1   1 . .   . . 1 .   1 . .  1 .   . . . . . 1 . .    -     . . . . . . 1 .
   10      26    . 1 . . .   1 .   . 1 .   . . 1 .   1 . .  1 .   . . . . . . . 1    C     . . . . . . . 1
    8      27    . 1 . . .   1 .   . 1 .   . . 1 .   1 . .  1 .   . . . . . . . 1    A     . . . . . . . 1
   -3 øvre 28    . . . . 1   1 .   . . 1   . . 1 .   1 . .  1 .   . . . . . . . 1    A     . . . . 1 . . .
   -3 nedre 29   . 1 . . .   . 1   1 . .   . . 1 .   1 . .  1 .   . . . . . . . 1    A     . . . . 1 . . .
   -4 øvre 30    . 1 . . .   . 1   1 . .   . . 1 .   1 . .  1 .   . . . . . . . 1    A     . . . . 1 . . .
   -4 nedre 31   . 1 . . .   . 1   . . 1   . . . 1   1 . .  1 .   . . . . . . . 1    A     . . . . . . . 1
   -7      32    . 1 . . .   . 1   1 . .   . . 1 .   1 . .  1 .   . 1 . . . . . .    A     . 1 . . . . . .
   -12     33    1 . . . .   1 .   1 . .   . . 1 .   1 . .  1 .   . . . . . . . 1    A     . . . . . . . 1
Gressbakken Nedre vest
    1      34    . . 1 . .   . . 1   . 1 .   . 1 .   . . 1   . 1 . .   . . . . . 1   B     . . . . 1 . .
    2      35    . . 1 . .   . 1   . 1 .   . 1 .   . 1 .   . 1 . .   1 . . . . 1    B     . . . . . . 1 .
    3      36    . . 1 . .   . 1   . . 1   . 1 .   . 1 .   . 1 . .   . . . . . 1   B     . . . . 1 . .
    4      37    . 1 . . .   . 1   . . 1   . 1 .   . 1 .   . 1 . .   . . . . . 1   -     . . . . 1 . .
Gressbakken Nedre øst
   16      38    . . 1 . .   . 1   . 1 .   . . 1 .   . 1 .  1 .   . . . . . . . 1    C     . . . . . . . 1
   21      39    . 1 . . .   . 1   . 1 .   . . 1 .   . 1 .  1 .   . 1 . . . . . .    C     . 1 . . . . . .
Nyelv Nedre vest
    1      40    1 . . . .   . 1   . . 1   . . 1 .   . 1 .  1 .   . . . . . . . 1    C     . . . . . . . 1
    5      41    . 1 . . .   1 .   . 1 .   . 1 . .   . 1 .  1 .   . . . . . . . 1    C     . . . . . . . 1
    6      42    . 1 . . .   1 .   1 . .   . . . 1   . 1 .  1 .   . . . . . . . 1    A     . . . . . . . 1
    7      43    . . 1 . .   1 .   . 1 .   . . 1 .   . 1 .  1 .   . . . . . . . 1    C     . . . . . . . 1
Bugøyfjord
    I      44    . 1 . . .   . 1   . 1 .   . . 1 .   . 1 .  . 1   . . . . . . . 1    B     . . . 1 . . . .
   II      45    . 1 . . .   . 1   . 1 .   . . 1 .   . 1 .  . 1   . . . . . 1 . .   B     . . . 1 . . . .
Sæleneshøgda
    I      46    1 . . . .   1 .   1 . .   . . 1 .   1 . .  1 .   . . . . . . . 1    A     . . . . . . . 1
   II      47    . . . . 1   1 .   1 . .   . . 1 .   1 . .  1 .   . . . . . . . 1    A     . 1 . . . . . .
  III      48    . . . . 1   . 1   . 1 .   . . . 1   1 . .  1 .   . . . . . . . 1    C     . . . . . . . 1
Advik
    a øvre 49    . 1 . . .   1 .   1 . .   . . 1 .   1 . .  1 .   . . . . . . . 1    A     . . . . . 1 . .
    a nedre 50   . 1 . . .   1 .   1 . .   . . 1 .   1 . .  1 .   . . . . . . . 1    A     . . . . . 1 . .
    b      51    . . 1 . .   . 1   1 . .   . . 1 .   . 1 .  . 1   . . . . . . . 1    B     . 1 . . . . . .
    j øvre 52    . . 1 . .   . 1   . . 1   . . 1 .   . 1 .  . 1   . . . . . . . 1    B     . 1 . . . . . .
Høybukt sør øst
    4      53    . . 1 . .   . 1   . . 1   . 1 . .   . . 1  1 .   . . . 1 . . . .    B     . . . 1 . . . .
Noatun neset
    I      54    1 . . . .   1 .   . 1 .   . . 1 .   . 1 .  1 .   . . . . . . . 1    C     . . . . . . . 1
Nesheim
    I      55    . 1 . . .   1 .   1 . .   . . 1 .   . 1 .  1 .   . . . . . . . 1    A     . . . . . . . 1
   II      56    . . 1 . .   1 .   1 . .   . . 1 .   . 1 .  1 .   . . . . . . . 1    C     . . . . . . . 1
Gravholmen
    I      57    . . 1 . .   1 .   1 . .   . . 1 .   . 1 .  1 .   . . . . . . . 1    C     . . . . . . . 1
Sandbukt
    1      58    1 . . . .   . 1   1 . .   . . 1 .   . . 1  1 .   . . . . . . . 1    C     . . . . . 1 .
    2      59    . . . . 1   . 1   . 1 .   . . 1 .   . 1 .  1 .   . . . . . . . 1    C     . . . . . . . 1
    3      60    . . 1 . .   1 .   . 1 .   . . 1 .   . 1 .  1 .   . . . . . . . 1    C     . . . . . . .
    4      61    . . 1 . .   1 .   . 1 .   . . 1 .   . 1 .  1 .   . . . . . . . 1    C     . . . . . . . 1
Slettnes
  hus i myra 62  . . . . 1   . 1   1 . .   . . 1 .   . 1 .  1 .   . . . . . . . 1    A     . . . . . . . 1
    1      63    . . 1 . .   1 .   1 . .   . . 1 .   . 1 .  1 .   . . . . . . . 1    C     . 1 . . . . . .
   23      64    . . 1 . .   1 .   1 . .   . . 1 .   . 1 .  1 .   . . . . . . . 1    C     . 1 . . . . . .
Hasvåg
    1      65    1 . . . .   1 .   1 . .   . . 1 .   . 1 .  1 .   . . . . . . . 1    C     . . . . . . . 1
    2      66    . . . . 1   1 .   1 . .   . . 1 .   . . 1  1 .   . . . . . . . 1    C     . . . . . . . 1
Risvåg
    A      67    1 . . . .   1 .   1 . .   . . 1 .   1 . .  . 1   . . . . . . . -    -     . . . . . . . 1
    C      68    . . . . 1   . 1   1 . .   . . 1 .   . 1 .  1 .   . . . . . . . 1    C     . 1 . . . . . .
    D      69    . . . . 1   1 .   1 . .   . . 1 .   . 1 .  1 .   1 . . . . . . .    -     . 1 . . . . . .
    Z      70    . 1 . . .   1 .   1 . .   . . 1 .   . 1 .  1 .   . . . . . . . 1    C     . . . . . . . 1
Mortensnes
   10      71    . . 1 . .   . 1   . 1 .   . . 1 .   . 1 .  1 .   . . . . . . . 1    C     . . . . . . . 1
   26      72    . 1 . . .   . 1   . 1 .   . . . 1   1 . .  1 .   . . . . . . . 1    A     . . . . . . . 1
Hellefjord Øvre
    1      73    . . 1 . .   1 .   1 . .   . . 1 .   . 1 .  1 .   . . . . . . . 1    C     . . . . . . . 1
    2      74    . 1 . . .   . 1   1 . .   . . 1 .   . . 1  1 .   . . . . . . . 1    A     . . . . . . . 1
    3      75    . . . . 1   1 .   1 . .   . . 1 .   . . 1  1 .   . . . . . . . 1    C     . . . . . . . 1
    4      76    . . . . 1   1 .   1 . .   . . . 1   1 . .  1 .   . . . . . . . 1    A     . . . . . . . 1
    5      77    . . 1 . .   1 .   1 . .   . . . 1   . 1 .  1 .   . . . . . . . 1    C     . . . . . . . 1
Hellefjord Nedre
   12b     78    . . . . 1   1 .   1 . .   . . 1 .   . 1 .  1 .   . . . . . . . 1    C     . . . . . . . 1
   21       9    . . . . 1   1 .   1 . .   . . 1 .   . . 1  1 .   . . . . . . . 1    C     . . . . . . . 1
Hellefjordbotn
   23      80    . . . . 1   1 .   1 . .   . . 1 .   . 1 .  1 .   . . . . . . . 1    C     . . . . . . . 1
Hellefjord Ytre
   28      81    . . . . 1   1 .   1 . .   . . . 1   . 1 .  1 .   . . . . . . . 1    -     . . . . . . . 1
   29      82    . . . . 1   1 .   1 . .   . . . 1   1 . .  1 .   . . . . . . . 1    A     . . . . . . . 1
   31      83    . . . . 1   . 1   1 . .   . . 1 .   1 . .  1 .   . . . . . . . 1    C     . . . . . . . 1
   33      84    . . . . 1   1 .   1 . .   . . . 1   1 . .  1 .   . . . . . . . 1    C     . . . . . . . 1
```

Var 1: Hearths
  A: no hearth
  B: one hearth
  C: two hearths
  D: three hearths
  E: charcoal concentration

Var 2: Depth
  F: deep (over 35 cm)
  G: shallow (under 35 cm)

Var 3: Size
  H: small (1-20 m²)
  I: medium (20-30 m²)
  J: large (30-70 m²)

Var 4: Form
  K: round
  L: oval
  M: rectangular
  N: square

Var 5: Orientation
  P: no orientation
  Q: length parallel to coast
  R: gable towards coast

Var 6: Terrain
  S: flat
  T: sloping

Var 7: Entrances / depressions in walls
  U: front
  V: one side
  W: two sides
  X: front and one side
  Y: front and two sides
  Z: back
  A1: all four sides
  B1: none

Table 1. Data matrix showing the registrations of structural/morphological variables on 84 excavated houses from the Late Stone Age and Early Sami Iron Age. Explanations to the variables are given at the bottom of the table. The numbering of rows and the lettering of columns refer to Figures 6 and 7. The right hand version of Var 7 is used in the analysis shown in Figure 7.

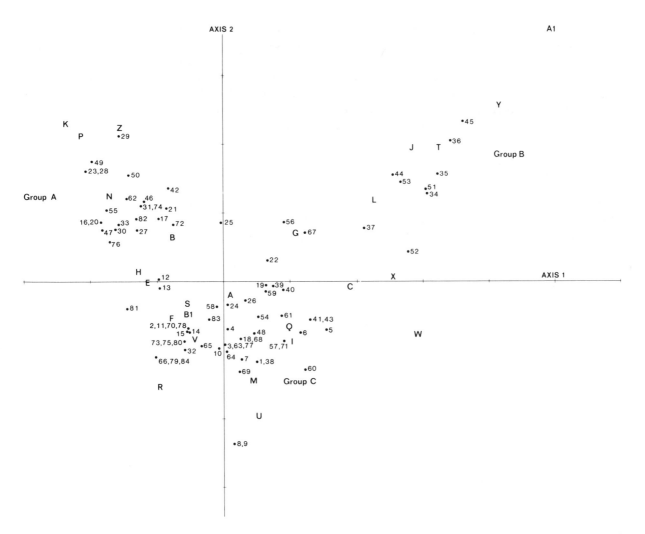

Figure 6. Multiple correspondence analysis plot of houses and form variables for the total sample, 84 x 27, investigated. For variable 7, only wall depressions are accepted as entrances.

of 84 excavated houses characterised by seven 'mixed' variables, each having a different number of values or categories. The identity of each unit – a single house – is thus retained in the analysis. As with correspondence analysis (CA), we are able not only to see how the units relate to the variables, but also how the units and variable categories relate to one another. Thus, close relationships between variable categories can be used to characterise groupings of house units. This is, of course, one of the most important aspects of CA/MCA. The categorisation of the values for each variable is a subjective judgement on the part of the researcher, and the basis for this categorisation was given under the description of each variable.

The data for the 84 houses are presented in Table 1. Each of the variables has two or more values. The values for each variable are rated as present (1) or absent (0), such that each variable has only one positive value. Two versions of variable 7 are given in Table 1. In the first version, only depressions are interpreted as entrances (main body of table). In the

other version, all likely features are interpreted as entrances (right-hand addition to table).

Before discussing the multiple correspondence analyses, an examination of the 84 x 27 matrix in Table 1 offers some illuminating insights into the present house typology. Although Gressbakken type houses are described as having an entrance passage in front towards the sea, it should be noted that of the 84 houses examined only two (no. 48 and 69) had only a front entrance. Neither of these houses – Sæleneshøgda III and Risvåg D – can be considered a 'typical' Gressbakken house. From Table 1, it can be clearly seen that if a house has a front entrance/depression, it also has a depression or possible entrance on the side, i.e. in this case in the gable end of a house. And, although Karlebotn types houses are described as having an entrance away from the sea, of the 18 excavated houses at the type site of Gropbakkeengen, only seven have possible entrances and only five of these are at the back of the house.

THE MULTIPLE CORRESPONDENCE ANALYSES

Several multiple correspondence analyses (MCA) (Bølviken et al. 1982; Bølviken & Schweder 1983; Solheim 1981) were performed on these data. Because of the nature of the variables, multiple correspondence analysis was used (Greenacre 1983:126–168). An initial MCA (Figure 6) was performed on data using strictly defined morphological features (depressions in walls) as 'entrances' in variable 7. Thus all 'entrances' that were unsure interpretations of certain 'features' (such as many small stones on a wall, few stones on a wall, a large rock (threshold) in the wall area, etc.) were rated as absent in the

first MCA analysis. In the second MCA (Figure 7), these were included, along with depressions in walls, as representing entrances.

Both multiple correspondence analyses of all 84 houses resulted in three clear groups and a number of outliers (Figures 6 and 7). In the first multiple correspondence analysis, the first two axes represent 26.03% of the variation – 16.49% and 9.53%, respectively (Table 2, left). In the second MCA the first two axes represent 26.29% of the variation – 16.47% and 9.82%, respectively (Table 2, centre). As can be seen from both MCA plots, there are three major clusters of houses (groups A, B, and C) and a number of outliers. As can be seen from the plots from the two different multiple correspon-

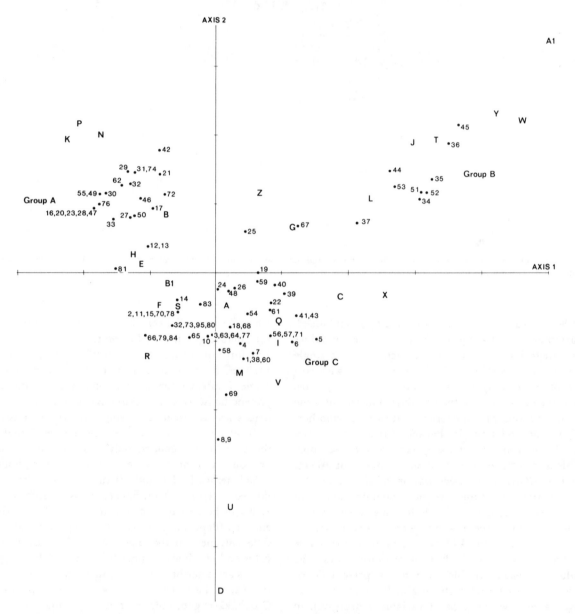

Figure 7. Multiple correspondence analysis plot of houses and form variables for the total sample, 84 x 27, investigated. For variable 7, all features interpreted as entrances are accepted.

Axis	1. MCA Expl. %	2. MCA Expl. %	3. MCA Expl. %
1	16.49	16.47	18.09
2	9.53	9.82	15.98
3	7.77	7.53	13.03
4	6.62	7.05	11.73
5	6.14	6.63	10.28
6	6.10	5.97	8.26
7	5.64	5.58	8.05
8	5.25	5.05	6.65
9	5.04	4.88	5.05
10	4.99	4.44	2.35

Table 2. Explanation percentages for the first 10 Axes of the three MCAs.

dence analyses, the position of the houses in the three clusters and the outliers remained relatively stable. Only house no. 52 (Advik øvre) and house no. 69 (Risvåg D, the potter's house) have changed groupings in the two MCAs. But it is clear from the second MCA plot that the clusters are no longer as tight as they were in the first plot; and there has been some internal rearrangement of some of the houses in each group. The effect of accepting all interpretations of entrances instead of just depressions is essentially minimal. Most variables or variable values remain stable and only four values move position. These are U: entrance in front; V: entrance on one side; W: entrance on two sides; and Z: entrance in back. These are four values of the variable entrance placement. It is this variable which shows most variation. This could be due either to a great amount of real variation in the data, or to the fact that this variable contains the greatest number of values (8) of any, i.e. that it is too subdivided in relation to the others. However, statistically, variation in the number of values per variable should only slightly effect the multiple correspondence analyses (L. Solheim, pers. comm.; Greenacre 1984:126-168). (See below.)

Group A represents 22 houses from nine different sites, and is dominated by houses from Gropbakkeengen (Figure 6). The inclusion of all possible entrances in variable 7 in the second MCA did not change the composition of this grouping of houses (Figure 7). The attributes associated with group A are a single hearth (B), round or square form (K, N), and, their correlate, no particular orientation with respect to the shore (P). Both small size (H) and a charcoal concentration (E) instead of a stone-lined hearth should also be included. One could also include the presence of a possible entrance away from the shore (Z), although, as can be seen from the first MCA plot, this attribute is not necessarily definitive for group A.

Group B is represented by seven houses in the first MCA (Figure 6), and by eight houses in the second MCA (Figure 7), from four localities. All of these houses are what could be called classic Gressbakken type houses and represent the most 'classic' sites for this type; and all are in Varangerfjord. The 'defining'

attributes which are mostly associated with this group are sloping terrain (T), length oriented with the sea (Q), and depressions or entrances on all sides (A1), the front and two sides (W), and, if depressions are strictly defined, on two sides only (W). Oval shape (L) is probably also most associated with this group. But it is interesting to note that neither size nor the number of hearths is of special importance for characterising this group.

Group C is the largest and most heterogeneous group, and is represented by 45 houses in the first MCA (Figure 6), and by 46 houses in the second MCA (Figure 7), from 18 localities. The inclusion of all possible entrances in the second MCA has caused house no. 69 (Risvåg D, the potter's house) to move into this group. Group C includes Gressbakken, Karlebotn, and Mortensnes type houses, and many 'mixtures' of these. The morphological attributes most closely associated with this group are rectangular shape (M), medium size (I), length oriented with the sea (Q), no hearths (A), flat terrain (S), and either no entrance (B1) or an entrance on one side only (V).

It would appear that group A includes what can be called Karlebotn houses, while group B represents Gressbakken houses. This latter group appears to be rather special, being primarily defined by the presence of depressions in house walls; and regionally distinct, being confined solely to the Varangerfjord area.

As can be seen from Table 1, the variables have differing numbers of values - from two to eight. The largest and most diversified variable is the one concerning the number and placement of possible entrances. Since it was believed that this could effect the significance, or weighting, of this variable, an MCA was performed in which the number of values that this variable could take was reduced to five. Thus, entrances on one side and on two sides were grouped together; as were entrances on the front and one side, the front and two sides, and on all sides. This left five values for this variable. It was also recognised that the house form values could be difficult to distinguish in a field situation (both excavation and survey) and were possibly not entirely discrete. Thus, the round and square forms were grouped, and the oval and rectangular forms were grouped.

This grouping of values for the entrance (all possible features accepted as entrances) and form variables resulted in an 84 × 22 matrix. An MCA of this matrix resulted in the plot (not shown here) where the first axis represented 21.02% of the variation and the second axis represented 12.03% of the variation - a total of 33.05%. In the MCA plot, the house groupings remained remarkably stable. Group A was unchanged. One house, Gressbakken Nedre Vest 4 (no. 37), was added to group B. Group C was somewhat more dispersed with some houses moving to a more outlying position. In general the house clusters remained constant, but there was a slightly different constellation of variables related to each group of houses. Also the number of variables related to groups A and B was, of course, reduced. The variables most closely related to group A were square/round form (V), no orientation (K), and entrance at the back (R). The variables most closely related to group B were large size (J), slope (P), and entrances in front and on one or both sides (U).

The variables were further manipulated in subsequent MCA analyses of the 84 houses. The terrain variables were removed as were some of those variables which were poorly represented (such as three hearths), but throughout the diverse manipulations (which will not be presented here) the three major house groupings remained essentially stable.

Variables			A	B	C	D	E	F	G	H	I	J	K	L	M	N	P	Q
Iversfjord																		
15	1		.	.	1	.	.	1	.	.	1	.	1	1	.	.	.	1
15A	2		.	1	.	.	.	1	1	.	.	.	1	1	.	.	.	1
59	3		.	1	.	.	.	1	1	.	.	.	1	1	.	.	.	1
17	4		1	.	.	.	.	1	.	.	1	.	1	1	.	.	1	.
18	5		.	1	.	.	.	1	.	1	.	.	1	1	.	.	1	.
19	6		1	.	.	.	.	1	.	1	.	.	1	1	.	.	1	.
20	7		.	.	1	.	.	1	.	1	.	.	1	1	.	1	.	.
24	8		.	1	.	.	1	.	.	1	.	.	1	1	.	.	.	1
26	9		.	1	.	.	.	1	1	.	.	.	1	1	.	.	.	1
28	10		.	1	.	.	.	1	.	1	.	.	1	.	1	1	.	.
32	11		.	1	.	.	.	1	.	1	.	.	1	1	.	.	.	1
Gropbakkeengen																		
59	12		.	.	1	.	1	.	1	.	.	.	1	1	.	.	.	1
56	13		.	.	1	.	.	1	.	1	.	.	1	1	.	.	.	1
51	14		.	1	.	.	.	1	.	1	.	.	1	1	.	.	.	1
12	15		1	.	.	.	1	.	1	.	.	.	1	1	.	1	.	.
10	16		.	1	.	.	1	.	1	.	.	.	1	1	.	.	.	1
-7	17		.	.	1	.	1	.	1	.	.	.	1	1	.	1	.	.
Gressbakken Nedre øst																		
16	18		.	.	1	.	1	.	.	1	.	.	1	1	.	.	.	1
21	19		.	1	.	.	.	1	.	1	.	.	1	1	.	1	.	.
Nyelv Nedre vest																		
1	20		.	.	1	.	1	.	1	.	.	.	1	1	.	.	.	1
5	21		.	.	1	.	1	.	.	1	.	.	1	1	.	.	.	1
7	22		.	.	1	.	1	.	.	1	.	.	1	1	.	.	.	1
Sæleneshøgda																		
III	23		.	.	.	1	.	1	.	1	.	.	1	.	1	.	.	1
Noatun neset																		
I	24		1	.	.	.	.	1	.	1	.	.	1	1	.	.	.	1
Nesheim																		
II	25		.	.	1	.	.	1	.	1	.	.	1	1	.	.	.	1
Gravholmen																		
I	26		.	.	1	.	.	1	.	1	.	.	1	1	.	.	.	1
Sandbukt																		
1	27		1	.	.	.	.	1	.	1	.	.	1	.	1	.	.	1
2	28		.	.	1	.	.	1	.	1	.	.	1	1	.	.	.	1
3	29		.	.	1	.	.	1	.	1	.	.	1	1	.	.	.	1
4	30		.	.	1	.	.	1	.	1	.	.	1	1	.	.	.	1
Slettnes																		
1	31		.	.	1	.	1	.	1	.	.	.	1	1	.	.	.	1
23	32		.	.	1	.	1	.	1	.	.	.	1	1	.	.	.	1
Hasvåg																		
1	33		1	.	.	.	.	1	1	.	.	.	1	1	.	.	.	1
2	34		1	.	.	.	.	1	1	.	.	.	1	.	1	.	.	1
Risvåg																		
C	35		.	.	.	1	.	1	.	1	.	.	1	1	.	.	.	1
Z	36		.	1	.	.	1	.	1	.	.	.	1	1	.	.	.	1
Mortensnes																		
10	37		.	.	.	1	.	1	.	1	.	.	1	1	.	.	.	1
Hellefjord Øvre																		
1	38		.	.	1	.	1	.	1	.	.	.	1	1	.	.	.	1
3	39		.	.	1	.	1	.	1	.	.	.	1	1	.	.	.	1
5	40		.	.	1	.	1	.	1	.	.	.	1	1	.	.	.	1
Hellefjord Nedre																		
12b	41		.	1	.	.	1	.	1	.	.	.	1	1	.	.	.	1
21	42		.	.	1	.	1	.	1	.	.	.	1	.	1	.	.	1
Hellefjordbotn																		
23	43		.	1	.	.	1	.	1	.	.	.	1	1	.	.	.	1
Hellefjord Ytre																		
31	44		.	.	1	.	.	1	1	.	.	.	1	1	.	.	.	1
33	45		.	.	1	.	1	.	1	.	.	.	1	.	1	.	.	1

Var 1: Hearths
A: no hearth
B: one hearth
C: two hearths
D: charcoal concentration

Var 2: Depth
E: deep (over 35 cm)
F: shallow (under 35 cm)

Var 3: Size
G: small (1–20 m^2)
H: medium (20–30 m^2)
I: large (30–70 m^2)

Var 4: Form
J: oval
K: rectangular

Var 5: Orientation
L: length parallel to coast
M: gable towards coast

Var 7: Entrances / depressions in walls
N: one side
P: front and one side
Q: none

Table 3. The data matrix for group C with entrances defines as depressions. The number of units is 45 and the number of variables is reduced to six, with a total of 16 values.

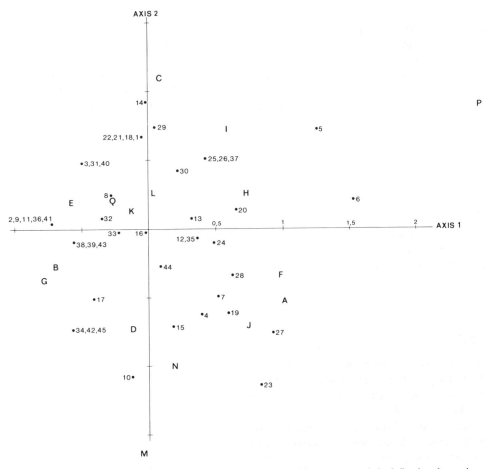

Figure 8. Multiple correspondence analysis plot of group C, the 45 x 16 matrix, with entrances strictly defined as depressions.

MULTIPLE CORRESPONDENCE ANALYSIS OF GROUP C

The 45 houses of group C, with depressions only defining entrances, were investigated further using multiple correspondence analysis, in an effort to reveal any internal structure in this group. When only these 45 houses are examined, six of the morphological attributes are no longer present and are thus removed from the analysis (Table 3). The values no longer present in the material are: three hearths (D), round shape (K), square shape (N), no orientation (P), and entrances/depressions in front and two sides (Y), and on all sides (A1). These represent those which are associated most with groups A and B, and the outliers.

In addition, five other variable values were removed. First removed were those which were poorly represented in group C: entrance/depression in the front only (U), in the back only (Z), and on two sides only (W). This removal also brings the number of values for this variable more into line with the number of values for the other variables. Secondly, the terrain variables, flat (S) and slope (T), were removed since, as mentioned earlier, an MCA of the

entire material with the terrain variables removed had shown that these did not significantly affect the established house groups. The remaining group C matrix is 45 x 16, representing 45 houses and six variables with a total of 16 values.

The MCA of group C resulted in the plot shown in Figure 8. The first two axes represent 34.07% of the variation: 18.09% and 15.98% respectively (Table 2, right). In group C there is no apparent clustering of houses. Nor do the variables show any clear clustering. As can be seen from the MCA plot (Figure 8), the variables do seem to exhibit a trend (vertically in the plot) having possibly most to do with size and number of hearths. However, it is clear that this trend is in many ways contrary to the way the variables should have grouped if they had followed the normative house type descriptions in use today. For example, depth is associated with the absence of a hearth rather than with the presence of two hearths as in the traditional typology.

Group C, which encompasses all houses other than those typical of the 'classic' Varangerfjord sites (especially Gropbakkeengen and Gressbakken), is extremely heterogeneous. An examination of the MCA plot for group C in relation to the location of the sites shows that this variation does not seem to be directly related to geographical differences or differences between outer coast and inner fjord. A similar examination of the radiocarbon-dated houses shows that there is no clear chronological structure in the spread of houses on the plot.

At present, it is perhaps difficult to say whether or not this heterogeneity is real or due to the amount of data at our disposal. However, one point seems obvious: when one comes away from the south side of Varangerfjord there is much variation in the morphological attributes of excavated Late Stone Age houses. An examination of the survey reports from the archaeological surveys conducted in connection with the Economic Map survey reveals a similar degree of variation in the combination of morphological attributes of unexcavated Late Stone Age houses.

CONCLUSION

Multiple correspondence analysis, which is correspondence analysis of an incidence matrix with three more categorical variables, was used in an investigation of a typology of Late Stone Age houses.

A preliminary perusal of the current house descriptions of the Mortensnes house type in comparison to actual excavated house plans revealed essentially the non-existence of this type as it has most recently been described in the literature. Only further excavations of so-called Mortensnes houses can reveal any pattern in structural morphology.

In addition, a preliminary perusal of the initial 84 x 27 matrix revealed discrepancies between the actual data and the house descriptions for particular aspects of both the Gressbakken house type and the Karlebotn house type.

The multiple correspondence analyses of the two 84 x 27 matrices resulted in three clusters of houses and a number of houses which could not be placed in any cluster (the outliers). Two of the clusters, group A and group B, were found to be Karlebotn type houses and Gressbakken type houses, respectively. It was found that the majority of these houses were from the classical type sites in Varangerfjord. The third cluster of houses, group C, was quite heterogeneous and was examined further using multiple correspondence analysis. There was no internal clustering within this group. It remained extremely heterogeneous in relation not only to structural/morphological characteristics but also chronology and geographical location. It would appear that as one moves away from Varangerfjord, both excavated and unexcavated houses show considerable variation in their combination of structural/morphological characteristics.

Acknowledgements

The initial work on house typology was begun in conjunction with a joint statistical-archaeological project entitled »Multivariate analysis in archaeology« at the University of Tromsø. The project was financed by The Norwegian Research Council for Science and the Humanities. I would like to thank Knut Helskog and Leiv Solheim for discussions and comments on the first draft of this article.

Find pattern of multistratified sites

Correspondence analysis as an explorative tool

By Reidar Bertelsen — University of Tromsø

INTRODUCTION

An earlier version of this paper has been published in *American Archaeology*, Vol 5 No 1, 1985. This version differs slightly, less emphasis being placed upon details concerned with the development of the archaeological hypothesis on transformation processes. The statistical discussion, however, is developed further.

The study of sites with complex archaeological stratification faces two major problems:

1. Isolation of stratification units from the accumulated web of depositions.
2. Differentiation between pre- and post-depositional transformations.

Traditionally, archaeologists use the term 'layer' for the units of a stratified site. This is not sufficient for a more detailed stratigraphical study, since we must also deal with cuts, post-holes, standing structures, etc. In this paper, 'unit' is used to denote all the features isolated by investigation of the cultural stratification of a site.

The term 'layer' is also found inappropriate here, since it suggests geological processes as close analogies. Our understanding of the formation processes of a site is dependent on a more complex model than nature can give us.

This paper concentrates on the first problem. It is a common experience for archaeologists that even the most minute excavation and documentation is bound to give us records that are far from the Pompeii model of a site. The reasons for this are partly the transformations of the material and partly our inadequate methods of analysis, or shall we say 'reading' ability.

From the comprehensive literature on stratigraphy and related fields, I shall mention only two works that have directed my interests into the line I will try to develop in this paper.

Edward C. Harris has developed a stratigraphic notation system that is consistent with an advanced understanding of archaeological stratification (Harris 1975a, 1975b, 1977 1979). To be successful, this system demands the maximum ability of the archaeologist to read similarities and differences in the web of stratification units. Along with the Harris notation system there also follows a well-developed terminology resting upon a long research tradition in this field. I will try to employ this terminology here.

The second work that has had an impact on my interests, is Michael B. Schiffer's studies of transformations, especially as formulated in his *Behavioral Archaeology* (1976).

Thirdly, but not least, it shall be mentioned that this work is an offshoot of a project I carried out together with Inger Marie Holm-Olsen and Przemyslaw Urbanczyk (Warszawa) on the stratigraphic analysis of north Norwegian settlement mounds (farm mounds). The empirical basis and a more comprehensive theoretical discussion can be found in the first report from this project (Bertelsen & Urbanczyk 1985a, 1985b). For a presentation of farm mound stratigraphy, see Holm-Olsen 1979.

STRATIFICATION UNITS

The research background for this work is the archaeological studies of the farm mounds of North Norway (Bertelsen 1979, 1984; Holm-Olsen 1981, 1983, 1985). These are settlement accumulations produced by households having a composite subsistence economy: cattle, fishing, hunting and some barley cultivation. Essential to the stratification is the architecture, being timber frame covered by thick grass turf, both in walls and roofs. This gives us accumulations consisting mainly of the following elements:

1. Collapsed turf houses (organic soil, wood and stones).
2. Dung accumulated inside byres and perhaps also outside openings.

3. Household waste such as food left-overs, ashes and different kinds of home industry remnants and by-products.
4. Water-transported humus and mineral particles from uphill areas.
5. Wind-transported particles that are trapped between the houses in the yard.
6. Natural soil accumulation.

The period of interest is mainly AD 1000-1800, because a majority of the farm mounds seem to start their build-up in the Viking period or a little later. However, the phenomenon can be traced back prior to the time of Christ (Bertelsen 1979, 1985; Jørgensen, R 1984). Physically the mounds are 1-3 metres deep covering an area of 1000-3000 m^2, but a few far more impressive mounds are known.

Observed today, the majority of the units of such accumulations are thin, extensive sheets of soil. For example, the Soløy farm mound which is to be discussed here gave a stratigraphic sequence of 58 units in a 3 by 3 metre trench only 1 metre deep. Most of the units were far wider than the trench, so one could observe only fragments of them. There is no reason to believe that our ability to read the stratigraphy was sufficiently advanced to allow us to assume that our sequence was close to the stratification reality. A process going on for ca 1000 years must have been a chain of more than 58 events and their accumulated deposits on this small part of the central area of the site.

Theoretically, one should expect that such events, if temporarily discrete, produced units with both bottom and top surfaces and a specific find pattern. These differences between units should be observable even if we have to operate within the limits of a trench. For the Soløy trench, there is a long series of factors we could suggest as reasons for our obvious mixing of the units. We shall not develop this point, only state that the factors are partly related to the abilities of the excavators, partly to the next theme of discussion, the transformations.

In this connection, we shall concentrate on the effects of the mixing of units. A perfect isolation would permit us to study the specific morphology and find content of the units, while a mixing deprives us of this opportunity. A total mixing would leave us with the aggregate of say 1000 years of cumulative events, unable to isolate any details. We shall not say that such data are without interest, but the information potential is rather limited. The records of any archaeological excavation are to be found somewhere on the axis between a maximally structured site with ideal isolation, and a total mixture.

TRANSFORMATIONS

Inspired by the way Michael Schiffer (1976) has systematised site formation processes, we have suggested a series of processes that affect the morphology of the units and the find distribution on the Soløy site (Bertelsen & Urbanczyk 1985a:133-146). The first category to be defined is what Schiffer calls cultural formation processes (1976:27-41). They are of four kinds:

S-A Processes (from systemic context to archaeological context).

A-A Processes (from one state to another state within archaeological context).

A-S Processes (from archaeological to systemic context).

S-S Processes (from one state to another state within systemic context).

Of the S-A Processes, I stipulate that discard will produce the highest number of finds, and that they will mainly be ecofacts. The A-A Processes do, of course, also distort the find distribution, mainly with the effect of mixing up structures. The A-S Processes we can imagine in this context are not so clear-cut. Most important of these processes is perhaps the cutting of grass turf on the site for construction of new buildings.

The major S-S Processes are:

1. Dogs and birds (esp. seagulls) manipulating the organic refuse.
2. Children's playing with broken objects.
3. Reuse of material, especially iron.

The cultural formation processes are not the only agent creating problems for the archaeologist. We must also consider the non-cultural (= natural) formation processes (Schiffer 1976:15):

1. Biological breakdown.
2. Chemical breakdown.
3. Physical breakdown.
4. Transport up or down caused by either physical or biological processes.

This list of transformation factors could definitely be made longer and more specific, but hopefully it has made it clear that one should expect so many and diverse cumulative events that it is possible to distinguish the stratification units on the 'fingerprints', although the forces that erase these fingerprints are formidable.

The effects of all these transformations are thus the same as those of inadequate unit isolation. The records of the Soløy excavation have to find a place somewhere on the axis between the unattainable, fully preserved and recorded structure and the total mixture. The individual stratigraphical units, however, are not likely to be on the same position of this axis, because they have been subject to different kinds and degrees of transformation.

STATISTICAL CLASSIFICATION

The discussion above leads me to the assumption that it is possible to find a residual pattern that can be correlated with a behavioural pattern of the past. The question is, can we find a method of evaluating the degree of patterning, or in other words the heterogeneity of the system of recorded stratification units, representing the web of stratigraphical units?

One way of solving such an evaluation problem would be through direct observation and judgement. This method is often employed, explicit or implicit, but it has the disadvantage of being coarse (the number of categories are often only two, preserved vs. disturbed), and even then the danger of inconsistency increases dramatically by the number of units. Another obvious solution is to apply a quantitative classification to the units. This solution has the advantage of consistency and of being detailed. On the other hand, it lacks the possibility of using as diverse criteria as could be considered through intuitive judgement. The criteria must be subject to measurement.

The material at hand in this case clearly invites a quantitative classification based on the find pattern of the units (Bertelsen & Urbanczyk 1985a). The reason for this is mainly the fragmentation of the units themselves within the limits of a 3 by 3 metre square. This yields rather rudimentary information on the morphology and other aspects of the structure of the units themselves.

The find content (artifacts and ecofacts) is perhaps the best preserved quality of the units. Clustering of finds within the units must also be viewed as an aspect of structure vs. mixture and should therefore be of relevance to the problem at hand. If the purpose of classification is interpretation of the units, a clustered distribution of finds will add another difficulty to the use of the data from a small trench, giving only fractions of the units. When we restrict ourselves to the objective of finding contrasts between any unit and the average find pattern (the entropy), we will not feel troubled by the possible clustering of finds within the units.

Observing the find content, we can define the total mixture as the average find pattern, and we will then suppose that a well preserved structure gives us few or no units with the average find pattern. Formally, we arrange our data in a matrix like this:

$$
\begin{array}{ccccc}
p_{11} & p_{12} & \cdots & p_{1b} & r_1 \\
p_{21} & p_{22} & \cdots & p_{2b} & r_2 \\
\cdot & \cdot & & \cdot & \cdot \\
\cdot & \cdot & & \cdot & \cdot \\
p_{a1} & p_{a2} & \cdots & p_{ab} & r_a \\
c_1 & c_2 & \cdots & c_b & 1
\end{array}
$$

The rows represents the relative frequencies of different find classes within each unit and the columns represent the relative frequencies of each find class in different units. The column marginals are $c_1 \ldots c_b$, and the row marginals $r_1 \ldots r_a$. The row column marginals can also be defined as the mean row profile (MRP) (Bølviken & Schweder 1983:chapter 3.2). Related to our problem we can say that the MRP is the find pattern of the total mixture. Defining it in this way, we adjust ourselves to the fact that we have to deal with fractions of the universe, and because of that will have to compare relative frequencies.

The multivariate statistical technique called correspondence analysis (CA) is specially designed as a tool for exploration of such data structures (Bølviken et al. 1982). The alternative, principal component analysis, would compare absolute frequencies. In CA, the unit profiles $(p_{11}/r_1 \ldots p_{1b}/r_1)$ are compared with the MRP by means of the chi square distance. Further discussion of the CA can be found in Bølviken et al. 1982; Greenacre 1984; Madsen 1985; Bølviken & Schweder 1983. Here we shall observe only that on the visual displays of the CA - the plots of two axes against each other - the MRP is the origin of the coordinate system.

Because of the properties of the CA, a plot of the units as projections on the plane defined by the two major axes (1st and 2nd) will show us the units as points at different distances from the origin. Supposing a structure of our data that is close to the total mixture, we shall then expect a plot with an increase in the density of points towards the origin. Supposing a better preserved structure, we shall expect an even distribution, two or more clusters at a distance from the origin, or even a distribution with a circular or semicircular pattern around the origin.

It is worth mentioning that the CA-plot has no capabilities that allow us to distinguish between units mixed by transformation processes and units mixed by inadequate archaeological methods.

Our data are as given in Table 1. We have the chronological sequence established as demonstrated by the Harris matrix (Figure 1). To prevent the time dimension from interfering with the definition of the axes, we will exclude from further analysis the following find classes: STEA, POTT, PIPE and GLAS as they are exclusive to specific periods of the ac-

	Excluded variables						Included variables										
UNIT	BONE	ORNA	GLAS	STEA	POTT	PIPE	FISH	BIRD	MAMM	SLAT	CLAY	SLAG	FLIN	META	IRON	SUM	INERT %
1	13	0	9	0	50	5	2	1	70	0	23	0	1	3	11	11	5.2
2	15	0	21	0	50	7	8	2	193	1	331	0	1	2	40	578	4.9
4	33	0	1	0	0	0	21	1	21	0	386	1	0	0	4	434	12.0
5	46	1	0	0	0	0	28	8	66	1	29	0	1	2	0	135	4.2
6	0	0	0	0	0	0	0	0	0	0	0	0	0	0	1	1	1.3
7	6	0	0	0	0	0	23	1	41	0	28	0	0	0	1	94	1.3
8	21	0	0	0	1	0	33	7	81	0	304	0	1	3	5	434	3.2
9	1	0	0	0	0	0	3	2	6	0	2	0	0	0	0	13	1.4
10	0	0	0	0	0	0	1	0	6	0	21	1	0	0	0	29	1.2
11	5	0	0	0	0	0	0	0	4	0	0	0	0	0	0	4	0.5
12	1	1	0	0	0	0	0	0	8	0	10	0	0	0	0	18	0.3
13	1	0	0	0	0	0	0	0	3	0	3	0	0	0	2	8	0.6
14	0	0	0	0	0	0	0	0	2	0	0	0	0	0	0	2	0.3
15	0	0	0	0	0	0	0	0	1	0	3	1	0	0	0	5	5.5
16	1	0	0	1	0	0	1	0	11	0	0	0	0	0	1	13	1.1
17	0	0	0	0	0	0	0	0	0	0	0	0	0	0	3	3	3.8
18	0	0	0	0	0	0	0	0	0	0	0	0	0	0	1	1	1.3
19	2	0	0	0	0	0	87	2	27	0	1	0	1	0	0	118	17.0
21	0	0	0	0	0	0	46	3	28	0	0	0	0	0	0	77	7.7
23	0	0	0	0	0	0	3	0	0	0	0	0	1	2	1	7	7.8
24	0	0	0	0	0	0	1	0	0	0	0	0	0	0	0	1	0.3
28	78	1	0	0	0	0	73	0	38	2	9	0	0	0	2	124	11.3
31	0	0	0	0	0	0	0	0	0	0	7	0	0	0	1	8	0.4
32	0	0	0	1	0	0	0	0	2	0	8	0	0	1	6	17	2.9
33	0	0	0	0	0	0	2	0	20	0	0	1	0	0	4	27	3.1
34	0	0	0	0	0	0	0	0	0	0	0	0	0	0	1	1	1.3
35	0	0	0	0	0	0	0	0	1	0	0	0	0	0	0	1	0.1
38	0	0	0	0	0	0	0	0	0	0	4	0	0	0	0	4	0.2
SUM							332	27	629	4	1169	4	6	13	84		
INERT %							35	3	12	1	19	7	3	6	13		

BONE: Unidentified bone fragments
ORNA: Decorated objects
GLAS: Glass from window panes
STEA: Steatite vessels
POTT: Pottery
PIPE: Clay pipes
FISH: Fish bones
BIRD: Bird bones
MAMM: Mammal bones
SLAT: Slate whetstones
CLAY: Fired clay
SLAG: Slag
FLIN: Pieces of flint
META: Metal fragments
IRON: Iron nails

Table 1. Data matrix showing the finds from the 1981 excavation at the Soløy farm mound. Along marginals are seen the sum and the inertia percentages of both the units and the variables. The variable labels are explained at the bottom of the table.

cumulation. The effect of material sensitive to time is demonstrated in Bølviken et al. 1982:51-52 (analysis by Holm-Olsen). BONE is taken out because I suppose that the information potential of this variable is embedded in the three main groups of bones (FISH, BIRD and MAMM). ORNA is not included in further analysis because this variable is not well defined and there are only three objects.

RESULTS

Before we go any further in the discussion of the plots, it is necessary to examine the diagnostics of the analysis. First of all, we can judge the general quality of our results from the upper part of Table 2. Here we find from the explanation percentage (Expl.%) that the CA-plot projected to the plane between the two major axes (Figure 2), represents appr. 71% of

the total difference between the units and the MRP. The rest of the differences are represented on the axes 3-6.

From the next section in Table 2 we can find the quality of each unit's representation. Because cumulative values (0-100) are given, we are especially interested in column 2, since this gives us the representation of each point on the plane between the two major axes. The units 6, 9, 10, 11, 12, 14, 15, 17, 18, 23, 32 and 35 are below 50%, but only the units 15 and 23 are so low that we in fact can say that they are not represented by the first two axes.

Likewise, we find from the last section in Table 2 that the variables BIRD, SLAG, FLIN and META are badly represented in the plot. This means that the structure in Figure 2 is defined mainly by the other variables. This observation is confirmed by the inertia percentages given along the marginals in Table 1.

Figure 2 exhibits a clustered distribution where we

		AXIS				
	1	2	3	4	5	6
EXPL.%	50	71	82	90	97	99
UNIT						
1	1	90	93	98	98	100
2	59	93	94	94	98	100
4	59	98	100	100	100	100
5	41	51	73	85	85	98
6	1	37	83	95	97	100
7	68	71	92	92	95	97
8	62	92	92	98	98	100
9	20	21	36	38	39	100
10	23	27	33	50	100	100
11	5	48	93	93	94	99
12	24	32	86	88	90	99
13	5	68	85	95	99	100
14	5	48	93	93	94	99
15	1	1	4	28	100	100
16	10	74	94	94	96	99
17	1	37	83	95	97	100
18	1	37	83	95	97	100
19	89	96	99	99	99	99
21	96	98	98	98	98	99
23	5	8	33	78	99	100
24	74	89	97	99	99	99
28	89	92	93	95	95	97
31	60	61	93	98	99	100
32	6	41	95	95	95	96
33	4	65	70	87	99	100
34	1	37	83	95	97	100
35	5	48	93	93	94	99
38	64	98	100	100	100	100
VAR						
FISH	89	97	100	100	100	100
BIRD	13	13	23	31	31	100
MAMM	15	70	99	99	99	100
SLAT	22	22	22	22	23	25
CLAY	81	100	100	100	100	100
SLAG	1	1	4	30	100	100
FLIN	4	8	21	73	95	95
META	0	12	27	79	99	99
IRON	3	58	92	99	100	100

Table 2. The cumulative explanation percentage of the first six axes (upper part) followed by the cumulative percentage of the total variation of the individual units (central part) and variables (lower part) explained by the axes.

can identify at least 5 or 6 groups. My suggestion is the following list:

On the 1st axis from + to –

1. 19, 21, 24, 28
2. 5, 7, 9
3. 2, 8, 10, 12
4. 4, 31, 38

On the 2nd axis from + to –

5. 6, 17, 18, 34
6. 1, 11, 13, 14, 16, 32, 33, 35

The units 15 and 23 are not included in the groups.

There is no cluster of units close to the origin, but the distances to group 2 and 3 are not great. This means that these units are close to the average find

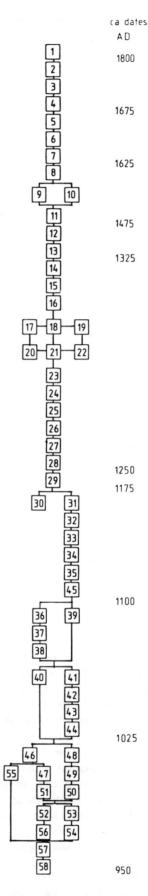

ca dates
A D

1800

1675

1625

1475

1325

1250

1175

1100

1025

950

Figure 1. The chronological sequence of the Soløy site shown as a Harris matrix.

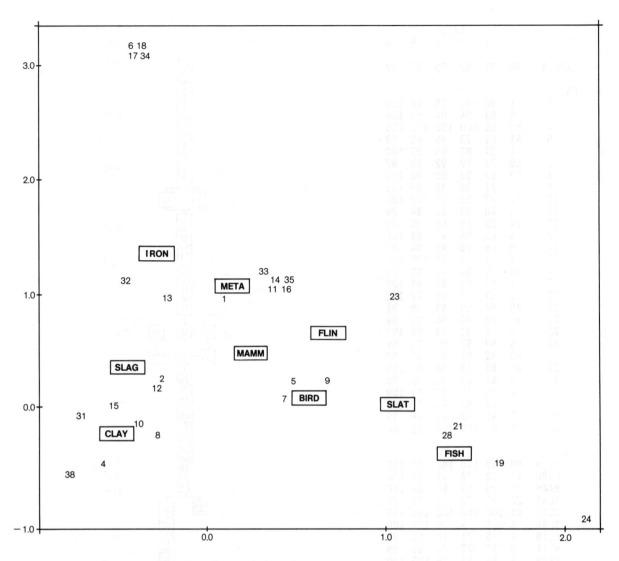

Figure 2. Plot of the first two principal axes from a correspondence analysis of the data in Table 1.

pattern. We find that they are relatively abundant on the variables MAMM and CLAY. Based on their position in the plot, we can also suggest that these two groups originally belonged to the groups 1 and 4. This suggestion is only hypothetical and we can test it only by means of independent variables, such as the result of different soil analyses.

Supposing a confirmation of our hypothesis, we can now sort out the units close to the origin and concentrate our further efforts on an interpretation of those units that probably have the best-preserved structure, or in other words: those stratigraphical units that are closest to the original stratification units. This is hopefully one step towards a better isolation of stratification units. Results of such a discussion are reported by Bertelsen & Urbanczyk (1985a:138-195, 1985b:228-250).

POSTSCRIPT

After the Sandbjerg symposium, T. Madsen has pointed out the problem of units with few finds. Some of these units are positioned far out on the axes of the CA-plot, and one might suspect that they have a strong effect on the definition of the axes. This could give an image of a structure that is far from what an analysis of a fuller material can give.

An analysis of the data excluding those units that have a row marginal less than 5 was performed by Madsen. The result revealed the same main structure as shown on Figure 2. This demonstrates that CA, as an explorative method, has a high stability. The reason for this is probably that even though CA is performed on relative frequencies, it is weighted according to the absolute values of the marginals.

Stylistic variation in the pottery of the Funnel Beaker Culture

By Anne Birgitte Gebauer — University of Aarhus

The aim of this study is to analyse form and decoration variation in the pottery of the Funnel Beaker Culture (TBK) from a small area in time and space, and to examine the relationships between style groups of pottery, human social units, and the patterned distribution of burial structures. The possible significance of the megalithic tombs is also considered.

Style has been defined as one aspect of formal variation in material culture, used to convey information about the personal and social identity of the maker or bearer (Wiessner 1984). This identification process is circular in nature, involving an interplay between the individual and the social environment. An individual's stylistic behaviour is generated from social expectations, and directed toward others in the larger social sphere. Specific information is transmitted concerning the social roles and affiliation of the individual. The responses to such transmissions, and the perceptions of these responses by the individual, are crucial to the maintenance of a self-concept and to a change in identity (Wiessner 1984; Voss 1982:45).

How individuals use material culture in social strategies depends on the framework of meaning within a particular historical context. Social and symbolic structures within the society define the compatibility of persons and artifact styles, and stylistic decisions are made relative to these structures. The frame of stylistic variation is the actual historical and cultural context (Hodder 1984:48).

Style can be used to transmit messages with varying degrees of specificity, ranging from vague associations to a distinct and invariant meaning that can be immediately decoded by the receiver. Usually, style operates at a semi-conscious level, evoking common associations among individuals. However, it may also be advantageous under certain conditions to conform to distinct expressions of group affiliation. Maintenance of a distinct style is related to selective pressures favouring both internal integration and external differentiation among groups conscious of their identity.

The conditions under which style takes on collective associations and yields information on social boundaries are frequently debated. In some studies it is suggested that insecurity, tensions, and competition between persons or groups may encourage stylistic imitation along certain dimensions (Conkey 1978, 1980, 1982; Hodder 1979, 1982a; Wiessner 1984).

Not all material culture, of course, plays an active role in social relations. Part of the variability in artifacts is 'normative' and caused by simple replication of traditional ways of doing things (Wiessner 1984; Gebauer 1984). However, it is unlikely that this should apply to the elaborate funeral pottery in this study, considering the ceremonial importance of pottery and the efforts invested in manufacturing the wide range of shapes and decorations.

In addition to the stylistic analysis of funeral pottery, this paper also considers the significance of megalithic tombs within the community. As observed by Hodder:

In some of these recent works on megalithic tombs there has been a tendency to be concerned mainly with generalisations, such as the use of megaliths as markers of territory, or of social and economic tensions. (1984:52)

Hodder criticises the weakness of the links between processes like territoriality, social stress and the imbalance between society and critical resources on one hand, and burials and megalithic monuments on the other. He stresses that the main problem with this type of explanation is its inability to account for the monuments in their own right, within a specific historical context.

The present paper investigates the significance of megalithic tombs within a local area through the stylistic analyses of pottery offerings made at the tombs. The hypothesis of territorial groups with a consciousness of identity related to the megalithic tombs would be supported, if distinct stylistic groupings could be demonstrated in pottery in relation to the tombs. Thus variation in style compared to the spatial distribution of tombs could reveal information on social structure (Hodder 1982b:171). If the

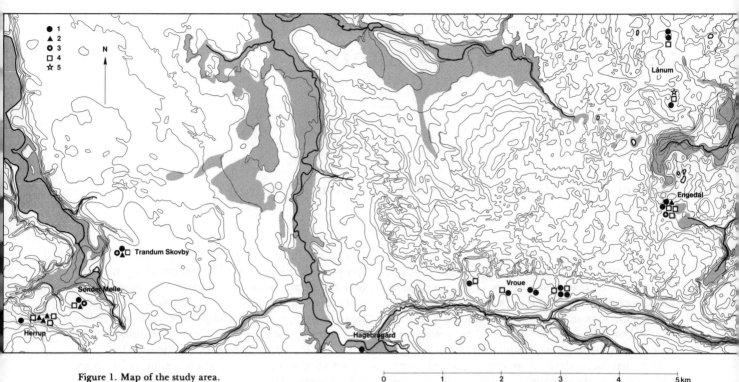

Figure 1. Map of the study area.
1: Megalithic tomb.
2: Mortuary house.
3: Simple inhumation grave.
4: Stone packing graves.
5: Unidentified structure.

identity of small local social units was expressed in ceramics, it can be expected that these units will appear in the funeral pottery, since this constitutes by far the most elaborate aspect of TBK material culture. It is essential here to use functionally equivalent sets of pottery to eliminate non-stylistic variation in the results (Ebbesen 1975; Gebauer 1977; Voss 1982:51).

Multivariate correspondence analysis (CA) is used here in a descriptive way to detect chronological and spatial patterns in the style attribute associations of the pottery (Bølviken et al. 1982; Madsen 1985:179ff). The capability of CA to display both units and variables in the same plot helps to detect those variables that are important in stylistic patterning. Further, principal coordinate analysis (PCA) (see Madsen this volume) is used to summarise the results of a series of CAs on various aspects of form and decoration extracted from the same basic pottery material.

THE STUDY AREA AND THE TOMBS

A small area between Viborg and Holstebro comprises the study region, referred to here as the Vroue area after one of the major sites (see map

Figure 1). Many archaeological investigations have been carried out in this area, and it has played an important role in recent discussions of the relationship between the TBK and the Battle Axe Culture, as well as in the study of mortuary houses and stone packing graves (Becker 1954:104, 1966, 1967, 1969, 1973; Davidsen 1978:82; Ebbesen 1975:198, 1978:site list A No 39-41, 44-46 and 102; Faber 1977; E. Jørgensen 1977a, 1977b, 1985; P.O. Nielsen 1979:57 and 63.

The pottery used in the analyses derives mainly from megalithic tombs. Pottery from two types of non-monumental structures related to burial rituals is also included, i.e. from mortuary houses and stone packing graves. The few simple inhumation graves are not considered, since they contained only a few pots.

The Vroue area covers 11.5 km from east to west and 5 km from north to south. An east to west oriented line of end-moraines from the last glaciation divides the area into northern and southern zones. To the north lies a relatively hilly terrain of moraine deposits cut by small valleys with numerous streams and wet areas. To the south lies a plain of diluvial sand.

Typically, the TBK sites are located on the slopes and terraces alongside the wet areas and streams. The higher elevations and locations at a distance from fresh water are avoided. The Vroue and Herrup sites are located on terraces below the hilly range formed by the glaciation (see Figure 1). Engedal and the two Lånum sites are situated on slopes close to rivers in the hilly northern part, whereas Hagebrogård is found on the southern plain close to the same stream as the Vroue sites.

Graves are usually found in clusters which include several different burial structures. On the whole, these clusters served as permanent burial grounds throughout the MN TBK (400 years). The composition of burial structures at each site appears in Table 1.

Megalithic tombs

Pottery offerings in connection with burials took place all through the EN TBK in Jutland (3100–2600 B.C.), but expanded in number of pots used as well as in the variety of pot shapes present, at the beginning of the MN TBK (2600–2200 B.C.). These rituals persisted to the end of the construction period of megalithic tombs, i.e. MN II/III (2400 B.C.) (Ebbesen 1978:118). A few of these pots came from inside the chamber as part of the grave goods, but by far the greatest number of pots were placed outside, at the kerb-stones on either side of the tomb entrance.

Different hypotheses have been put forth to explain the pottery at the tomb entrances and its relationship to the burials in the chambers. In tombs where pottery is found both in the chamber and at the entrance, there is a clear contemporaneity between the two deposits, with the same range of pot shapes and decorations found in both (Ebbesen 1978:125). Formal and chronological similarity indicate that the pottery in both areas is functionally related and was probably used at burial ceremonies (Kjærum 1970:52). Furthermore, the limited chronological

variation suggests that only a few ceremonies took place at each site (Kjærum 1970:50; Koch & Gebauer 1976:22 and Figure 16–17; Gebauer 1979:142).

Although the majority of the pottery in front of tombs can be considered as offerings, some of it may have been grave goods cleared from inside the chamber. Clearing of the chamber is indicated by non-ceramic artifacts, human bones, and refittable fragments of pottery between the two areas. Cleared goods can also be distinguished from the pottery offerings by their position directly at the entrance or at some distance from the kerb stones, and at a higher stratigraphic level than the rest of the pottery (Forssander 1936; Thorvildsen 1946:91; Berg 1951:41 ff.; Kjærum 1970:26 and 52; Koch & Gebauer 1976:19; Ebbesen 1978:118 and 129 ff.).

Mortuary houses

A mortuary house is a rare North Jutland type of structure that has variously been interpreted as a grave, a temple related to burial rituals, or as a sanctuary with no direct relation to funeral rites (Becker 1969, 1973; Faber 1977; Kjærum 1955, 1967; Langballe 1985; Marseen 1960). Often, mortuary houses occur in close spatial relationship to megalithic tombs and in some cases share constructional features with these (Kjærum 1955:20; Marseen 1960:49). No definite indications of interments have ever been found, but two mortuary houses contained structures that may be interpreted as graves (Kjærum 1955:24, 1966:328; Marseen 1960:41 and Figure 5). A very short period of use can be inferred from the following points: the houses were destroyed by fire, they lack floor layers, the pottery is almost completely intact, and its stylistic variation is very limited. The assumption of long-term use as temples with series of successive ceremonies certainly does not seem warranted. It is likely that only a single major ceremony took place in each mortuary house.

Name of site	Type of structure	Number of vessels	MN TRB periods	Site numbers		
Herrup 1	Mortuary house	30	II	18.02.09	sb. 628	anlæg 26
Herrup 2	Stone pack. grave	7	III/IV	18.02.09	sb. 628	anlæg 18R, 21, ?
Sdr. Mølle	Megalithic tomb	13	I	18.02.09	sb. 645	
Trandun Skovby	Mortuary house	23	I	18.02.09	sb. 646	
Hagebrogård	Megalithic tomb	46	I–II	13.01.16	NM Jour. No. 635/61	
Engedal 1	Mortuary house	18	I	13.01.01	sb. 141	
Engedal 2	Megalithic tomb	32	I–V	13.01.01	sb. 138	
Engedal 3	Megalithic tomb	26	II–V	13.01.01	sb. 137	
Vroue 1	Megalithic tomb	26	I–III/IV	13.01.16	sb. 88	
Vroue 2	Megalithic tomb	20	II–III/IV	13.01.16	sb. 5	
Vroue 3	Megalithic tomb	37	II–III/IV	13.01.16	sb. 21	
Vroue 4	Megalithic tomb	75	I–V	13.01.16	sb. 20	
Lånum 1a	Megalithic tomb	52	I–III/IV	13.01.13	sb. 39	
Lånum 1b	Megalithic tomb	53	I–V	13.01.13	sb. 40	
Lånum 2	Megalithic tomb	29	II–III/IV	13.01.13	sb. 48	

Table 1. Sites included in the analyses, their pottery content and dating according to MN TRB chronology.

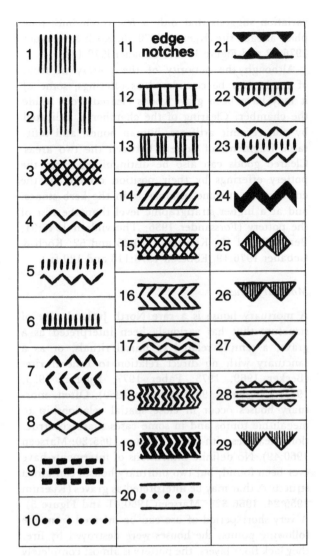

Figure 2. Designs included in the correspondence analyses.
Unbounded designs:
  1: Continuous lines or rows of strokes.
  2: Discontinuous lines or rows of strokes.
  3: Cross-hatching.
  4: Zigzag lines.
  5: Row of vertical strokes bounded by a zigzag line.
  6: Groove with lateral chasing.
  7: Row of chevrons.
  8: Lozenges made of zigzag lines.
  9: Checkerboard.
  10: Rows of pits.
  11: Edge notches.
Bounded designs:
  12: Band with transversal hatching.
  13: Band with metope design.
  14: Band with oblique hatching.
  15: Band with cross-hatching.
  16: Band with chevrons.
  17: Band with zigzag lines.
  18: Band with transversal zigzag lines.
  19: Band with zigzag bands.
  20: Band with row of dots.
  21: 'Zipper' band.
  22: Band with contours of a straight line and a zigzag line and filling of transversal strokes.
  23: Band of two zigzag contour lines and transversal strokes.
  24: Band of chevrons.
  25: Band of lozenges.
  26: Band of triangles.
  27: Single band of triangles without filling.
  28: Group of lines bounded by two bands of triangles without filling.
  29: Band of triangles without base line.

The pottery found in the mortuary houses forms a selection of the range of pottery found at megalithic tombs. Pedestalled bowls and clay ladles are particularly common. Artifacts of stone and amber are generally absent, with the exception of a set of 13 transversal arrowheads from Herrup 26. The mortuary houses may be the foci for lavish pottery offerings, comparable to those at the tombs, and performed in relation to burials here. On the other hand, they may also be regular burials containing both interment and offerings in one structure. This interpretation is supported by similarities with EN inhumation graves which have wooden superstructures (Fischer 1976:54; Liversage 1981:55; Madsen & Nielsen 1977:33; Madsen 1979:309). In either case, mortuary houses are indeed closely related to burial rites. The pottery found here is likely to exhibit stylistic motifs similar to the ceramics from the megalithic tombs.

Stone packing graves

Stone packing graves are the second type of non-monumental structure included in this study. This special type of inhumation grave has a local North Jutland distribution (Becker 1960, 1963, 1967; Ebbesen 1978; E. Jørgensen 1973, 1977a:180 ff.; Madsen 1976; S.V. Nielsen 1952). These graves are found in pairs or small clusters, together with a structure that was probably a mortuary house where grave goods were deposited. Stone packing graves are often found in kilometre-long rows, probably along Neolithic paths. The longest row is 1.7 km long (Ebbesen 1978:128; E. Jørgensen 1973, 1977a:204), and the rows tend to radiate from megalithic tombs. Early stone packing graves sometimes contain pottery (MN II-IV) (Becker 1967). However, the majority of the graves belong to MN V, when stone tools, often of excellent quality, are the most common type of grave goods, and when pottery only rarely occurs (P.O. Nielsen 1979:57; E. Jørgensen 1977a:180).

THE MULTIVARIATE ANALYSES OF THE FUNERAL POTTERY

Analyses of material with both time depth and spatial distribution poses problems of simultaneous control of both temporal and geographical variation. The five-period chronology for MN TBK does not provide sufficient criteria for separating the pottery according to time periods (J. Winther 1926, 1928, 1935, 1938, 1943; Mathiassen 1939:36, 1944:86 ff.; Berg 1951; Becker 1954, 1955; Ebbesen 1975:11; Gebauer 1977). Instead, each site is used as a unit for the analyses, irrespective of chronology. Pottery assemblages from both megalithic tombs and houses are used in the same analyses.

A separate correspondence analysis of each pot shape is impossible to carry out, since the number of units and variables becomes far too small. Instead, a series of analyses are performed on the decoration of each zone of the pot, i.e. rim, neck and bottom zone, irrespective of the basic pot form. It was expected that the zone analyses would eliminate or reduce the functional variation caused by a correlation between decoration and decoration zones. Apart from zone analyses of the decoration, a series of studies was also carried out on the total amount of bounded designs and decoration techniques from each site. Pedestalled bowls and clay ladles are analysed separately, since their decoration is structured differently from that of other vessels.

Similar designs made by different techniques are considered as one. Designs and decoration techniques are analysed separately, since it is assumed that the two aspects reflect different levels of decision making. Though some designs are made more readily using specific techniques, the two aspects of decoration generally represent independent choices in the decoration process. Secondary designs, such as accessory details or double contour lines, were not

study are shown in Figure 2 for the designs, Figure 3 for the techniques, and Figure 4 for the pot shapes.

The following CA analyses are referenced here:

1-3	Rim, (Figure 5a, Table 2) neck (Figure 5b, Table 3) and bottom (Figure 5c, Table 4) zone designs from all sites.
4	Bounded designs from all sites.
5-7	Rim, neck and bottom zone decoration techniques from all sites.
8	Decoration techniques from all zones from all sites (Figure 5d, Table 5).
9	Pot shapes from all sites (Figure 5e, Table 6).
10-12	Rim (Figure 7a, Table 7), neck (Figure 7b, Table 8) and bottom (Figure 7c, Table 9) zone designs from early sites.
13	Bounded designs from early sites (Figure 7d, Table 10).
14-16	Rim, neck and bottom zone decoration techniques from early sites.
17	Decoration techniques from early sites (Figure 7e, Table 11).
18	Pot shapes from early sites (Figure 7f, Table 12).
19-20	Rim (Figure 8a, Table 13) and bottom (Figure 8d, Table 14) zone designs from the later sites.
21	Bounded designs from late sites (Figure 8b, Table 15).
22	Hatchings from late sites (Figure 8c, Table 16).
23-24	Rim and bottom zone decoration techniques from late sites.
25	Decoration techniques from late sites (Figure 8e, Table 17).
26	Pot shapes from late sites (Figure 8f, Table 18).

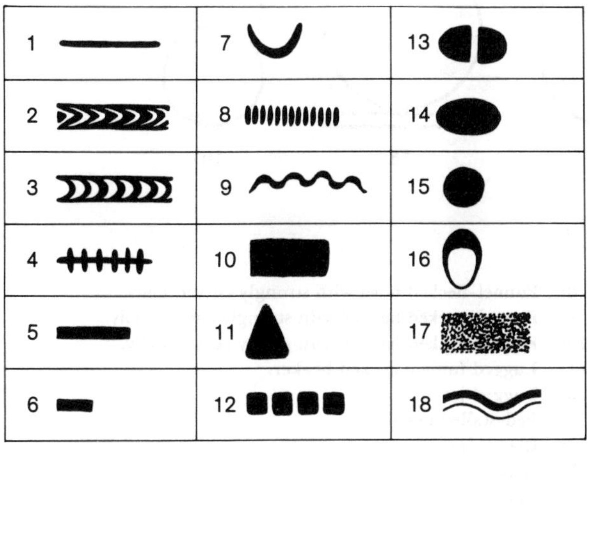

Figure 3. Decoration techniques included in the correspondence analyses.

1: Grooves.
2: Stab-and-drag.
3: Stamped lines.
4: Lines with transversal hatching.
5: Chisel stamp.
6: Spatula stamp.
7: Arc-shaped stamp.
8: Whipped cord.
9: Cardium.
10: Rectangular stamp.
11: Triangular stamp.
12: Denticulate stamp.
13: Bi-denticulate stamp.
14: Oval stamp.
15: Round pits.
16: Stab-and-drag pits.
17: 'Brushing out' – removal of clay from pot surface.
18: Moulded lines of clay added to pot surface.

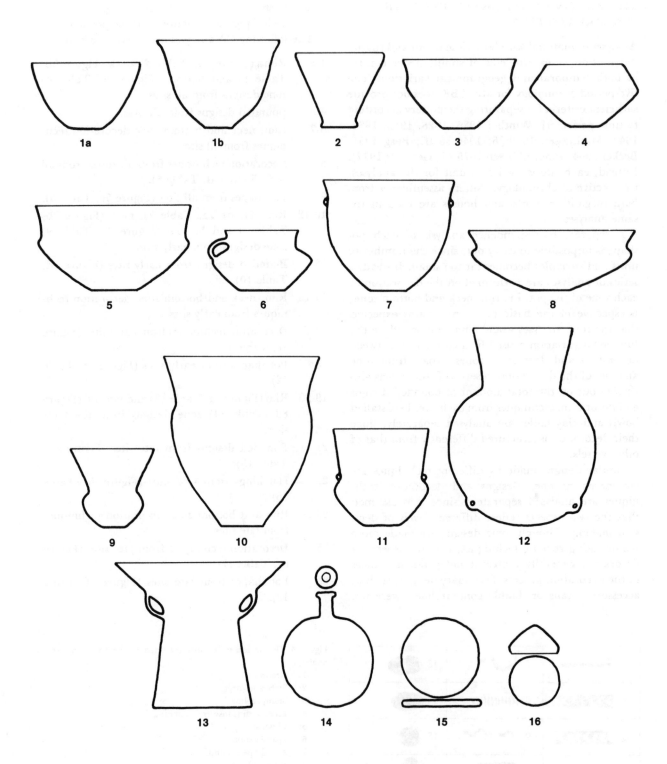

Figure 4. Pot shapes included in the correspondence analyses.

1a-b: Unsegmented bowl.
2: Unsegmented beaker.
3: Bi-segmented vessel with cylindrical or concave upper part.
4: Double conical vessel.
5: Ledged vessel.
6: Tri-segmented shouldered vessel.
7: Funnel-necked bowl with gently curved belly.

8: Funnel-necked bowl with strongly curved belly.
9: Funnel-necked beaker with strongly curved belly.
10: Funnel-necked beaker with gently curved belly.
11: Lugged funnel-necked beaker.
12: Lugged jar.
13: Pedestalled bowl.
14: Clay ladle.
15: Clay disc.
16: Clay lid.

CA of attributes from all sites

(Figure 5a–e, Table 2–6). A mutual trend in all these analyses is the distinction between a closely related group of sites, and another more loosely associated group of sites. This distinction appears on the first axis of each analysis. From available contextual information, it is clear that the distribution along the first principal axis reflects a division of time. To clarify this division, all sites were ranked according to the average of their coordinates on the first principal axis in each of the analyses (Figure 6). This rank order shows an early group of 3 mortuary houses and 2

	1	3	4	5	8	7	2	9	29	26	*	24	23	10	22	Inertia %
Herrup 26	12	0	2	1	2	1	0	3	1	0	0	0	2	0	0	15
Sdr. Mølle 1	2	0	3	1	0	0	2	0	0	0	1	0	0	0	2	5
Trandum Skovby 2	2	0	8	0	3	0	3	0	3	0	1	0	0	1	3	8
Hagebrogård	20	1	6	6	0	0	3	1	0	0	1	0	1	1	0	19
Vroue 1	1	0	8	1	1	0	0	0	3	3	3	3	1	3	0	5
Vroue 2	0	1	2	0	1	1	0	0	0	0	2	4	1	5	0	7
Vroue 3	2	1	6	2	1	2	0	0	0	0	9	3	0	2	0	4
Vroue 4	3	5	11	0	4	5	6	0	0	5	7	5	2	1	1	6
Engedal 1	6	0	0	0	0	0	5	2	2	0	2	0	0	2	1	7
Engedal 2	0	1	4	0	4	2	3	0	4	0	6	0	0	3	1	5
Engedal 3	1	0	0	0	0	1	0	0	1	0	1	0	0	2	0	3
Lånum 1a	1	1	6	0	4	5	2	0	0	1	8	1	0	1	0	4
Lånum 1b	0	1	10	0	3	4	10	0	0	3	11	2	0	11	0	7
Lånum 2	0	0	0	0	0	4	2	0	0	2	6	2	0	2	0	6
Inertia %	23	3	4	7	3	5	5	8	8	5	6	6	3	7	8	

* = 12,14,15: single bands filled with hatching

Table 2. (Figure 5a) Data matrix for rim designs at all sites. Attribute numbers correspond to Figure 2.

	*	5	9	4	1	**	***	25	2	24	12	26	Inertia %
Herrup 26	1	2	1	0	3	1	1	0	0	0	0	0	9
Trandun Skovby 2	0	0	0	1	2	1	0	5	1	1	0	0	4
Sdr. Mølle 1	0	0	0	1	2	1	0	0	0	1	0	0	5
Hagebrogård	2	4	4	4	3	1	0	0	0	1	0	0	21
Vroue 1	0	0	0	0	1	0	3	4	2	0	2	2	11
Vroue 3	0	0	0	0	0	0	0	1	1	1	1	1	4
Vroue 4	0	1	0	0	0	0	0	4	2	3	3	0	9
Engedal 1	2	1	0	2	1	0	0	0	0	0	0	0	13
Engedal 3	0	0	0	1	1	0	1	1	0	2	0	0	5
Lånum 1a	0	0	0	0	2	1	0	2	1	3	2	2	5
Lånum 1b	0	0	0	0	2	1	0	8	1	0	0	3	9
Lånum 2	0	0	0	0	0	0	0	3	1	1	0	2	5
Inertia %	11	9	11	10	5	4	10	11	5	6	9	8	

* = 12–17: Horizontal bands type 12–17 arranged in horizontal groups
** = 12,14,15: Single bands filled with hatching
*** = Single triangles

Table 3. (Figure 5b) Data matrix for neck designs at all sites. Attribute numbers correspond to Figure 2.

	1	2	15	14	16	21	6	26	4	2	Inertia %
Herrup	3	3	1	0	7	12	0	2	3	4	27
Sdr. Mølle 1	2	2	1	0	1	3	0	2	4	1	3
Trandum Skovby 2	2	5	2	0	2	1	0	3	1	1	5
Hagebrogård	10	7	5	2	3	7	0	1	5	1	6
Vroue 1	2	3	0	2	0	1	0	2	2	3	5
Vroue 2	0	4	0	0	0	0	1	0	1	0	8
Vroue 3	2	5	0	0	0	0	0	1	2	0	5
Vroue 4	13	9	7	3	1	3	3	3	11	4	5
Engedal 1	2	0	1	0	2	2	0	1	0	1	7
Engedal 2	5	7	1	0	0	1	0	2	4	2	4
Lånum 1a	10	9	1	0	0	1	0	2	5	6	8
Lånum 1b	7	8	6	6	1	3	6	6	11	5	12
Lånum 2	2	4	0	1	0	0	1	1	4	3	4
Inertia %	6	13	6	9	19	21	12	4	4	6	

Table 4. (Figure 5c) Data matrix for bottom designs at all sites. Attribute numbers correspond to Figure 2.

	1	5	6	7	9	3	12	15	18	8	4	Inertia %
Herrup	25	21	16	8	1	0	0	0	2	9	0	13
Sdr. Mølle 1	12	11	7	7	0	1	0	0	0	1	0	7
Trandum Skovby 2	24	13	9	12	0	3	5	1	2	2	0	5
Hagebrogård	48	26	12	10	8	2	0	2	0	4	0	8
Vroue 1	24	9	6	0	4	9	15	4	3	0	0	6
Vroue 2	13	5	3	0	0	5	1	4	4	0	0	8
Vroue 3	14	7	2	0	5	4	11	4	4	0	0	5
Vroue 4	57	10	15	5	5	6	15	3	0	1	8	6
Engedal 1	20	9	1	2	2	0	0	4	1	0	5	9
Engedal 2	20	3	7	3	5	0	13	1	1	4	1	3
Engedal 3	2	0	0	0	0	0	9	1	2	0	0	10
Lånum 1a	38	6	5	7	2	1	16	0	1	1	0	4
Lånum 1b	35	1	10	2	9	3	29	12	2	8	2	11
Lånum 2	13	0	4	1	5	2	15	2	0	0	1	6
Inertia %	3	13	4	10	5	8	24	8	8	8	10	

Table 5. (Figure 5d) Data matrix for decorational techniques at all sites. Attribute numbers correspond to Figure 3.

	13	14	6	9	10	8	7	4	5	3	2	1	11+12	Inertia %
Herrup 1	8	2	4	3	0	1	2	0	0	0	0	5	2	9
Sdr. Mølle 1	1	2	2	1	1	2	1	0	0	0	0	2	0	4
Trandum Skovby 2	5	3	5	1	0	3	1	0	0	0	0	0	2	8
Hagebrogård	11	4	8	2	5	3	2	2	3	0	0	2	0	5
Vroue 1	5	2	2	1	3	1	3	0	1	3	0	1	1	3
Vroue 2	3	1	2	0	0	0	0	0	1	2	0	1	0	4
Vroue 3	2	1	0	0	3	2	1	1	1	2	2	0	0	8
Vroue 4	5	4	4	12	4	2	6	0	5	8	0	1	0	11
Engedal 1	5	4	0	1	0	2	1	0	0	0	0	3	2	10
Engedal 2	3	0	3	2	1	0	1	1	0	1	3	0	0	12
Lånum 1a	5	3	3	8	6	1	1	0	8	1	1	1	0	7
Lånum 1b	3	3	4	1	1	0	7	2	5	0	1	0	0	10
Lånum 2	1	2	1	1	5	0	0	1	5	0	0	1	0	9
Inertia %	5	3	5	8	8	6	7	5	10	11	14	9	8	

Table 6. (Figure 5e) Data matrix for pot shapes at all sites. Attribute numbers correspond to Figure 4.

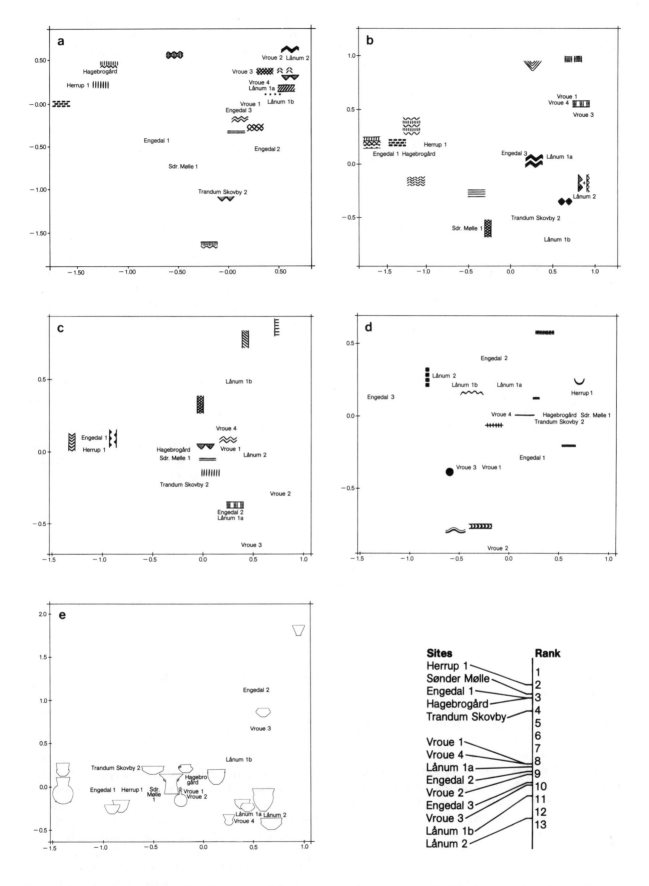

Figure 5. Correspondence analyses of attributes from all sites. a: Rim designs. b: Neck designs. c: Bottom designs. d: Decoration techniques. e: Pot shapes.

Figure 6. Average rank order of sites based on their position on the first principal axis of the various correspondence analyses of designs, techniques and pot shapes.

megalithic tombs, and a late group of 9 megalithic tombs. The early group contains pottery from MN I, whereas the majority of the pottery in the later group can be dated to MN II.

Ordering sites according to coordinates on the first principal axis cannot be interpreted in terms of an actual dating order for the sites. The rank order reflects the average chronological variation in pottery found at each site. The early sites contained only MN I pottery, although the megalithic tomb at Hagebrogård did contain a few later pots. This homogeneity is partially related to the shorter period of use for the mortuary houses, in contrast to the general pattern of substantial successive deposits at the megalithic tombs.

It is obvious that, among the later tombs, the order on the first axis in each analysis depends on the amount of pottery at each site, dating earlier or later than MN II. Vroue 4 for example contained a majority of MN II pottery, but also a small amount of MN I and MN III-IV pottery. Thus, Vroue 4 has a position in the rank order as the 'earliest' site in the late group. Vroue 2, containing only MN II pottery, is in the middle of the rank order; Lånum 2 with MN II ceramics and a large quantity of MN III-IV pottery is determined to be the 'youngest' site in the sequence.

An assessment of stylistic variation as a function of the number of pottery deposits at each tomb is difficult. Pottery in MN I style at the later tombs creates a special problem here. Do these pots represent primary use of the tomb in MN I, or are they a stylistically old-fashioned part of a deposit laid down early in MN II? If these early pots date the construction and primary use of the tomb, then these tombs and their pottery should be included in the analysis of the early group of sites. However, no simple criteria permit an unequivocal division of pottery into MN I and MN II styles respectively. For subsequent analyses, the bipartite division of sites was maintained according to the rank order of the sites on the first axis of each analysis.

A substantial part of the MN III/IV pottery, on the other hand, has to be separated from the late group of tombs in order to diminish variation over time. This can be done safely by removing all pottery that has an overall decoration carried out with denticulated stamps, combs, or cardium (Marseen 1960; Kjærum 1970:45; Ebbesen 1978:72). A few pots from MN V are also present. However, due to their small number and scarce decoration, they have no influence on the analyses.

The CAs on pottery from all sites thus provide a chronological dichotomy of an early homogeneous group of 5 sites with MN I style pottery, and a later heterogeneous group of 9 sites containing largely MN II style pottery. In the analyses that follow, stylistic variation will be explored separately at the early and the late sites, as well as within the MN III/IV pottery.

CA of attributes from the early sites

(Figure 7a–f, Table 7–12). The early sites consisted of 3 mortuary houses: Herrup 26 (30 vessels), Trandum Skovby (23 vessels) and Engedal 1 (18 vessels); and 2 megalithic tombs: Sdr. Mølle (13 vessels) and Hagebrogård (46 vessels). A total of 181 vessels thus formed the data base.

The analyses of the designs in the rim and neck zones, as well as the total amount of bounded designs, indicate an association between Hagebrogård and Herrup 26 on the one hand and between Trandum Skovby and Sdr. Mølle on the other hand. Engedal 1 stands alone, although it shows some similarities to Hagebrogård and Herrup 26 (Figure 7a–c).

Among the neck designs (Figure 7b), checkerboard patterns were found only at Herrup 26 and Hagebrogård. Zigzag lines alternating with rows of vertical strokes and various combinations of horizontal bands are restricted to these two sites and Engedal 1. Trandum Skovby and Sdr. Mølle are characterised by a general absence of designs typical of Herrup 26, Hagebrogård and Engedal 1. This division is further supported by the exclusive presence at Trandum Skovby of various designs with lozenges, a feature not included in the CA, as its uniqueness would obscure other patterns of variation completely.

Bounded designs reflect the same spatial associations (Figure 7c). Bands filled with one row of chevrons, 'zipper' bands, and bands consisting of two lines of chevrons filled with a row of vertical strokes are characteristic of Herrup 26, Hagebrogård and Engedal 1 (Figure 2: 16, 21 and 23). These designs are either absent, or occur only once or twice, at Trandum Skovby and Sdr. Mølle. On the other hand, bands of triangles, bands of lozenges, and bands filled with vertical strokes between one straight contour line and one contour line of chevrons are found exclusively at Trandum Skovby (Figure 2: 26 ,25 and 22). Engedal 1 contained a small number of designs characteristic of both groups.

As the analysis of rim designs include many bounded designs (Figure 7a), the results are not completely independent of the analysis of bounded designs alone. However, when the unbounded rim designs are considered alone, they independently support the twofold division. Characteristic of Hagebrogård and Herrup 26 are designs made of one row of vertical strokes, one row of vertical strokes underlined by a line of chevrons, checkerboard patterns, and notches at the edge of the rims (Figure 2: 1, 5, 9 and 11). A typical bounded rim design at these sites is two lines of chevrons filled with vertical

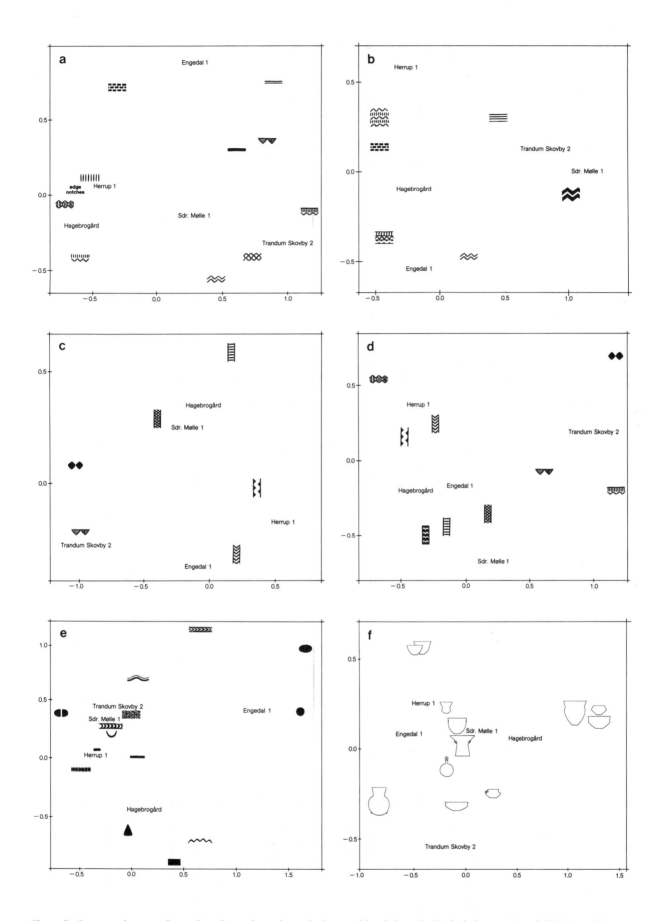

Figure 7. Correspondence analyses of attributes from the early sites. a: Rim designs. b: Neck designs. c: Bounded designs. d: Bottom designs. e: Decoration techniques. f: Pot shapes.

101

	*	**	11	26	9	23	18	15	***	18	22
Herrup 1	12	3	1	1	3	2	2	1	0	0	0
Hagebrogård	19	6	4	0	1	1	0	7	1	0	0
Engedal 1	6	0	1	2	2	0	0	0	2	4	1
Sdr. Mølle 1	1	1	0	0	0	0	0	2	1	1	1
Trandum Skovby	1	10	0	3	0	0	3	0	2	3	3

```
*   = Row of short vertical strokes
**  = 1-3 horizontal lines.
*** = Single bands filled with hatching.
```

Table 7. (Figure 7a) Data matrix for rim designs at the early sites. Attribute numbers correspond to Figure 2.

	1	4	*	9	**	24	Inertia %
Herrup 1	3	0	3	1	1	0	19
Hagebrogård	3	4	4	4	3	1	11
Engedal 1	1	2	1	0	2	0	18
Sdr. Mølle 1	2	1	0	0	0	1	32
Trandum Skovby 2	2	1	0	0	0	0	19
Inertia %	21	13	15	15	13	22	

```
*  = Alternating zigzag lines and rows of horizontal strokes
** = Horizontal group of simple bounded designs like 12,14,15,16,21.
```

Table 8. (Figure 7b) Data matrix for neck designs at the early sites. Attribute numbers correspond to Figure 2.

	15	12	16	21	26	25	Inertia %
Herrup 1	1	2	7	12	0	0	30
Engedal 1	1	0	2	2	1	0	6
Hagebrogård	5	3	3	7	1	1	13
Sdr. Mølle 1	1	2	1	3	2	0	13
Trandum Skovby 2	2	0	2	1	3	1	39
Inertia %	14	13	9	14	36	14	

Table 9. (Figure 7c) Data matrix for bottom designs at the early sites. Attribute numbers correspond to Figure 2.

	16	21	15	12	19	25	26	23	22	Inertia %
Herrup 1	8	12	1	3	1	2	2	2	0	19
Trandum Skovby 2	2	1	4	1	0	5	4	0	3	46
Sdr. Mølle 1	1	1	2	3	1	0	2	0	1	15
Hagebrogård	4	10	7	4	1	0	1	1	0	15
Engedal 1	2	3	1	2	0	0	1	0	1	5
Inertia %	5	15	11	7	5	26	9	5	16	

Table 10. (Figure 7d) Data matrix for bounded designs at the early sites. Attribute numbers correspond to Figure 2.

	5	6	7	10	11	9	3	15	18	8	14	2	17	13	Inertia %
Herrup 1	21	16	8	1	2	1	0	0	2	9	0	0	0	1	16
Sdr. Mølle 1	11	7	7	0	0	0	1	0	0	1	1	0	0	1	11
Trandum Skovby 2	13	9	12	0	1	0	3	1	2	2	0	2	2	0	18
Hagebrogård	26	12	10	9	5	8	2	2	0	4	0	0	1	0	20
Engedal 1	9	1	2	1	0	2	0	4	1	0	2	1	0	0	35
Inertia %	1	5	5	12	4	10	5	18	4	8	13	7	5	4	

Table 11. (Figure 7e) Data matrix for decorational techniques at the early sites. Attribute numbers correspond to Figure 3.

	13	14	6	9	10	8	7	1	11+12	4	5
Herrup 1	8	2	4	3	0	1	2	5	2	0	0
Sdr. Mølle 1	1	2	2	1	1	2	1	2	0	0	0
Trandum Skovby 2	5	3	5	1	0	3	1	0	2	0	0
Hagebrogård	11	4	8	2	5	3	2	2	0	2	3
Engedal 1	5	4	0	1	0	2	1	3	2	0	0

Table 12. (Figure 7f) Data matrix for pot shapes at the early sites. Attribute numbers correspond to Figure 4.

strokes (Figure 2: 23). Horizontal lines of chevrons as well as straight horizontal lines are frequently found at Trandum Skovby (Figure 2: 4 and 1). Typical bounded rim designs here are simple bands with various fillings, bands of triangles, and bands filled with vertical strokes between one straight contour line and a contour line of chevrons (Figure 2: 26 and 22).

The bottom designs display no spatial variation. Only the common bounded designs like bands filled with cross hatching, transversal strokes, chevrons, or 'zipper' designs are used at the bottom zone (Figure 2: 15, 12, 16 and 21). The inter-site variation turns out to be partly dependent on the frequency of various pot shapes at mortuary houses and megalithic tombs. Carinated vessels, for instance, and hence designs typical of these, i.e. bands of triangles, are more important at megalithic tombs than at mortuary houses.

Generally, only a few decoration techniques are common at all of the early sites: grooves, chisel, spatula, and arc-shaped stamps (Figure 7d). Spatial variation occurs in the employment of special stamps in the rim and neck zones, and to some degree in the total number of decoration techniques used at each site. The analyses of the techniques display the same association between Hagebrogård and Herrup 26 and between Trandum Skovby and Sdr. Mølle as seen in the design analyses. The analysis of techniques at the bottom zone, however, supports only the association between Hagebrogård and Herrup 26. Engedal 1 deviates from other sites in low frequencies of three common techniques: arc-shaped stamps, spatula chasing, and whipped cord, as well as by the presence of round pits, oval stamps and stab-and-drag designs.

Thus, analyses of both designs and decoration techniques reveal two local sub-styles at Hagebrogård - Herrup 26 and at Trandum Skovby - Sdr. Mølle respectively. Engedal 1 remains isolated, but shares many characteristics with Hagebrogård and Herrup 26. Interestingly, the spatial patterning of sub-styles does not follow the geographical distribution of sites. Sdr. Mølle lies closer to Herrup 26 than to Trandum Skovby, but both Trandum Skovby and Sdr. Mølle are located less than 2 km from Herrup 26, while the Hagebrogård tomb lies about 5 km away.

Different rules clearly applied when different parts of the pots were decorated. Local ceramic traditions were primarily reflected in the decoration of the rim and neck zone of the pots, while bottom designs were 'neutral' in this respect and varied according to pot shape.

CA of attributes from the later sites

(Figure 8a-f, Table 13-18). Sites containing predominantly MN II style pottery include 9 megalithic tombs with a total of 350 pots. Out of these pots, 61 pieces are decorated in Ferslev style and they are sorted out for a separate analysis (see below). Included in the current analyses are: Vroue 1 (24 vessels), Vroue 2 (19 vessels), Vroue 3 (25 vessels), Vroue 4 (70 vessels), Engedal 2 (25 vessels), Engedal 3 (18 vessels), Lånum 1a (40 vessels), Lånum 1b (45 vessels), and Lånum 2 (23 vessels).

The analyses of the rim designs and the total amount of bounded designs (Figure 8a-b), indicate stylistic differences between the Vroue and Lånum sites, particularly with regard to the various kinds of hatching in the bounded designs. A CA of hatchings at each site (Figure 8c) produced a clear division between the Lånum sites versus the Vroue sites and Engedal 2.

The Lånum sites are characterised by oblique and transversal hatching as well as by triangular bands and linear bands filled with transverse zig-zag lines (Figure 2: 14, 12, 26 and 18). Typical rim designs include horizontal lines and rows of chevrons. At the two Lånum 1 sites, rim designs of 1-2 zig-zag lines and lozenges made of zigzag lines occur frequently (Figure 2: 4 and 8).

The Vroue sites are characterised by cross-hatching, bands of chevrons, and designs made of more than two zigzag lines. Bands of lozenges, and triangles also occur frequently.

Engedal 2 contains all three kinds of hatching, but cross hatching is dominant as at Vroue. The other design analyses, however, relate Engedal 2 more closely to Lånum 1a, since these two sites share a high frequency of rim designs of 1-2 zigzag lines, lozenges made of zigzag lines, and bands of triangles (Figure 2: 4, 8 and 26).

103

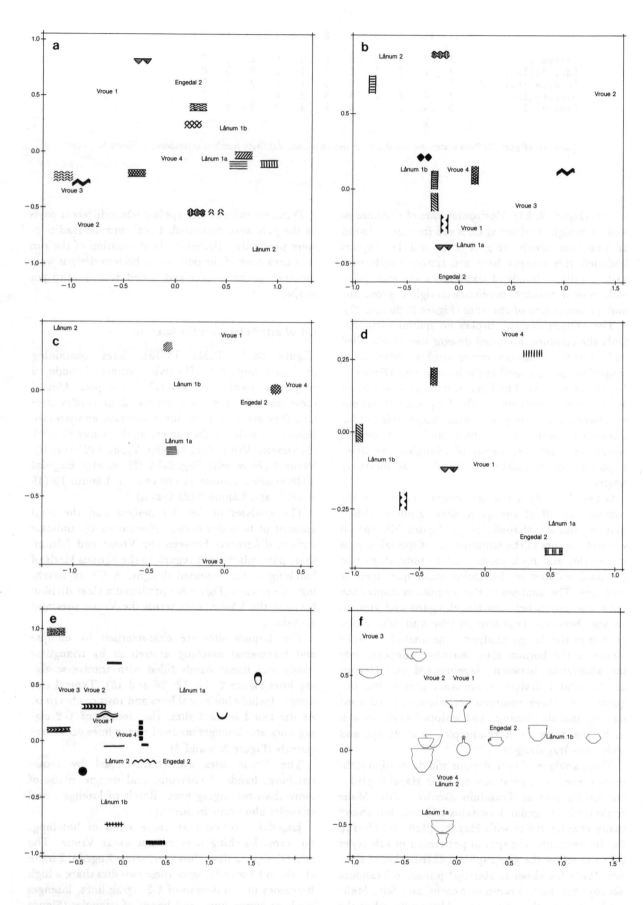

Figure 8. Correspondence analysis of attributes from the later sites. a: Rim designs. b: Bounded designs. c: Hatchings. d: Bottom designs. e: Decoration techniques. f: Pot shapes.

	*	**	8	7	24	23	26	14	15	12	***	Inertia %
Vroue 1	4	2	1	0	4	1	6	0	1	0	0	13
Vroue 2	0	0	1	1	5	1	0	0	2	0	0	17
Vroue 3	1	5	1	2	3	0	1	0	1	0	0	18
Engedal 2	4	0	4	1	1	0	4	2	1	0	1	8
Lånum 1a	5	0	4	5	1	0	0	4	1	0	2	13
Lånum 1b	8	0	4	3	0	2	3	0	1	4	6	14
Lånum 2	0	0	0	4	0	2	0	1	0	1	2	15
Inertia %	5	19	4	8	17	6	12	11	4	9	7	

```
*    = 4a: 1-2 zigzag lines.
**   = 4b: More than 2 zigzag lines.
***  = 1: Group of horizontal lines.
```

Table 13. (Figure 8a) Data matrix for rim designs at the later sites. Attribute numbers correspond to Figure 2.

	15	21	14	26	2	1	Inertia %
Vroue 1	0	1	1	3	2	4	10
Vroue 4	6	2	2	3	6	20	15
Engedal 2	1	1	0	1	4	3	7
Lånum 1a	1	1	0	1	8	7	21
Lånum 1b	6	6	6	4	2	3	47
Inertia %	11	13	23	10	24	19	

Table 14. (Figure 8d) Data matrix for bottom designs at the later sites. Attribute numbers correspond to Figure 2.

	14	15	12	21	24	23	26	25	18	Inertia %
Vroue 1	1	1	0	1	4	1	10	3	1	11
Vroue 2	0	2	0	0	5	1	0	0	0	25
Vroue 3	1	1	0	0	3	0	2	0	1	8
Vroue 4	3	10	1	3	4	2	6	3	1	7
Engedal 2	2	2	0	1	1	0	6	0	0	7
Lånum 1a	4	2	0	1	2	0	4	0	0	9
Lånum 1b	4	7	4	2	1	2	10	3	4	13
Lånum 2	2	0	1	0	0	2	1	1	0	18
Inertia %	11	9	11	3	29	12	11	7	8	

Table 15. (Figure 8b) Data matrix for bounded designs at the later sites. Attribute numbers correspond to Figure 2.

	1	2	3
Vroue 1	3	0	5
Vroue 2	0	0	3
Vroue 3	0	1	1
Vroue 4	4	3	21
Engedal 2	3	3	10
Lånum 1a	3	4	4
Lånum 1b	12	9	14
Lånum 2	2	1	0

```
1: Oblique hatching
2: Transversal hatching
3: Cross-hatching
```

Table 16. (Figure 8c) Data matrix for hatchings at the later sites.

	1	5	6	9	15	4	12	3	8	7	16	2	18	17	Inertia %
Vroue 1	23	8	6	4	3	2	7	7	0	0	0	2	3	0	9
Vroue 2	11	5	3	0	4	0	1	3	0	0	0	0	0	2	13
Vroue 3	13	7	2	0	3	0	1	2	0	0	0	2	2	1	13
Vroue 4	13	6	14	5	3	4	8	6	1	3	1	0	0	1	9
Engedal 2	10	2	8	3	1	1	4	0	4	3	2	0	1	0	10
Lånum 1a	13	6	5	1	0	0	3	1	1	6	4	0	1	0	21
Lånum 1b	35	1	9	3	11	9	3	3	8	2	0	2	2	0	19
Lånum 2	11	0	4	2	2	1	5	1	0	0	0	0	0	0	7
Inertia %	4	11	5	4	6	7	6	5	11	13	12	5	4	8	

Table 17. (Figure 8e) Data matrix for decorational techniques at the later sites. Attribute numbers correspond to Figure 3.

	13	14	6	9	10	8	7	1	4	5	3+4	Inertia %
Vroue 1	5	2	2	1	3	1	3	1	0	0	3	7
Vroue 2	3	1	2	0	0	0	0	1	0	1	2	11
Vroue 3	2	1	0	0	3	2	0	0	0	0	2	18
Vroue 4	5	4	4	12	4	2	5	1	0	5	5	9
Engedal 2	3	0	3	2	1	0	1	0	1	0	1	9
Lånum 1a	5	3	3	8	6	1	1	1	0	4	0	10
Lånum 1b	3	3	3	1	1	0	6	0	2	1	0	22
Lånum 2	1	2	1	1	5	0	0	1	1	1	0	14
Inertia %	5	3	5	13	13	11	15	5	12	6	12	

Table 18. (Figure 8f) Data matrix for pot shapes at the later sites. Attribute numbers correspond to Figure 4.

A CA of neck designs shows a dispersed pattern with no significant clustering of sites. 19 designs were recorded originally, but only five designs occur at more than two sites. Even these designs occur in small numbers at only a few sites.

A CA of the bottom zone designs produced no significant pattern (Figure 8d). Again it is the distribution of pot shapes at each site that influences the result. Thus, the first principal axis distinguishes between (1) sites where vertical grooves and hence funnel-necked beakers are predominant (Vroue 4, Engedal 2, Lånum 1a. Figure 4: 9), and (2) sites with a majority of band designs at the bottom zone, and hence pots like funnel-necked bowls and carinated vessels (Vroue 1 and especially Lånum 1a (Figure 4: 7, 6 and 5).

In general, the analyses of designs from the late sites produced a distinction between the Vroue sites and the Lånum sites. This distinction appears most clearly in the filling of bounded designs, but is also present in rim designs and bounded designs in general.

The analyses of decoration techniques from each zone reveal the same pattern as the analyses of the total number of decoration techniques from each site (Figure 8e). Only the latter are discussed here, however, since they are based on more reliable material. The plot of the two first principal axes shows a cluster of the Vroue 1, 2 and 3 sites. Close to the centre lies Lånum 2 and Vroue 4, with Engedal 2. Lånum 1a lies isolated in the neighbourhood of Engedal 2, while the second axis discriminates between Lånum 1b and the other sites.

From known contextual information, it is evident that the first axis reflects time variation. Sites with MN I style pottery (arc-shaped stamps and whipped cord) are distinguished from sites containing only MN II style or very little MN I style pottery.

The degree of variability, and the number of characteristic variables at each site, also influence the pattern in the plot. Vroue 4 and Lånum 2 lie close to the centre, since neither site has any specific characteristics. Vroue 4 contains all kinds of techniques, while Lånum 2 includes only the most common decoration techniques.

The very homogeneous cluster of Vroue 1, 2 and 3 is separated by the occurrence of stab-and-drag, stamped lines, chisel chasing, moulded lines, and brushed-out designs (Figure 3: 2, 3, 5, 18 and 17). The Lånum sites, on the other hand, form a less homogeneous group, but generally contain more spatula chasing, cardium, pit stabs, and lines with transversal hatching (Figure 3: 6, 9, 15 and 4). Engedal 2 and Lånum 1a share a broad range of techniques from both MN I and II.

Thus, the CA of decoration techniques clearly reveals chronological variation at the first axis reflecting differences in the amount of MN I style pottery found at each site. Spatial variation is manifested by the cluster of Vroue 1, 2 and 3 sites, and the similarities between Engedal 2 and Lånum 1a.

A CA of pot shapes from each site shows a clustering of the Vroue 1, 2 and 3 sites versus the Lånum sites, with Vroue 4 and Engedal 2 in an intermediate position (Figure 8f). The Vroue 1-3 sites contained many pedestalled bowls, funnel-necked bowls with strongly curved bellies and bi-segmented vessels (Figure 4: 13, 8 and 3). None or very few of the following pot shapes were present at Vroue 1-3: funnel beakers, funnel-necked bowls with gently curved bellies, biconical vessels and ledged vessels (Figure 4: 9, 7, 4 and 5).

The Lånum sites have relatively few of the characteristic pot shapes of Vroue 1-3. Instead there are many funnel beakers, ledged vessels, biconical vessels, storage vessels, carinated vessels, and clay ladles. At Lånum the composition of pot shapes varied among the sites, especially with respect to the funnel-necked pot shapes. Engedal 2 and Vroue 4 at the centre of the plot are uncharacteristic with regard to pot shapes.

PCA of CA results on designs and decoration techniques from late sites

(Figure 9a-b, Table 19-20) A coherent picture of the variation described by the CAs of MN II style designs and techniques can be given by a PCA based on the coordinates of the first and second axes of the CAs (Madsen 1985:200).

A PCA based on the CA's of designs show a similar differentiation between the Lånum sites and the Vroue sites as the CA's. However, the distinction found in the PCA is less clear than in the CA's of rim designs and hatching (figure 8 A and C) as this analysis include the more mixed pattern in the CA's of bounded designs and bottom designs especially.

A PCA based on the CAs of the decoration techniques produces a pattern very much like the one given by the CA of the total number of techniques from each site (Figure 8e, 9b). Yet the PCA gives a more distinct pattern, since it also takes other CAs into consideration. Lånum 1a and Engedal 2 are found to oppose the cluster of Vroue 1-3 sites with the neutral sites Lånum 2 and Vroue 4 in the middle, with Lånum 1b isolated.

CA of pedestalled bowls

(Figure 10) A separate CA of the decoration on pedestalled bowls was made with the individual vessels as units. The results show three stylistic groups of pedestalled bowls. They are distinguished mainly by the following elements: (1) horizontal lines of arc-shaped stamps, (2) alternating horizontal zigzags and horizontal rows of short vertical strokes, and (3) horizontal stamped lines.

The first principal axis shows a clear chronological trend. From known contextual information, designs No. 1 and 2 can be ascribed to MN I and design No. 3 to MN II. The general trend through time is towards a more frequent use of supplementary designs, and the employment of a wider range of designs.

16 pedestalled bowls are characterised by design no. 1: 10 from the early, and 6 from the later sites. On the bowls from the early sites, the characteris-

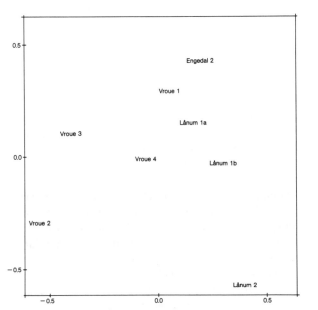

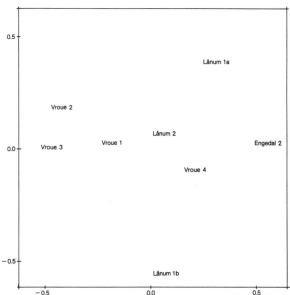

Figure 9. Principal coordinate analyses (PCA) based upon first and second principal axes coordinates from CAs of the later sites. a: PCA of design analyses. b: PCA of technique analyses.

	Rim 1. axis	Rim 2.axis	Bounded 1.axis	Bounded 2.axis	Bottom 1.axis	Bottom 2.axis	Hatching 1.axis	Hatching 2.axis
Vroue 1	9.32	10.52	10.09	9.74	10.00	9.89	10.04	10.26
Vroue 2	9.14	9.34	11.39	10.63	*	*	*	*
Vroue 3	9.00	9.64	10.64	9.88	*	*	9.97	9.19
Vroue 4	9.95	9.90	10.03	10.11	10.20	10.32	10.44	10.03
Engedal 2	10.10	10.60	9.95	9.41	10.36	9.65	10.19	9.95
Lånum 1a	10.48	9.93	10.09	9.61	10.59	9.70	9.68	9.76
Lånum 1b	10.55	10.18	9.59	10.11	9.19	9.91	9.74	10.03
Lånum 2	10.84	9.10	9.32	10.87	*	*	8.93	10.30

Rim refers to CA of Table 13.
Bounded refers to CA of Table 15.
Bottom refers to CA of Table 14.
Hatching refers to CA of Table 16.

Table 19. (Figure 9a) Data matrix for PCA of CA design analyses from late sites.

	Bottom 1.axis	Bottom 2.axis	Neck 1.axis	Neck 2.axis	Rim 1.axis	Rim 2.axis	Total 1.axis	Total 2.axis
Vroue 1	216.00	166.00	146.00	165.00	173.00	202.00	174.00	218.00
Vroue 2	257.00	157.00	*	*	138.00	226.00	149.00	243.00
Vroue3	*	*	87.00	190.00	129.00	215.00	147.00	246.00
Vroue 4	237.00	202.00	202.00	230.00	307.00	208.00	216.00	206.00
Engedal 2	200.00	278.00	271.00	207.00	227.00	140.00	258.00	181.00
Lånum 1a	248.00	208.00	276.00	184.00	162.00	146.00	276.00	242.00
Lånum 1b	132.00	194.00	189.00	264.00	213.00	251.00	184.00	146.00
Lånum 2	222.00	149.00	233.00	109.00	220.00	185.00	195.00	180.00

Bottom, neck and rim refer to CAs of data not shown in tables here.
Total refersto CA of Table 17.

Table 20. (Figure 9b) Data matrix for PCA of CA technique analyses from late sites.

tic design is usually combined with a horizontal row of vertical dashes at the rim, while other designs are rare (Figure 11). This very typical MN I feature is never found on pedestalled bowls from the later sites. Instead these have supplementary designs of bands of lozenges, triangles, and chevrons as well as linear designs of lozenges and chevrons.

Design no. 2 is found on 11 pedestalled bowls, including 3 from the late sites. Included are two vessels with only half of the defining design, either horizontal zigzags or rows of vertical strokes. Supplementary designs occurred only on two pots as vertical rows of chevrons.

Design no. 3 is found on 14 pots, of which two belong to the early sites. The defining design is combined with 1-4 supplementary designs; zigzag lines and bounded designs of chevrons and triangles being the most common (Figure 11).

Stylistic variation among pedestalled bowls shows the same chronological trend as seen in other CA analysis. However, stylistic groupings of pedestalled bowls according to their main designs do not correspond entirely with the division into early and late sites, since some of the later sites contain a propor-

tion of MN I pottery. The pattern of supplementary designs in the plot, however, suggests a bipartition of design group no. 1. This division does correspond with the pattern of early and later sites.

The amount of intra-site variability is different from site to site. At some sites, the pedestalled bowls appear to be stylistically homogeneous, while at other sites they turn out to be rather different. Thus stylistically homogeneous pedestalled bowls are found in the mortuary houses of Herrup 26 and Trandum Skovby, while at Engedal, the mortuary house contained dissimilar bowls. The latter case is remarkable, since mortuary houses most probably embodied only one episode of pottery deposition.

Among the megalithic tombs, Vroue 1-3 are notable for the complex and homogeneous decoration of their pedestalled bowls. The similarity of the Vroue 1-3 sites is unique compared to other late sites, including the neighbouring Vroue 4 tomb. The supplementary designs typical of Vroue 1-3 are not restricted to these sites, but they occur only in small numbers and more dispersed elsewhere.

To conclude, the analyses of pedestalled bowls produce three distinct design groups, two from MN

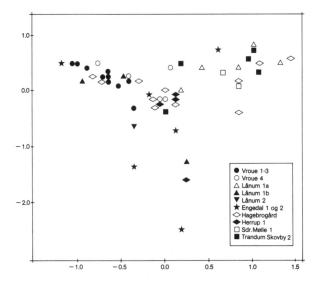

Figure 10. Correspondence analysis of pedestalled bowls from early and late sites.

I and one from MN II. The association pattern of the supplementary designs suggests that some of the bowls in design group no. 1 are later than the others. Furthermore, there is a clear tendency for decorations to become more complex through time, as the importance of supplementary designs increases with regard to the basic designs. A local sub-style including Vroue 1, 2 and 3 can be distinguished. This sub-style does not include the neighbouring Vroue 4 tomb, and it is probable that it served to symbolically differentiate people interred in the Vroue burial ground. Lånum 1a, 1b, and 2 share some stylistic features, but have no distinct sub-style of their own. Otherwise, stylistic variation cross-cuts the spatial distribution of the sites.

CA of MN III/IV pottery from the late tombs

(Figure 13, Table 21-22) The Ferslev style, dating to MN III/IV, is defined as pottery decorated using only one technique, either denticulated stamp, cardium or comb (Kjærum 1970:45; Ebbesen 1978:72). A total of 68 pots are decorated in the Ferslev style: Herrup (7 vessels), Vroue 1 (2 vessels), Vroue 2 (1 vessel), Vroue 3 (12 vessels), Vroue 4 (5 vessels), Engedal 2 (7 vessels), Engedal 3 (8 vessels), Lånum 1A (12 vessels), Lånum 1B (8 vessels), Lånum 2 (6 vessels).

The frequency of these pots at the individual sites is shown in Table 22. The Herrup site contains a series of stone packing graves, while the others are megalithic tombs. The number of variables recorded is limited due to the small number of pots available, the high degree of fragmentation, and the few designs in use. The two reliable CAs are based on (1) bounded designs from all three pot zones pooled together, and (2) the distribution of pot shapes at each site (Figure 13a-b).

The design analysis showed a tripartite distribution of sites, according to the localities of Lånum, Herrup, and Vroue-Engedal. The Lånum group is characterised by the frequent use of simple bands with oblique hatching and bands of lozenges (Figure 2: 14 and 25). In addition, simple bands filled with chevrons and bands of triangles are also found here, while designs like simple cross-hatched bands and bands filled with metope designs are absent (Figure 2: 18, 26, 15 and 13).

Figure 11. Pedestalled bowl design no. 1-3 and supplementary designs.

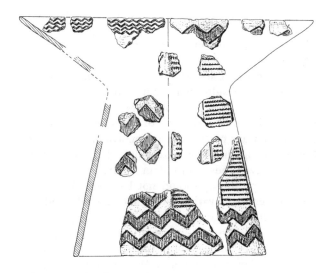

Figure 12. Pedestalled bowl from Vroue 3 (after E. Jørgensen 1977: Abb.164).

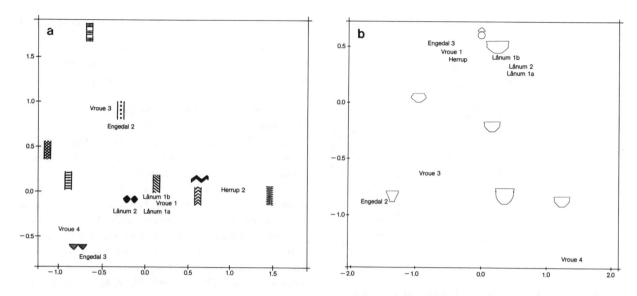

Figure 13. Correspondence analyses of a: bounded designs, b: pot shapes from MN III/IV pottery at the late sites.

Vroue 3, Vroue 4, Engedal 2, and Engedal 3 are characterised by the presence of rare, bounded designs like the metope bands, while designs typical of the Lånum sites occur infrequently.

Herrup is characterised by chevron bands, double bands of triangles, and a high frequency of obliquely hatched bands (Figure 2: 24, 28 and 14). Most other designs and the use of cardium are absent at Herrup.

The distributional pattern of pot shapes among the sites reveals the same uniformity within the Lånum group. All three sites contain four tripartite ledged vessels as well as very uniform bipartite ledged bowls (Figure 4: 3 and 5). A variety of pot shapes are found in small numbers at the other sites. The stone packing graves at Herrup contain only various beaker shapes, while both bowls and beakers are found at the megalithic tombs.

EVALUATION OF THE CA AND PCA IN THE PRESENT STUDY

The use of CA in stylistic studies of funnel beaker pottery has worked quite successfully. The simultaneous plotting of both analytical units and variables makes it possible to explore the significance of individual variables in relation to the units.

Time is clearly reflected in the first principal axis of many of the analyses. This could be expected in advance, because such a linear monotonic factor as time will dominate less distinctive patterns like spatial variation (Bølviken et al. 1982). Functional variability is also reflected in some analyses, e.g., between bottom designs and pot shapes. Spatial variation, which is the focus of this study, also appeared quite clearly in some analyses. In addition,

different patterns of distribution in the analyses of decoration on the individual rim, neck, and bottom zones revealed aspects of the structuring principles of decoration.

The major problem in this study turned out to be the small number of samples available for each analysis. Originally, the complete registration included 476 vessels. However, as this information was split up according to sites and pot zones in order to analyse both inter-site variation and structure of decoration, the numbers of observations per unit became extremely small. In addition, differences in the degree of variation within the individual sites sometimes obscure the results. Indeed, a variable that is not particularly significant may at a small site be singled out by the analysis as an important feature giving this site a special 'deviant' status. Very rich sites on the other hand may behave as 'neutral' in a CA plot simply because they contain a wider range of variation.

Small sets of data with many types of variation may produce results that include more or less random elements. It is therefore important that several CAs based on different sets of variables repeatedly produce similar patterns. This replication is a strong argument against the possibility that these CA analyses have produced random results.

Yet the possibility should not be overlooked that the differences in variation at each site will tend to produce similar patterns in the CAs. This problem concerns only the late sites with the rich collections from Vroue 4 and Lånum 1b. However, the pattern of variation found in CAs from the late sites is independently supported by analyses of hatchings and of pedestalled bowls.

	14	16	20	12	15	13	26	24	25	28	Inertia %
Herrup	7	3	0	0	0	0	0	5	1	5	25
Vroue 1	1	1	0	0	0	0	0	0	1	0	4
Vroue 3	3	0	1	1	1	3	1	2	2	0	17
Vroue 4	2	0	0	1	1	0	4	0	2	0	14
Engedal 2	3	1	0	0	0	2	1	0	1	0	9
Engedal 3	1	0	0	0	0	0	4	1	1	0	12
Lånum 1a	4	2	0	0	0	0	2	2	3	0	4
Lånum 1b	9	1	1	0	0	0	1	0	4	1	8
Lånum 2	6	1	0	1	0	0	2	0	2	0	5
Inertia %	5	7	5	6	7	20	19	11	4	17	

Table 21. (Figure 13a) Data matrix for bounded designs in MN III/IV pottery. Attribute numbers correspond to Figure 2.

	7	3	5	16	4	2	Inertia %
Herrup	0	0	3	2	2	1	5
Vroue 1	0	0	1	0	1	0	5
Vroue 3	1	0	1	0	1	2	12
Vroue 4	1	3	0	0	0	0	27
Lånum 1A	0	2	4	2	0	0	7
Lånum 1B	1	0	4	1	0	0	8
Lånum 2	0	1	4	0	0	0	8
Engedal 3	0	0	0	1	1	0	9
Engedal 2	0	0	0	0	1	2	19
Inertia %	10	26	13	10	15	25	

Table 22. (Figure 13b) Data matrix for pot shapes in MN III/IV pottery. Attribute numbers correspond to Figure 4.

The PCA proved to be an adequate way of amalgamating the information from the set of CAs, and to produce an overview in one summary plot. This method resulted in similar, but more distinctive patterns than the CAs.

EVALUATION OF STYLISTIC VARIATION WITHIN THE VROUE AREA

Many factors cause stylistic variability in pottery, particularly temporal and spatial differences. While the general trend of chronological variation is known from other contexts, spatial variation can be distinguished only when related to the geographical distribution of the sites. Furthermore, a lack of information about the production process of pottery, as well as basic social structure, prevent a decoding of spatial variation into various components originating in different aspects of societal organisation.

In the following pages, structuring principles will be considered through time at the local level, and in relation to the general chronology of MN TBK. Further, spatial variability in the Vroue area is discussed, and the significance of stylistic clusters in relation to site distribution is evaluated.

Chronological variation in the pottery from the Vroue area

Time variation is clearly seen in connection with the techniques of decoration. The CA of the total number of techniques at all sites demonstrates the frequent use of a recurrent set of techniques in MN I, as opposed to the sporadic use of several techniques in MN II (Figure 5d). No single technique is limited to one time period alone, but there are significant quantitative differences in frequencies of technique use through time.

Five techniques are used repeatedly at all the early sites: grooves, chisel and spatula chasing, arc-shaped stamps, and whipped cord (Figure 3: 1, 5, 6, 7 and 8). Other techniques like rectangular and triangular stamps and cardium impressions are found only at a few sites (Figure 3: 10, 11 and 9).

At the late sites, only grooves and denticulated stamps are present everywhere (Figure 3: 1 and 12), but techniques such as lines with transversal hatching, stamped lines, cardium, pits, moulded lines and stab-and-drag are commonly used (Figure 3: 3, 9, 15, 18 and 2). Chisel and spatula chasing are continued from the early phase, while the arc-shaped stamp only rarely occurs and whipped cord is absent.

111

In the MN III/IV, the denticulate stamp and cardium are used exclusively.

The chronological variability in designs can be illustrated through an ordering of their frequency (Figure 14). The employment of designs reflects a conservative tradition with a long-term use of most designs. Like decoration techniques, the range of variation changes from the repeated use of relatively few designs in MN I to a more dispersed pattern utilising many designs in MN II, ending with a small repertoire of designs in MN III/IV.

The decoration of the MN I pottery is highly structured with bottom designs related to certain pot shapes, and specific designs related to each pot zone. Simple designs composed of a few elements are used as rim zone designs. Overall neck zone designs are formed by permutations of the rim zone designs into new, complex patterns. Bottom zone designs are composed of vertical grooves and bands. Bounded designs occur rarely only, except in the bottom zone. Most bounded designs are simple bands with straight contour lines.

The MN II designs represent a continuation from MN I and the beginning of many Ferslev style designs. Only a few designs are specific to this period. New types primarily include bounded designs like chevrons and lozenge bands. Triangle bands are much more common than before. Most bounded designs are filled with hatchings, instead of the chevrons or 'zipper' designs typical of MN I. A completely new set of mostly bounded neck zone designs is introduced. In the bottom zone there is a change from simple straight bands to chevron, lozenge and triangle bands, with hatching as the dominant filling.

The Ferslev style in MN III/IV clearly represents a reduced repertoire of the MN II style. Bounded designs predominate and hatching is almost the only type of filling. The distinction between the decoration in different pot zones is minimal. The structure of decoration breaks down, and the range of variation is strongly reduced with respect to both designs and techniques. There is no relationship between bottom zone designs and different pot shapes. In addition, pot shapes are less distinctive than previously.

Chronological variation in Vroue area and the five period system

The tombs and mortuary houses of the Vroue area contained pottery dating from MN I, MN II and MN III/IV. Apparently the local chronology here included fewer distinguishable phases than the general MN TBK chronology with five periods and the subdivisions of MN I (a–b) and MN IV (a–b) (Ebbesen 1978:75). However, it should not be forgotten that although designations of style correspond nominally to designations of time periods, it is not possible to build a definitive chronology on the basis of style (P.O. Nielsen 1982:152). When applying the MN TBK chronology as a general frame of reference, regional and functional variation must also be taken into consideration. Chronological studies within a specific area based on style should have local data as their starting point. The local sequence should be evaluated in relation to relevant parts of the general chronology – not vice versa (Ebbesen 1978:72ff; Gebauer 1977).

The conservative tradition evident in the pottery of Northern Jutland, with the long term use of designs,

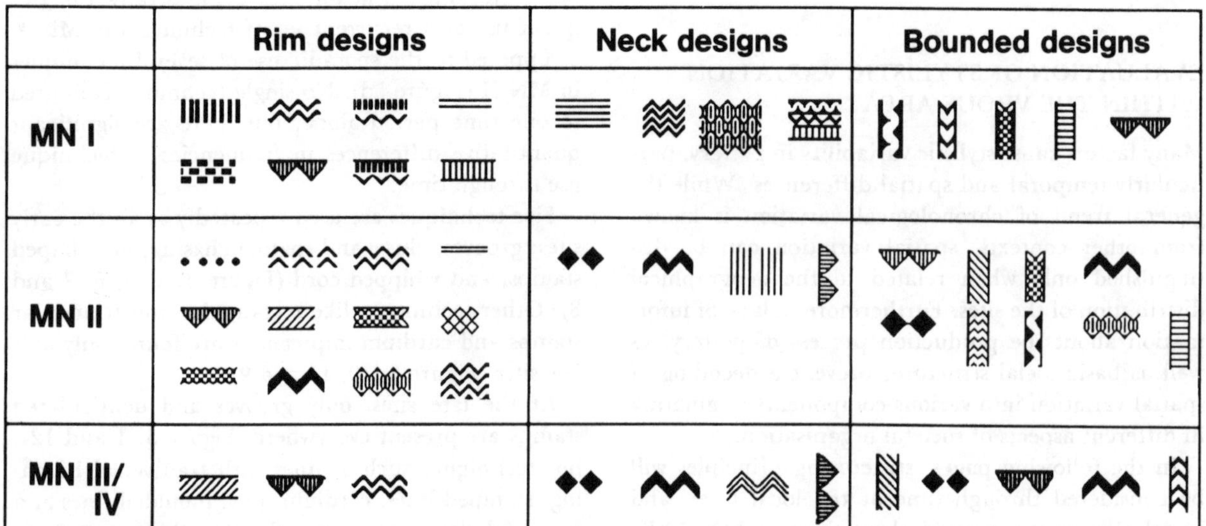

Figure 14. Chronological variability in designs in the Vroue area from MN I-III/IV. Designs are listed according to their frequency reading from top left.

has previously been described by Kjærum (1966:331) and Ebbesen (1978:75ff). As noted by both authors, the only characteristic, self-contained styles are the MN I and the Ferslev style proper. The intermittent stage of MN II and the early Ferslev style have few features of their own, and the existence of MN IV style pottery is purely hypothetical. MN V style is represented only by a few pots in this area (Davidsen 1978:Figure 43 and Figure 59; Ebbesen 1978:Figure 94).

Ebbesen (1979:48 ff.) recently analysed the pottery from Troldebjerg and described the designs that define the Troldebjerg style. He found this style at 24 other sites including settlements, tombs, mortuary houses and bogs scattered over most of Denmark (Ebbesen 1979:Figure 82). Hence, the Troldebjerg style was considered to represent a distinct time period within Denmark, although overlaps with Fuchberg and Klintebakke style were considered possible.

It is, however, evident from Ebbesen's survey that apart from Troldebjerg itself, pottery in Troldebjerg style constitutes only a minor element at the sites he mentions. The Troldebjerg style is also difficult to define in relation to the Fuchberg and Virum styles on the one hand, and to the Klintebakke style on the other. The range of variation in the Troldebjerg style is broad, and it overlaps considerably with the others. The question is then whether the Troldebjerg style represents a distinct period outside Langeland. Although a few pots and sherds can be recognised at sites in other areas, this does not justify the presence of a distinct time period in those areas. Clearly, the chronology should be established using local materials.

The Troldebjerg style was found chiefly in band-decorated bowls, pedestalled bowls and clay ladles. With regard to the band-decorated bowls, there is considerable stylistic overlap with the Virum, Fuchsberg and Klintebakke styles. A genuine Troldebjerg style thus occurs only on pedestalled bowls and clay ladles outside Langeland.

Find contexts do not support a chronological distinction between MN Ia and MN Ib. The mortuary house at Herrup 26 containing both MN Ia and Ib style pottery was a wooden structure that burned down before any repair would have been necessary. The pottery was arranged in two groups at the rear of the house and seems to have been undamaged when the house caught fire, nor had a distinct floor level formed. Herrup 26, then, most likely contained only a single pottery deposit and thus cannot support any temporal distinction between MN Ia and Ib.

In addition, the distribution of pottery in front of megalithic tombs does not support the hypothesis that Troldebjerg style pottery constituted separate deposits from Klintebakke style deposits. At Borre the pedestalled bowls with zigzag lines (MN Ia) were placed together with the majority of the pedestalled bowls (and the MN I pottery in general) to the right of the entrance (Koch & Gebauer 1976). At Hagebrogård the four pots that Ebbesen refers to MN Ia were placed on both sides of the entrance and formed part of concentrations of MN Ib pottery (E. Jørgensen 1977a). At the Vedsted dolmen, three pots found in front of the kerb-stones were dated to MN Ia (Ebbesen 1979:26). These pots were deposited immediately to the right of the entrance like the majority of the pottery.

A contemporaneity of Troldebjerg and Klintebakke style is supported by the combination of MNIa and MNIb elements on the same vessel: for example a pedestalled bowl with Troldebjerg design combined with inside rim decoration of arc-shaped stamps, a diagnostic MNIb design (Borre pot No. 148). On other pedestalled bowls, the Troldebjerg design is carried out with arc-shaped stamps and whipped cord typical of MNIb (E. Jørgensen 1977a, Hagebrogård No. 1003-1004).

In Jutland at least, combinations of MNIa and Ib elements indicate a contemporary use of the two styles of pedestalled bowls and clay ladles. Variation in decoration of the two pot shapes is attributable to their ceremonial importance (see below). Regional variation in the decoration of pedestalled bowls has long been recognised (Schwabedissen 1953:61 Figure 25; Kjærum 1966:331; Ebbesen 1978:178 note 63).

The MN I style in the Vroue area displays a mixture of the local EN style in North Jutland (Volling) and the south Danish styles of late EN and earliest MN (Virum and Fuchberg) (Becker 1954:54; Andersen & Madsen 1978; Ebbesen & Mahler 1980). Related to Volling and in contrast to the South Danish styles, the Vroue MN I style has a preference for a variety of stamps rather than cord impressions. Overall neck zone designs from Volling style are combined with bottom zone designs of vertical grooves and bands typical of the Virum and Fuchberg styles (E. Jørgensen 1977a:30, abb.26m, Nr.25).

As noted earlier, the MN II style in the Vroue area represents a transitional phase between the MN I and the Ferslev styles, with very few characteristics of its own. Several Ferslev designs are introduced but, unlike the Ferslev style proper, these designs were not carried out by an overall use of the denticulate stamp. A similar distinction between early Ferslev style (MN II) and Ferslev style proper (MN III) is suggested by Kjærum (1970:45), Ebbesen (1978:76) and Eriksen (1984:57). As observed by P.O. Nielsen (1982:153), MN II style proper (Blandebjerg) is largely an East Danish tradition and only a few of its elements can be seen in the Vroue pottery. Indeed, the local MN II style here, as in North Jutland in general, represents a continuation of many MN I elements combined with early Ferslev style and a few elements from the Blandebjerg style.

Characteristic of the MN III is a separation of neck and belly zones by a narrow hatched band or a group of horizontal lines. This horizontal design serves as the starting point for the bottom zone designs. The presence of this division distinguishes both the Ferslev style and the MN III style proper (Bundsø) from the MN II style (Kjærum 1970:45; Eriksen 1984:57). It suggests that the beginning of both styles was synchronous. Both styles also include many of the same designs, and use only one or few techniques of decoration. Denticulate stamp and cardium are characteristic of Ferslev style, while grooves and stab-and-drag are typical of MN III (Marseen 1960; Kjærum 1970:45; Ebbesen 1975:50-52, 1978:72-77).

As pointed out by P.O. Nielsen (1982:153), the MN IV style was probably a local phase in southeastern Danmark. Definite MN IV style pottery is rare in North Jutland (Davidsen 1978:113 ff.). Continuous use of Ferslev style pottery is indicated here until MN V (Ebbesen 1978:186).

Geographic variation in the pottery from the Vroue area

Pottery decoration is highly structured. A common conceptual scheme seems to have prescribed the appropriate decoration for each pot shape and for each zone of the pot. Such strict regulations left little room for geographic or individual variability. The layout and composition of designs was defined by standards. Only at a very simple level were local or individual preferences in designs or techniques apparently acceptable. Spatial variation is seen primarily in different categories of filling of bounded designs, i.e. areas that were already defined by the overall structure of decoration for that specific pot shape. Also, the results of the zone analyses show that geographic variability is confined to the upper part of the pot in the rim and neck zone.

The degree and character of geographic variation changed through time. The most exclusive distributions of stylistic features are found at the early sites, and include neck designs and some rim designs, in particular. Generally, only minor details were involved in the spatial variations like the various filling of simple straight band designs or different contour lines for the same bounded design (Figure 2: 22 and 23). However, quite visible variation is reflected in the neck designs. Distinctive patterns of decoration define two sub-styles that cross-cut the geographical site distribution, and distinguish between Trandum Skovby and Sdr. Mølle on the one hand and Herrup and Hagebrogård on the other. Engedal 1 shares stylistic features with the latter, but otherwise stands alone.

At the later sites, spatial variation is more subtle, less exclusive in distribution, and less obvious to the observer. The most exclusive variability is seen in different kinds of hatching, and in the distribution of rim designs and bounded designs. The stylistic variation seen here corresponds to the spatial pattern of the four Vroue sites in contrast to the three Lånum sites. Two clusters characterised by differences in decoration of pedestalled bowls, in rim designs, and in techniques of decoration partly cross-cut this spatial pattern. They consist of Vroue 1-3 on the one hand and Engedal and Lånum 1a on the other hand.

The MN III/IV pottery from the late sites and Herrup show stylistic differentiation between Lånum, Vroue-Engedal and Herrup. The use of denticulate stamps typical of this period constrains variation in the filling of bounded designs. Instead, spatial variation is found in the relative distribution of different shapes of bounded designs, in the range of variation at each site, in the pot shapes, and in the use of cardium.

Spatial variation in pot shapes appears during all three phases. This variation is found most markedly in relation to different burial structures, i.e. mortuary houses, megalithic tombs and stone packing graves, most likely reflecting differences in the ceremonies at each of these structures.

The composition of pot shapes also varies among individual sites. The mortuary house at Herrup 26 thus contained several band-decorated bowls and small funnel beakers. Trandum Skovby had only one band-decorated bowl and one funnel beaker, but several funnel-necked bowls with strongly curved belly and carinated vessels. At Vroue, tombs 1-3 show a similar, limited variation in pot shape with a high frequency of pedestalled bowls. Vroue 4 on the contrary contained a wide range of formal variation. Vroue 4 was the only site to contain several clay discs. The MN II pot shapes at Lånum differ from those at Vroue in composition, yet show considerable inter-site variation. In MN III/IV, on the other hand, the Lånum sites contain highly uniform pot shapes compared to the Engedal and Vroue sites.

The marked variation in the choice of forms in pottery deposits, even among neighbouring sites of the same type, indicates that pot shapes served as another aspect of differentiation in the burial ceremonies. Cultural standards prescribed certain pot shapes for specific ceremonies. The choice of other pot shapes and perhaps their frequency may have been decided according to local traditions.

An example of such prescriptions can probably be seen in the pedestalled bowls. They are the only shape present at all sites (except the stone packing graves), and obviously were an obligatory part of rituals at megalithic tombs and most mortuary houses. Only a limited number are found at causewayed camps or at settlement sites. The special status of pedestalled bowls is also apparent from their high level of stylistic variability both locally (Vroue 1–3) and regionally (Schwabedissen 1953:61; Kjærum 1966:331).

Two kinds of geographic, stylistic variation characterised by different degrees of specificity and visibility are found in the Vroue area. Distinctive sub-styles are related to individual tombs or mortuary houses at Herrup-Hagebrogård and Sdr. Mølle-Trandum Skovby in MN I, and at Vroue 1–3 in MN II. These sub-styles are characterised by exclusive distributional patterns and/or uniform combinations of decoration elements that produced highly pronounced differences in the pottery. Sub-styles appear where specific combinations of elements cross-cut the spatial distribution of sites. This kind of stylistic variation in pottery likely represents a symbolic differentiation among neighbouring sites, but apparently persisted only through one style period.

Vague stylistic groupings on the other hand are found among the main burial areas over a considerable period of time (MN II–III/IV). This variation is characterised by frequency differences in the distributional pattern of decoration details. It is recognisable only on close inspection and does not affect the general impression of the pottery styles.

It is assumed that these contrasting spatial patterns can be related to a tribal social structure. A tribal structure for the TBK society is generally accepted, although disagreements prevail concerning the degree of organisation above the local community level (Madsen 1982; Andersen 1981; Voss 1982; Tilley 1984). A tribal society is lineage-based and small scale. Local communities consist of one or more lineage groups (Service 1962; Tilley 1984). Individual households are the minimal units of production and consumption. A number of households may form a lineage group, linked by a common ancestor or ancestors, with an elder or elders at the head of the group. Lineage groups or branches are the basic units within which the appropriation of labour takes place.

I would argue that these local communities are responsible for the vague stylistic groupings seen in the Vroue area. Common stylistic features in the pottery thus resulted from traditional agreement among potters. Vague stylistic variation with low visibility was the result of internal group coherence. No demonstration of external differentiation was intended at this level.

The distinct sub-styles, on the other hand, may have signalled a we/they dichotomy between neighbouring or competing lineage groups at Herrup, Sdr. Mølle, Trandum Skovby and Hagebrogård in MN I. At Vroue this differentiation probably concerned lineage groups within the same local community. The distinct sub-styles thus served to mark out differences between competing local lineages, and to stress social divisions. These lineages probably formed social networks across the local communities, and this behaviour may serve to explain the spatial stylistic pattern that cross-cuts the distribution of the burial grounds. Competition among lineage groups may also explain the fluctuating constellations of sub-styles through time. The status of different lineages within the local communities varied according to their social and economical capability.

THE FUNCTION OF MEGALITHIC TOMBS WITHIN THE VROUE AREA

Spatial stylistic variation suggests that clusters of monumental and non-monumental burial structures served as burial grounds for local communities. Evidence of long-term stylistic traditions related to each burial ground indicates that they were used continuously by the same local communities. Thus the distribution of burial grounds is probably indicative of the spacing of social units as well (Figure 1). The constant relationship between local communities and burial ground suggests a rather unvarying man-land relationship, and this fixed spatial pattern points to strong territorial structures among the local communities.

Unfortunately very little is known of settlement sites in the area. At Vroue a MN V settlement was situated along the river beneath the burial ground (E. Jørgensen 1985:6). A close relationship between the dead and the living was a typical feature of the TBK, and the co-occurence of burials and settlements close to a wet area was quite common (Madsen 1982). Other settlements were likely located in the vicinity of Engedal and Lånum 1 and 2. While settlements might shift over the four hundred years of MN TBK, the burial grounds apparently remained as sacred places that asserted permanence, continuity, and stability in contrast to the less certain world of the living.

These public monuments may well have served as symbolic markers of social territories (Renfrew 1973, 1976; Chapman 1981; Madsen 1982). The stable spatial organisation suggests a balanced relationship between social groups and resources. It seems unlikely that the symbolic value of the burial grounds is related to economic stress and pressure on critical resources.

It seems evident that symbolic demarcation of territories should be connected to burial grounds in general, rather than the individual tombs. The latter were related to lineage groups within the local community, as suggested by the distribution of sub-styles. The repetition of small, equivalent units at the Vroue burial ground (Vroue 1–4) also suggests a segmented lineage structure (Figure 15). The variety of

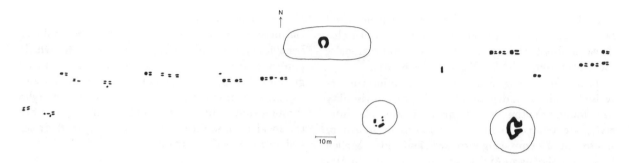

Figure 15. The Vroue I burial ground.

burial structures, as well as the composition of the pottery deposits, may be seen as a competitive display in which economic surplus was converted into symbolic capital or personal prestige. An elaborate ancestor cult served to identify the social with the sacred order, and the legitimate social domains of elders and certain lineages within society.

Vroue 4 in this connection may be seen as an example of a tomb related to a dominant lineage. It contained a minimum of 75 pots dating from MN I-V. The number of episodes of pottery deposition is difficult to estimate, but it is likely that at least 4 depositions took place. The number of MN I style pots suggests a deposition in MN I, or the beginning of MN II, before the major deposits in MN II. Subsequently small depositions followed in MN III/IV and V. The pottery deposits at Vroue 4 were larger than the deposits at Vroue 1-3; they also included the maximum amount of stylistic variability in decoration, technique, and pot shape.

The Vroue 1-3 tombs contained much less pottery, probably resulting from only two episodes of deposit in MN II and MN III/IV. The pottery is decorated according to a distinct sub-style, clearly seen in the pedestalled bowls. The short-term use of Vroue 1-3, the homogeneity of the pottery, and the distinctive decoration of the pedestalled bowls, suggest that a clear separation was made between these sites and Vroue 4 in relation to the primary burials during MN II.

Pottery offerings may be looked upon as destruction of social wealth (Tilley 1984:141). In this sense the differences in the amount of pottery offered may be seen as an expression of hierarchical differentiation among lineage groups. However, ranking by the size of pottery deposits alone may lead to serious misinterpretation. Other aspects of the funeral rites may also signify various social distinctions, some of which may be difficult to recognise archaeologically (Tainter 1978; O'Shea 1981:51). For instance, it is difficult to estimate the prestige related to repeated burials in an old lineage tomb like

Vroue 4, as opposed to the investment connected with the construction of new tombs such as Vroue 1-3. Moreover the size and composition of pottery depositions may in part be prescribed by religion.

When the Vroue tombs were reused in MN III/IV, no distinction was made between the pottery at Vroue 1-3 and at Vroue 4. However, differences in the patterns of use continued. Vroue 4 was reused again in MN V, as the only megalithic tomb in this burial ground.

Thus megalithic tombs, as well as non-monumental burial structures, served as expressions of the social order, and as substantiation of kin relationships and political power in TBK society.

CONCLUSIONS

Stylistic analyses of pottery offerings at burial structures within a small local area in central Jutland showed two patterns of geographic variation:

(1) Sub-styles characterised by exclusive distributional patterns and/or uniform combinations of decoration elements that produced pronounced differences in the pottery. Primarily, different categories of the fill of bounded designs are involved and this stylistic variation is reflected especially at the rim and neck zone of pots as well as in pedestalled bowls. Sub-styles cross-cut the geographical distribution of sites but spatial configurations change from one style period to the next (MN I/MN II). Short-term substyles are related to individual burial structures or competing lineage groups.

(2) Less pronounced stylistic groups are found among the main burial areas over a considerable period of time (MN II-III/IV). This variation is characterised by frequency differences in the distributional pattern of decoration details.

Monumental and non-monumental burial structures in the study area were clustered in several major burial areas. Each major burial area seems to be in use throughout MN TRB, i.e. a span of some 400 years. Obviously the burial area as a whole, rather than the individual tomb, served as the ceremonial focal point. Individual tombs are likely related to lineage groups, as suggested by the distribution of short-term sub-styles and the repetition of small, equivalent units at Vroue. Long-term stylistic traditions related to each burial area indicate that they were used by the same local community. The stable spatial organisation suggests a balanced relationship between social groups and resources. It seems unlikely that the symbolic value of the burial grounds was related to economic stress or pressure on critical resources. These clusters of public monuments may have served as symbolic markers of social territories, but legitimisation of intra-group structure may have been just as important.

Acknowledgements

I acknowledge with thanks the post-doctoral research grant at Århus University and the facilities provided at the Institute of Prehistoric Archaeology, Moesgård, which enabled me to carry out research for this study. Pottery and site information were kindly made available to me by the original excavators: Carl Johan Becker, Ole Faber and Erik Jørgensen. The paper has been improved by many helpful conversations with friends and colleagues at Moesgård. In particular, I would like to thank Niels H. Andersen, Helle Juel Jensen, Torsten Madsen and Peder Mortensen. Torsten Madsen also helped with the completion of the multivariable statistics. The final version has benefited greatly from careful readings by Torsten Madsen and T. Douglas Price.

The distribution and exchange of prestige artefacts in Sweden

A factor analysis of Early Bronze Age metalwork

By Thomas B. Larsson — University of Umeå

The aim of this paper is to study large scale distribution patterns of metalwork from the Early Bronze Age in Sweden. The investigation has been carried out by means of factor analysis using the SPSS package (program PA2) at UMDAC, University of Umeå, Sweden. The results of the analysis will be interpreted archaeologically in terms of exchange and social organisation, with special reference to archaeological problems, such as ethnicity, culture and cultural boundaries (Barth 1969; Gregory 1982; Hodder 1982; Narroll 1964).

My main concern is interpretation - to correlate multivariate analysis of data with prehistoric society. I will therefore not make any evaluation of the computer technique itself, or comment upon the relevance of factor analysis in archaeology (Binford 1972a; Forsberg 1984, 1985; Neustupny 1973).

MATERIAL CULTURE AND SOCIAL REPRODUCTION

To begin with, I find it worth while to stress the symbolic dimension of bronze metalwork, as a complement to the utilitarian functions associated with the physical form of different types of artefacts. In many cases, the symbolic meaning of material culture has priority over the utilitarian function, I think (Højlund 1979; Larsson 1984, 1986). Together with developing social complexity the need for symbolic functions in society increases as a means to legitimate and reproduce structures of dominance and inequality in the spheres of production (Larsson 1986). Material culture, ideology and the reproduction of the social order form a structure actively used in this process by the dominant groups or classes to impose their own consciousness on the whole of society, in order to hide the exploitation on which their dominance and supremacy rely (Bloch 1983:29; Larsson 1986). The continuous conflicts and contradictions caused by human action in the immediate labour process, as well as participation in social activities that reproduce the values, ideas and rules on which the society relies, lead to ad hoc solutions, which, seen in a historical perspective, are the basic force behind social evolution (Rey 1977). Depending on the actual relations of production, the ideological expressions that reproduce the conditions of surplus appropriation are manifested through the use of symbols. Consequently, symbolic messages take material forms - concrete objects are used to materialise and emphasise the abstract ideological conceptions on which the social formation is founded. Certain artefacts become signifiers of the social order (Shanks & Tilley 1982:132).

The Early Bronze Age in South Scandinavia is a period during which social stratification combined with competition for symbolic prestige objects (bronze artefacts) becomes accentuated and clearly recognisable in the archaeological record. The archaeological documentation for this is copious (Aner 1956; Broholm 1944; Jensen 1982; Kristiansen 1978, 1982, 1984; Larsson 1986; Moberg 1956; Welinder 1977).

A function of Early Bronze Age metalwork as indicator of group affiliation can also be expected to be 'visible' in the archaeological record, especially if it was a time of social stress and competition. Consider in this respect Hodder's statement:

I would suggest generally that, as competition over resources and conflict between groups increase in the Baringo area, there are greater advantages in groups overtly stressing their differences (Hodder 1982c:26).

Therefore, another background for the symbolic meaning of material culture is the fact that groups of people, at various levels of organisation - from villages to entire ethnic complexes - express their particular identity in relation to others by the active use of artefacts, as well as through their customs, values and languages.

In this paper the Early Bronze Age metalwork is viewed as having a symbolic function as a signifier of the social structure and order, and also as an

	V1	V2	V3	V4	V5	V6	V7	V8	V9	V10	V11	V12	V13	V14
U1	80	20	12	88	84	14	55	32	13	16	76	8	46	54
U2	26	12	1	37	35	3	25	10	3	8	26	4	13	25
U3	18	4	4	18	17	5	10	7	5	10	11	1	8	14
U4	27	0	1	26	21	6	8	11	7	15	10	1	18	9
U5	16	6	2	20	22	0	9	6	7	9	10	2	8	14
U6	19	3	1	21	19	3	11	7	3	5	12	1	11	11
U7	36	12	1	47	36	12	20	25	3	5	35	8	27	21
U8	15	4	1	18	14	4	12	4	3	6	10	3	10	9

V1: Type A V5: Single find V9: Edge-form III V13: No wear
V2: Type B V6: Hoard find V10: Flange-hight I V14: Wear
V3: Decorated V7: Edge-form I V11: Flange-hight II
V4: Undecorated V8: Edge-form II V12: Flange-hight III

U1: Scania U4: Västergötland/Bohuslän/Dalsland U7: Uppland/Södermanland
U2: Blekinge/Småland U5: Öland U8: Värmland/Västmanland/Närke
U3: Halland U6: Östergötland

Table 1. Data matrix of 14 attributes associated with flanged axes in eight regions of Middle and South Sweden. Labels for the units and the variables are explained below the table.

expression of group identity and affiliation. While the former function is related to the vertical profile of society, the latter is more associated with the horizontal basis, i.e. the spatial organisation of society into groups of different sizes.

The specific way in which the two aspects of symbolism are manifested through bronzes in a given region during the Early Bronze Age is dependent on many factors:

1. The development of an exchange system.
2. The existence of a widespread ideological framework.
3. Social and economic developments.
4. Contradictions between groups and classes with different relations towards the labour process.
5. The material culture conformity within regional communities.
6. The cultural differences between communities.

To analyse exchange systems and socio-spatial organisation, as reflected in the distribution of bronze works of various types, I have chosen Early Bronze Age tools and weapons, i.e., flanged axes, palstaves, shaft-hole axes, socketed axes, swords, daggers, and spearheads (Larsson 1986).

A FACTOR ANALYSIS OF FLANGED AXES

The flanged axe is a type of artefact that can be related to the notion of 'tool', used as a working implement, more than any other type from the Early Bronze Age period. This does not mean that the symbolic function is reduced; the utilitarian quality in combination with the great number of axes found in Middle and South Sweden (471 with provenance; Larsson 1986:28) make the flanged axes most suitable when looking for cultural boundaries of basic nature, in the same manner as one can use the socketed axes for the Late Bronze Age (Baudou 1953, 1956; Larsson 1984).

The data matrix for the flanged axes is given in Table 1. The variables, representing 14 different aspects of the flanged axes, are as follows:

V1 and V2 divide the axes into two categories: type A and type B. The first type is the most common, with an edge that continues to the neck without a marking- or stop ridge, while the second type is usually chisel-shaped, with a rather marked hold for the shaft. The two types are shown in Figure 1.

V3 and V4 concern style in the way they divide the axes into decorated and non-decorated ones. A good representative of decorated axes of the continental Unetice type is the axe from Grävle, Torslunda parish on Öland (Oldeberg 1974:No. 2057; Åberg 1923:39).

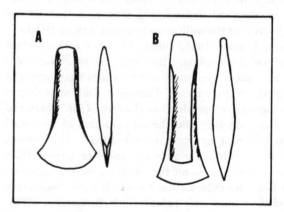

Figure 1. Two main types of flanged axes used in the factor analysis.

Another example is the axe from Knivinge, Vreta Kloster parish in Östergötland (Oldeberg 1974:No. 2318; Montelius 1917:No. 795).

V5 and V6 indicate the find circumstances: V5 represents single finds and V6 hoard finds. Because of the very few flanged axes found in burials, it has not been considered meaningful to include these as a special variable.

V7, V8 and V9 are related to the form of the edge. They indicate whether the edge is straight (V7), slightly convex (V8) or extremely convex (V9). A measurement of convexity is attained by using the ratio between the height (h) and the width (w) of the edge in the way illustrated in Figure 2. If the height of the edge is only one fourth of the width, or less, the axe belongs to V7. If the height is between one fourth and one half of the width, it belongs to V8. Edges that have a ratio over one half belong to V9.

V10, V11 and V12 account for the maximal thickness of the axes, i.e. the height of the flanges (Figure 3): V10 = 1–10 mm; V11 = 11–20 mm; V12 = >21 mm.

V13 and V14 indicate whether the axe shows clear signs of wear or not. This distinction is difficult to make from the drawings in Oldeberg's publication (1974), which is the main source that I have used. The main focus of interest, when trying to decide whether an axe shows obvious signs of wear, is whether the edge is symmetric or asymmetric in shape. To take some examples from the catalogue compiled by Oldeberg (1974): No. 48, 85, 184, 386, and 475 are flanged axes from the province of Scania that show signs of wear on the edge, while No. 2318, 2335, 2728, and 2761 from the provinces of Östergötland and Södermanland do not show any marked signs of wear, judging from the drawings. V13 and V14 must, however, depending on the circumstances mentioned above, be treated with caution, as I have not examined the axes personally.

The main purpose of the factor analysis of the flanged axes is to investigate whether regional variations exist in Sweden according to the 14 variables, or whether the distribution of axes is homogeneous for the entire area under study. Consequently, the units are eight regions in Middle and South Sweden, from Scania in the south to Uppland in the north. In four units (U2, U4, U7 and U8), two or three adjoining provinces with a low number of axes have been merged to form a larger region .

As can be seen from Table 2, two factors were identified in the flanged axe material, with factor 1 being unipolar and factor 2 bipolar. For factor 1, the loadings range from 0.57 to 0.99, signalling a high degree of mutual correlation between the 14 variables, while factor 2 with its positive and negative loadings, varying between –0.53 and 0.79, indicates differences in the correlation between the vari-

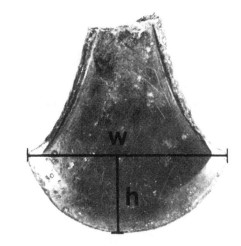

Figure 2. Photograph of the edge of a flanged axe showing the measurements (w and h) used to determine the edge shape.

Figure 3. Photograph showing the flange height thickness measurement (t).

ables; a difference in another dimension compared to factor 1. The factor scores for the eight regions under study are listed in Table 2. The very high value recorded for Scania for factor 1 should here be noted. The greatest difference in factor scores for factor 1 is between Scania (U 1) and Östergötland (U 6). For factor 2, the greatest difference in factor scores is between Västergötland/Bohuslän/Dalsland (U 4) and Uppland/Södermanland (U 7). Evidently it is not the same dissimilarities that create the polarisation between Scania and Östergötland indicated by factor 1, and the polarisation between West Sweden and the northern provinces, indicated by factor 2.

To make it easier to evaluate these discrepancies, the most important variables and cases, according to the loadings and scores, of the two factors are marked with asterisks in Table 2. From this it can be seen

| | Loadings | | | Scores | |
	Factor 1	Factor 2		Factor 1	Factor 2
V1	* 0.99	0.03	U1	* 2.30	* 0.50
V2	0.90	−0.17	U2	−0.06	−0.54
V3	0.86	* 0.46	U3	−0.54	* 0.59
V4	* 0.99	−0.09	U4	−0.26	* 1.47
V5	* 0.99	0.03	U5	−0.48	* 0.60
V6	0.85	*−0.28	U6	−0.70	−0.37
V7	0.96	−0.08	U7	* 0.41	*−1.80
V8	0.93	−0.21	U8	−0.67	−0.45
V9	0.77	* 0.59			
V10	0.57	* 0.79			
V11	* 0.99	−0.13			
V12	0.82	*−0.53			
V13	0.97	−0.06			
V14	0.96	−0.02			

Table 2. Loadings and factor scores from a factor analysis of the data in Table 1. Asteriks indicate units and variables considered to be diagnostic.

that the most relevant variables for explaining factor 1 are V1 (flanged axes type A), V4 (undecorated), V5 (single find) and V11 (flange height II). However, as most variables have quite high loadings for factor 1, it is clear that they are all of importance; the ones marked are those of greatest significance only.

Comparing the number of axes in each case with the factor scores, the correlation is very high for factor 1. It may therefore safely be assumed that factor 1 is strongly related to the frequency variations between the eight cases.

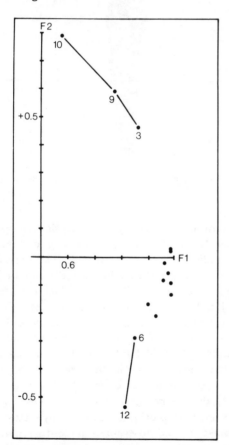

Figure 4. The loadings of the 14 variables plotted against factor 1 and factor 2. Variable numbers of the highest and lowest loading for factor 2 have been marked.

For factor 2 there is one positive and one negative range of loadings as well as factor scores. The positive range of loadings is explained by V10 (flange heights I), V9 (edge form III) and V3 (decorated). These are features typical of axes designed more for display than for practical labour. The negative range of loadings have V12 (flange height III) and V6 (hoard find) as specially significant attributes. e

The other variables are more or less uncorrelated with factor 2, having loadings around zero.

The variables most typical of the positive and the negative sides of factor 2, mentioned above, indicate two types of flanged axes, characterised by very different features: one 'exclusive' type with decoration and extremely convex edges – to a large extent of Central European origin (Unetice type), and one 'simple' type with high flanges, often associated with hoards.

The factor loadings for the two factors are plotted against each other in Figure 4, and the dominant variables for the positive and negative sides of factor 2 are marked and joined by a line. One should note the cluster of variables located between 0.90 and 1.00 on the axis of factor 1, rather uncorrelated with factor 2, but accounting for most of the variance in the material as a whole. Together these variables represent the 'ordinary' or average type of flanged axes, often found in Sweden, while factor 2 divides the axes into two classes according to qualitative aspects; factor 1 measures quantity and factor 2 quality.

Turning to the spatial distribution, we can best illustrate how these quantitative and qualitative dimensions are related to the eight regions by plotting the factor scores from the two factors against each other (Figure 5). Scania (U 1), West Sweden (U 4) and the northern provinces (U 7) are the three extremes in both quantitative and qualitative terms.

The quantitative picture is totally dominated by Scania, where appr. 50% of all flanged axes from Sweden are found (Larsson 1986). The great number of axes in Scania, of both luxury and

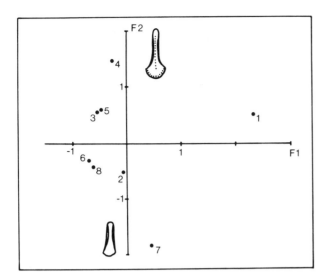

Figure 5. Factor scores for the eight provinces plotted against factor 1 and factor 2.

utilitarian types, are probably the main reason for its rather neutral position between West Sweden and Uppland/Södermanland on factor 2. However, together with Västergötland/Bohuslän/-Dalsland, Halland and Öland, Scania is more related to variables 3, 9 and 10, than to variables 6 and 12.

The regional variations in the distribution of flanged axes can best be illustrated by an isometric mapping of the two factors. Starting with factor 1 (Figure 6), the quantity of axes in southern Sweden is revealed by isometric curves, based on the factor scores. There is one high peak for Scania and

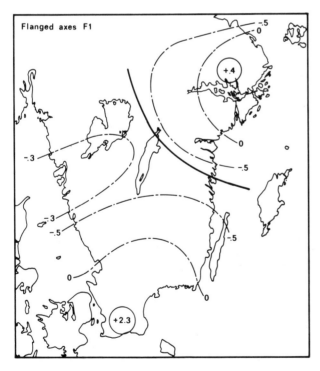

Figure 6. Map of southern Sweden. Curves denote the variation in factor scores for factor 1.

one lower peak for Uppland/Södermanland, while the maximum depression between these peaks runs through the province of Östergötland.

Considering the fact that the great majority of the earliest bronzes are imports from Central Europe, it must be assumed that the internal circulation of bronzes within Scandinavia was mainly a south to north process. If the circulation and exchange of Early Bronze Age flanged axes could simply be explained as a diffusion from a 'core area' in Denmark/Scania to the Lake Mälaren Valley in the north, in line with the 'random drift hypothesis' (Binford 1972b:295), the lowest figures would be expected for Uppland/Södermanland.

However, as this is not the case, a possible explanation of the trend in Figure 6 is that we are dealing with two poles in an exchange network: one centre in the 'core' of the Nordic Bronze Age culture in Denmark/Scania, and another centre at the northern periphery in the Lake Mälaren Valley. This kind of spatial patterning is often associated with prestige goods exchange, contrary to what is found in 'down-the-line-exchange' (Renfrew 1984:149, Figure 4).

Another possibility is that the exchange focused upon raw materials, like copper and tin, and that the relatively large number of axes in the Lake Mälaren Valley indicate a manufacturing centre. Both ways, however, the crucial question is how the circulation spheres in which raw materials or ready made artefacts moved were organised to supply a regional centre in Uppland/Södermanland without a general fall-off pattern from south to north. Apart from direct access to bronze, i.e. a local extraction of raw materials, this could only happen by a direct exchange connection with regions rich in bronze; an exchange system that linked areas together, more or less irrespective of the distance between them.

The border position of the province of Östergötland (Figure 6) in the distribution of flanged axes in southern Sweden during the Early Bronze Age is surely no coincidence. During historic times the northern part of this province constituted the border between Götaland and Svealand (the woodlands of Kolmården). It is indeed quite possible that this known border region might have its origin way back in the Bronze Age, based on natural, geographical conditions (the hilly forest belt), as well as on deep-rooted traditions of tribal territories. Without making any venture into the area of place-name research, it can be noted that modern literature on the subject makes it clear that Östergötland means the eastern part of the land of the Götar tribe (Franzén 1982:10).

If we turn to the qualitative dimensions indicated by factor 2, the picture is somewhat different (Figure 7). Regions like Blekinge/Småland (U2), Östergötland (U6), and Värmland/Västmanland/-Närke (U8) seem to be peripheral in this context, with a mixture of axes with both prestige and non-prestige

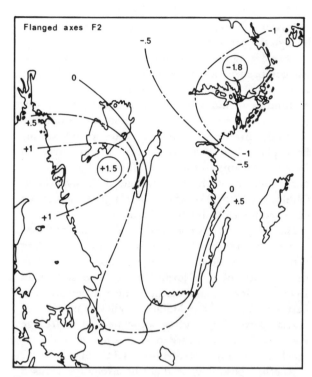

Figure 7. Map of southern Sweden. Curves denote the variation in factor scores for factor 2.

attributes. Axes with 'prestige attributes' (factor 2, positive scores) are of notable significance in Scania (U1), Halland U3), Öland (U5) and, in particular, Västergötland/Bohuslän/Dalsland (U4). Even if the total number of axes of the luxury type is greatest in Scania, the relative 'importance' of this type is far greater in West Sweden than in any other part.

Another area of interest here is Öland (U5), which forms the outpost for the circulation and consumption of luxury flanged axes in the eastern part of southern Sweden. If the coastal zone of Scania, where the majority of the flanged axes are found, had the status of 'hinterland' to the powerful centres in Denmark, the relatively low factor scores noted for Scania in comparison with West Sweden and Öland (where the total number of axes are low) might be expected. Scania would thus be a socio-political buffer zone in the junction between three centres: Denmark, Västergötland and Öland. It is also possible that the emphasis placed on quality in Östergötland and Öland relates to an unstable and competitive social situation in these regions. That is, competition for power and prestige was greater here during the beginning of the Bronze Age compared to Scania, and consequently, the symbolic function of flanged axes, perhaps used by dominant groups within these regions to manifest and strengthen their supremacy, was greater.

Looking at Figure 7, it is clear that the 'cultural drift theory' cannot be successfully applied to this pattern either. If Denmark is taken to be the starting point from which the axes are spread by

exchange or trade, the factor scores for Halland and Blekinge/Småland would have been much higher than they in fact are, and moreover, the extremely high value for West Sweden makes this theory completely invalid. The only way to explain the pattern noted for factor 2 and yet retain the idea of cultural drift is by making West Sweden the core area whence flanged axes of a certain type drifted towards Halland and Scania. However, this argument leaves Öland on the east coast of Sweden in an inexplicable position, since there are very low scores for Småland, which lies geographically in between.

It is quite clear that we must seek other explanations when dealing with this particular type of distribution. We must consider an exchange system that interlinked certain areas of particular 'status' in the circulation of metalwork irrespective of distance; a form of 'long-distance trade' that is typical of a prestige goods system (Friedman & Rowlands 1977:245, Figure 6.3).

With the position of Uppland/Södermanland in the quantitative distribution of flanged axes (or raw materials) shown in Figure 6 in mind, the existence of a direct long-distance exchange must indeed be considered. Also, when looking at the negative score on factor 2 for this region, related to quite different attributes (the shape and design of the axes), the need for cultural manifestations as expressed by, for example, a particular type of flanged axe, is rather evident. The existence of long-distance exchange of goods, in combination with the use of axes of a particular type, is a feature that might be taken to indicate cultural differences between the groups in the Lake Mälaren Valley (Svear) and the other tribes of southern Sweden (Götar).

The difference between Västergötland/Bohuslän/Dalsland (U4) and Öland (U5), in contrast to Uppland/Södermanland (U7), expressed by the factor scores for factor 2 (Figure 7), separates the Lake Mälaren Valley from the rest of Sweden, and, further, tends to divide southern Sweden into one western and one eastern area, in which Västergötland and Öland are the two core areas.

With the results of the factor analysis as a starting point, some general remarks concerning the Early Bronze Age exchange system in Sweden can be made. Figure 8 illustrates this in a schematic way. To make the model comprehensible, the black nodes are defined as different social units (e.g., tribes, lineages or territorial clans): A to E. The thick line coming from outside to unit D marks the input of goods in the system (bronze artefacts and/or raw materials), while the circles connecting the units within this hypothetical 'culture' indicate the exchange of goods, in the form of gifts and commodities (Gregory 1982:12; Larsson 1986). The arrows indicate the direction of the exchange, where the flow of goods above the base

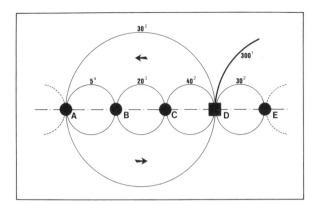

Figure 8. Model illustrating an exchange system involving five social units (A–E). The larger figures indicate the amount of metalwork in circulation and the smaller differences in time.

line goes from D to A, and below the base line in the reverse direction .

If we assume that 300 flanged axes (or the raw material for manufacturing 300 axes) are 'imported' to unit D, which is the core area in this model (Denmark/Scania in the Nordic Bronze Age), the goods are then distributed further by exchange to adjacent units. 30 items are exchanged to unit E (Öland; U5) and 40 items are passed by exchange to unit C (West Sweden; U4). Unit C, which is in an exchange relationship with unit B, passes half of its 40 items to unit B (Östergötland; U6) which in turn, in its relations with unit A (Uppland/Södermanland; U7) on the periphery of the culture complex, passes 5 of its 20 items to unit A (Figure 8).

This chain of exchange, from D to A, with a steady decrease in the number of items in circulation when moving from centre to periphery, is a phenomenon which can be identified by using 'fall-off curves' (Hodder 1974, 1982c:47).

As can be seen from Figure 8, there is also a long-distance direct connection between units D and A (between Denmark/Scania and Uppland/Södermanland) that does not involve units B or C. Goods travelling in this channel are usually of particular prestige character; symbols of great importance for either A or D, and it is also likely that the exchange of these goods may have taken the commodity form (Gregory 1982:23). If Uppland/Södermanland were located at the periphery of the Nordic Bronze Age culture during its earliest phase, with respect to material culture and ideology, the connections with Denmark/Scania via exchange of prestige goods could have been of utmost importance for a local élite as a way of legitimising and sustaining its influence and power.

Because of the remote location of the Lake Mälaren Valley in relation to the main routes in bronze distribution, and also due to the lack of its own resources of copper and tin, the maintenance of a long-distance exchange line with the core area in South Scandinavia must surely have been valuable. As a consequence of this direct connection, unit A in my model (the Lake Mälaren Valley) ends up with a total of 35 items. This is almost as much as in unit C, but the nature of the exchange between D-C and D-A is quite different.

This system of exchange can explain the quantitative distribution of flanged axes illustrated in Figure 6. The need to express group affiliation, i.e. differences between communities and conformity within communities, indicated by Figure 7, can also be verified. The differences in material culture (in this case flanged axes) are regarded as different 'dialects' within a symbolic 'language', which the tribal formations in southern Sweden used to express their identity and the social structure within each community. The latter may of course have varied from area to area and the particular function of certain types of artefacts (as symbols) might have altered between, for example, Scania, Västergötland and Uppland.

A FACTOR ANALYSIS OF WEAPONS AND TOOLS

In the following, the study of the Early Bronze Age flanged axes will be supplemented by an analysis of both weapons and tools. The structures observed when dealing with the flanged axes only, and the

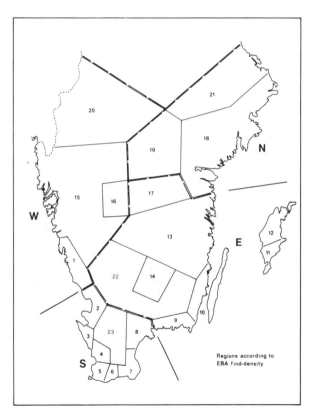

Figure 9. Regional division of southern Sweden according to the distribution of Early Bronze Age metalwork (cf. Larsson 1986:24).

125

Table 3:

		1	2	3	4	5	6	7	8	9	10	11	12	13	14	15	16	17	18	19	21	22	23
Flanged axe	A	.	2	5	9	22	10	16	6	1	2	.	.	.	1	16	3	1	1	.	3	.	3
–	B	13	13	14	20	26	10	38	26	6	32	16	9	12	5	17	4	17	31	8	37	6	11
Palstave	A	24	18	28	19	15	5	30	12	13	23	8	10	10	3	10	9	3	14	7	5	13	11
–	B	1	1	6	5	5	2	4	7	4	8	.	3	.	1	.	.	.	1	2	.	6	2
–	C	.	.	1	1	1	1	1	2	.	1	.	.	.	.	.	.	.	.	.	.	.	.
Shafthole axe	A	.	4	1	2	7	2	.	1	1	.	.	.	.	.	3	2	3	.	1	4	.	.
–	B	1	1	.	.	.	1	1	5	.	.	1	.	.	.	.	.	1	.	1	.	1	.
–	C	3	.	.	.	1	.	.	1	.	2	.	.	.	.	.	.	.	.	.	1	2	.
–	D	.	.	.	.	.	.	.	1	1	.	.	.	.	.	.	.	.	.	.	1	.	1
–	E	.	.	.	.	.	1	1	.	.	.	.	1	1	1	.	.	.	.	2	3	.	.
Socketed axe	A	.	.	.	1	1	.	1	.	1	.	.	.	4	2	.	2	.	1	2	1	1	1
–	B	1	1	1	.	.	.	.	1	.	.	.	.	.	2	1	3	4	2	4	4	1	1
–	C	.	.	.	.	.	.	1	.	1	1	.	1	.	.	2	1	2	4	1	2	1	.
–	D	1	5	1	3	1	1	.	.	.	6	.	1	.	.	.	5	1	.	.	.	2	.
–	E	.	1	.	1	3	1	.	1	.	2	1	1	.	.	.	1	.	1	.	3	.	.
–	F	2	.	2	.	.	.	.	.	1	.	.	.	.	.	1	.	1	.	2	.	.	.
Sword/dagger	A	10	21	15	7	32	14	34	16	7	10	3	7	4	6	12	26	4	4	3	2	9	3
–	B	4	7	5	6	4	7	29	10	2	7	4	1	3	4	1	3	4	2	1	1	7	5
–	C	2	3	5	1	2	3	8	.	.	3	1	.	2	1	1	1	.	.	.	.	5	.
–	D	1	2	1	2	3	.	3	2	.	2	1	.	1	.	1	.	1	.	.	1	2	.
–	E	.	2	3	7	6	1	11	1	2	5	.	1	.	1	2	3	.	1	.	5	3	1
–	F	1	5	6	2	6	3	14	4	4	2	.	3	1	.	3	3	1	3	1	1	2	1
Spearhead	A	1	1	1	1	1	2	8	4	3	11	.	7	.	2	1	6	3	.	2	4	.	1
–	B	.	.	.	.	2	.	.	.	.	.	.	.	.	.	1	.	1	2	1	1	.	.
–	C	.	1	2	.	2	.	6	1	.	2	1	5	1	.	1	3	1	3	.	4	1	1
–	D	1	.	.	1	2	1	1	1	.	3	.	.	.	1	1	.	1	.	.	3	.	.
–	E	7	.	.	1	.	1	3	.	.	.	1	.	.	.	5	.	.	1	.	.	.	1
–	F	.	2	5	1	1	4	5	6	2	5	1	3	2	1	1	1	.	1	2	3	2	2
–	G	.	1	.	1	.	.	1	1	1	1	.	1	1	.	.	.	.	1	.	.	1	.
–	H	.	4	1	1	1	3	4	2	6	8	.	1	.	3	1	2	.	5	.	5	.	1

Table 3. Data matrix of the frequency of 30 tool and weapon types counted in 22 different regions of Middle and South Sweden. The geographical position of the regions is seen in Figure 9.

		Factor scores					Factor loadings		
		Factor 1	Factor 2	Factor 3			Factor 1	Factor 2	Factor 3
Flanged axe	A	0.29	0.73	2.64	Region	1	0.85	0.10	−0.37
–	B	3.51	−3.52	1.43	–	2	0.88	0.37	−0.01
Palstave	A	2.75	0.98	−3.73	–	3	0.89	0.26	−0.29
–	B	0.03	0.34	−0.99	–	4	0.92	−0.09	−0.05
–	C	−0.60	−0.13	0.03	–	5	0.82	0.25	0.42
Shafthole axe	A	−0.35	−0.12	0.66	–	6	0.78	0.33	0.46
–	B	−0.51	−0.23	−0.03	–	7	0.92	0.17	0.13
–	C	−0.57	−0.12	−0.34	–	8	0.93	−0.06	0.18
–	D	−0.62	−0.21	−0.17	–	9	0.81	0.26	−0.33
–	E	−0.51	−0.32	−0.08	–	10	0.92	−0.21	−0.12
Socketed axe	A	−0.40	−0.36	−0.43	–	11	0.89	−0.38	−0.01
–	B	−0.30	−0.34	−0.10	–	12	0.81	0.03	−0.22
–	C	−0.47	−0.43	−0.07	–	13	0.92	−0.21	−0.18
–	D	−0.44	0.01	0.20	–	14	0.83	0.22	0.20
–	E	−0.52	−0.25	0.14	–	15	0.78	0.02	0.39
–	F	−0.60	−0.20	−0.20	–	16	0.62	0.64	0.20
Sword/dagger	A	2.02	3.60	1.90	–	17	0.79	−0.46	0.27
–	B	0.67	0.56	0.26	–	18	0.85	−0.47	0.00
–	C	−0.26	0.44	−0.28	–	19	0.85	−0.21	−0.21
–	D	−0.44	−0.17	−0.10	–	21	0.70	−0.62	0.24
–	E	−0.14	0.23	0.05	–	22	0.79	0.34	−0.34
–	F	0.01	0.51	−0.11	–	23	0.93	−0.14	−0.17
Spearhead	A	0.02	0.03	−0.06					
–	B	−0.59	−0.37	0.04					
–	C	−0.31	−0.26	−0.17					
–	D	−0.51	−0.27	0.28					
–	E	−0.46	−0.16	−0.10					
–	F	−0.03	0.01	−0.39					
–	G	−0.55	−0.14	−0.34					
–	H	−0.11	0.16	0.08					

Table 4. Factor scores and loadings from a factor analysis of the data in Table 4.

126

suggested interpretations, can thereby be set in their functional context when studied in relation to other Early Bronze Age artefact types.

In this analysis I have chosen a finer regional sub-division of southern Sweden, into 23 regions (Figure 9), in line with the framework used in my thesis (Larsson 1986:Figure 8).

In this case a Q-mode factor analysis was used (Nie et al 1975:469; Rummel 1970:446; Stephenson 1953). Compared to the R-mode technique used in the study of the flanged axes, the cases (regions) are treated as variables and placed on the horizontal axis in a Q-mode analysis. This inverted version is perhaps the most accurate when trying to find patterns of similarity between geographical regions or areas (Rummel 1970:446).

Region 20 has been removed from this study because of its extremely low numbers for all types of metalwork. In experimental runs it could be noted that this region tended to disrupt the structures in the material. When it was removed the patterns became much clearer.

The cases (here artefact types) were also further subdivided into types according to the scheme used by Oldeberg (1976) and by myself (Larsson 1986:26-51) In all, the bronzes were divided into 30 sub-types - two types of flanged axes, three types of palstaves, five types of shaft-hole axes, six types of swords/daggers, six types of socketed axes and eight types of spearheads (Table 3).

Three factors with an eigenvalue larger than 1.0 were identified, and it is fairly evident that swords/daggers, flanged axes and palstaves are the key features when trying to explain the similarities and differences between the 22 regions under study.

The factor loadings and factor scores are shown in Table 4. Spearheads, shaft-hole axes and socketed axes have low factor scores for all three factors, which means that they explain only a minimal part of the variation in the entire material. Figures 10, 11, and 13 show the plotted factor loadings for the three factors and seven of the 22 regions have been marked by numbers (regions 1, 6, 7, 16, 17, 18, and 21).

The relationship between factor 1 and factor 2 is not governed by quantity or quality, as in the case with the flanged axes discussed above. Instead, factor 1 is tied up with the interrelationship of swords/daggers, flanged axes and palstaves in each region, i.e., a region with a homogeneous equipment of these three types has a high loading on factor 1, independently of whether the proportional relationship is 5-5-5 or 40-40-40.

This relationship can be further emphasised by a multiple regression analysis (a correlation calculation dealing with more than two dimensions) of the six regions with loadings higher than 0.90. (regions 4, 7, 8, 10, 13, and 23). The correlation coefficient is, as expected, very high: r = 0.93. Conversely, the

correlation between the regions with the lowest loadings for factor 1 is much lower: r = 0.51 (regions 6, 15, 16, 21, and 22 with loadings less than 0.80). It should also be noted that the correlation between factor loadings and the number of artefacts found is extremely low for all three factors: factor 1, r = 0.21; factor 2, r = 0.17; factor 3, r = 0.27.

From these complementary calculations it is quite clear that factor 1 gives a measurement of the homogeneity in bronze assemblages in each region. Turning to factor 2, the marked distribution along the y-axis seen in Figure 10 separates the data in two directions: one positive side where swords/daggers are of major importance, and one negative side dominated by flanged axes. Transferring this observation to the spatial dimension, we can clearly observe a polarisation between northeastern and southwestern Sweden (Figure 14); the difference between Uppland and Västergötland noted for the flanged axes (Figure 7) is very accentuated here, due to the difference in function between swords/daggers and flanged axes.

The third dimension in this material, factor 3, tends to separate the metalwork with reference to swords/daggers and flanged axes on the one side (positive loadings) and palstaves on the other (negative loadings), as illustrated in Figure 11.

We shall now consider the spatial dimension in greater detail. In Figure 12 I have marked the regions in southern Sweden according to their different degrees of homogeneity in the occurrence of swords/daggers, flanged axes and palstaves as given by factor 1. There are two areas with a great unifor-

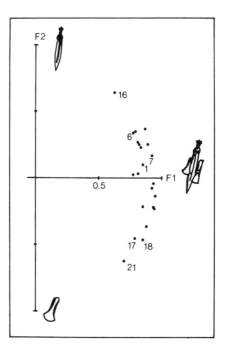

Figure 10. Factor loadings for the 23 regions plotted against factor 1 and factor 2. Seven regions are marked by numbers.

mity in metalwork assemblage; one in Scania consisting of regions 4, 7, 8, and 23, and another in eastern Sweden, consisting of regions 10 and 13 (Figure 9). There are also two areas where the fluctuation between the three types of artefacts, rather than the homogeneity, is the main characteristic. The larger of the two consists of regions 15, 16, 17, and 23, and the smaller area with low loadings for factor 1 is region 21. All other regions on the mainland and on the island of Gotland have loadings ranging between 0.80 and 0.90, forming an intermediate, 'neutral' zone with an average type of relationship between the different types of bronze work. This picture (Figure 12) is further refined when we turn to factor 2 and factor 3, since these dimensions measure the 'status' of each region in relation to only one or two of the three main types of metalwork (Figures 10 and 11). For example, factor 2 marks out those regions in which swords/daggers or flanged axes play the dominant role. Region 16 is thus dominated by swords/daggers, while region 21, on the other hand, has a greater proportion of flanged axes compared to swords/daggers. The fact that these regions are related more either to swords/daggers or flanged axes implies that the artefact assemblages are not very homogeneous. This is also confirmed when looking at the loadings for factor 1 (Figure 12). Therefore, regions with a marked homogeneity in artefact assemblages and high loadings for factor 1 will not play any significant role in factors 2 and 3, and vice versa.

When the loadings for factor 2 and factor 3 are plotted against each other (Figure 13), regions with a homogeneous assemblage will centre around

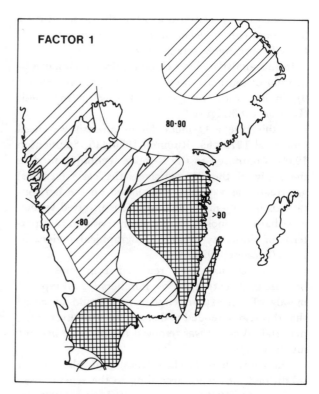

Figure 12. Map of southern Sweden showing the factor loadings for factor 1 for the different regions: less than 0.80, 0.80–0.90, more than 0.90.

the origin, while regions with a more asymmetrical relationship between the three types are to be found in peripheral positions (like regions 1, 6, 16, and 21), depending on which one of the three types is the most important in that particular region.

It is clear that the flanged axes can be regarded as the main type of bronze artefacts, giving northeastern Sweden its particular profile during the Early Bronze

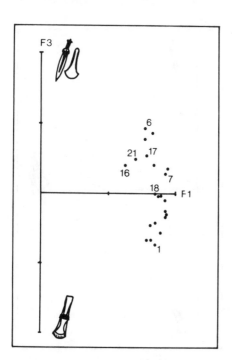

Figure 11. Factor loadings plotted against factor 1 and factor 3. The same regions as in Figure 10 are marked by numbers.

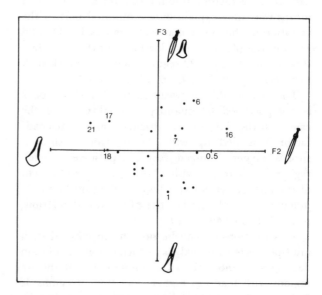

Figure 13. Factor loadings plotted against factor 2 and factor 3. The same regions as in Figure 10 are marked by numbers.

Age. If we add to this the earlier result from the analysis of flanged axes, it is also possible to specify the particular type of flanged axe that is characteristic of this part of Sweden, namely an axe with high flanges. In contrast the characteristic form of western Sweden is the axe with a very convex edge and low flanges, often decorated.

Combining the results of the two factor analyses, it is obvious that the difference in the bronzework equipment between the western and the northern regions is not just a matter of variation in axe design, but also expresses at a 'higher level' the access to, and use of, weapons vs. tools. At the 'tool-level', two main types of flanged axes divide southern Sweden into two large blocks (Figure 7), and this division is further underlined when turning to the spatial relationship between weapons (swords/daggers) and tools (flanged axes), as illustrated in Figure 14. The border zone, running between the southern part of region 10 and Lake Vättern, marked in black in the middle of the figure, is the dividing line between tool and weapon dominance, according to the loadings recorded for factor 2 (Table 4). Factor loadings between 0.10 and 0.30 are marked by thin hatching for both the positive and the negative side, loadings between 0.30 and 0.50 are indicated by dense hatching, and finally loadings above 0.50 are marked by cross-hatching. The tool centre is located in region 21 and the weapon centre in region 16. Again, this picture very closely resembles the one shown in Figure 7.

The significance of this polarisation into two core areas and their hinterlands - one centre in Uppland and another in Västergötland (Falbygden) - must, in my opinion, be interpreted as an indication of cultural differences between groups using bronze metalwork (among other things) to express their own traditions and identity, i.e., an indication of social organisation on the macro-scale.

This differentiation of weapons and tools, as an indicator of social organisation in space, cannot fruitfully be applied in Scania, because of the high frequencies of all types of bronzework in this area of Sweden. In the regions north of Scania, where this 'wealth' in bronzes rapidly decreases, the tools are distributed along an eastern route, while weapons are channelled in a northwestern direction towards Falbygden in Västergötland.

Again, the pattern of distribution of both weapons and tools does not describe a 'fall-off' curve that can be associated with a gradual diffusion due to time or other unintentional spread (random drift). Instead, the pattern reveals a prestige goods pattern, of the type outlined above (Figure 8). In this case, the goods that passed from the main centre to the regional centres (from D to A in Figure 8) can be divided into two categories: weapons (to region 16) and tools (to region 21). The area with loadings between 0.30 and 0.50 on the positive side in Figure 14 - regions

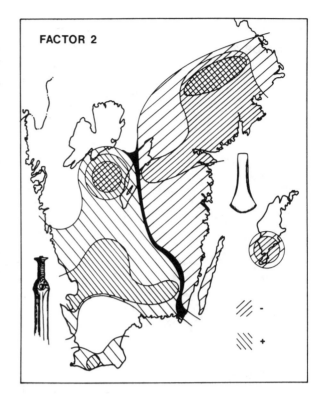

Figure 14. Density map showing factor loadings for factor 2. Light hatching 0.10-0.29, dense hatching 0.30-0.49, cross-hatching >0.49, for both positive and negative loadings, based on the standard deviation. Non-hatched areas have loadings around zero (-0.09-0.09).

2 and 22 - could be explained as a result of a 'fall-off' distribution, comparable to the exchange lines between D-C-B in Figure 8. The peak in weapon distribution for region 16 cannot be explained in that way; it necessitates an assumption of long distance exchange connections.

Another possibility is that the long-distance exchange was a two step procedure: from Denmark/Scania to Västergötland (1) and from Västergötland to Uppland (2), where the more ordinary and common types, like flanged axes, were passed further on to Uppland, while luxury prestige goods like swords were less likely to be passed any further. If this was the case, we would also expect that a proportion of the more common axes were distributed from region 16 to the adjacent region 15 in a form of gift exchange between groups and local lineages in western Sweden. Looking at Figure 15, which shows the loadings for factor 3 (the positive side is related to swords/daggers and the negative side to palstaves), it is evident that a dividing line separated regions 15 and 16 from the rest of southern Sweden.

In the southernmost part of Sweden, there are two smaller areas with positive loadings (regions 5-8 and region 14), while the general tendency is negative, showing the importance of palstaves. The positive loadings for Uppland (region 21) must also be noted.

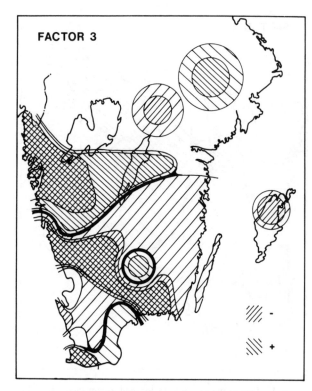

FACTOR 3

Figure 15. Density map showing factor loadings for factor 3. Light hatching 0.10-0.19, dense hatching 0.20-0.29, cross hatching >0.29, for both positive and negative loadings, based on the standard deviation. Non-hatched areas have loadings around zero (-0.09-0.09).

If we take swords/daggers and flanged axes together and contrast them with palstaves, which was the third logical step for the computer to take when structuring this material, the expected short-distance exchange of flanged axes from region 16 to region 15 can easily be inferred. The artefact assemblage in region 15 is strongly governed by both weapons and tools, whereas region 16 is the real centre when looking only at the weapons (Figure 14).

Also, when looking at weapons and tools separately, region 15 is more or less uncorrelated to both. This indicates that the relationship between weapons and tools is very homogeneous in region 15, but the number of weapons is less than in region 16 and the number of tools is less than in region 21.

Given a certain number of weapons and tools distributed by long-distance exchange to region 16, where the consumption of most of the weapons took place, then many tools were passed on in exchange to region 21, while only a smaller number of weapons and tools were distributed to adjacent groups. This spread created a more homogeneous relationship between the two types of artefact, even if the actual number of items in circulation was restricted in region 15.

With palstaves, swords/daggers and flanged axes considered as the main features in studying the Early Bronze Age metalwork in Sweden, the regional emphasis put on the different types is shown in

Figures 14 and 15. Swords/daggers and flanged axes have been discussed above and their functions as symbols expressing cultural differences and similarities are particularly evident for the western and northern regions. The palstave, when contrasted with the other types, is spatially related to a large area consisting of Regions 1, 3, 9, 13, 22, and 23 (negative hatching in Figure 15) and two smaller areas, one in Närke (region 19) and the other located in North Gotland (region 12). The major importance of the palstave in the artefact assemblages is to be found in a belt reaching from region 9 to region 1. Between the Scanian coastal zone, and Västergötland, there is only one region with positive loadings for factor 3, and that is central Småland (region 14). It is, therefore, quite possible that this area should be regarded as another 'core area' in the exchange system regulating the distribution of bronze works, together with region 16 and region 21 (Larsson 1986:Figure 60).

CONCLUSIONS

Irrespective of the exact relationship between the structure of metalwork dispersal and the different prehistoric social units that characterised the social formations in Sweden during the Early Bronze Age, the factor analyses presented in this paper make it clear that significant structures can be separated, and that the patterns may be explained in terms of social organisation. The difficult part is to label the areas of various size according to anthropological concepts, such as tribes, sub-tribes, lineages and clans, when relating the identified structures to known organisational units within 'primitive' communities. Therefore, I have avoided any detailed interpretation of the spatial patterns outlined here as well as using an unsigned check-list approach to classify the Early Bronze Age society in Sweden as a tribal or chiefdom-organised society.

To conclude, the first analysis showed that the distribution of flanged axes in general shows a 'fall-off' pattern from two geographical extremes – Scania and the Lake Mälaren Valley – where the maximum depression runs through the province of Östergötland. As these early bronze axes to a large extent are European imports, the observation made here cannot simply be explained as a steady 'down the line' spread from south to north; if so, the quantitative minimum would be expected for the Lake Mälaren Valley. Instead, the pattern is more characteristic of a prestige goods exchange system, interlinking certain regions (e.g. central places) with a particular status. The qualitative variable marks a division of southern Sweden into a northern, a western and a southeastern area, in which the polarisation is most accentuated between the northern and the western. Again, Östergötland is located at the junction point. Altogether, this is interpreted as a sign of social organisation in space, where group affiliation and boundaries between groups at a particular level of organisation are expressed by metalwork symbolism.

The second analysis strengthens our already noted cultural difference between the northern and the western regions. It is quite possible to discuss this phenomenon in terms of two political centres of two tribal formations, one in Uppland and the other located in Västergötland. The distribution of Early Bronze Age weapons and tools, as shown in Figure 14, further emphasises the prestige goods character of the exchange system, which may be interpreted as the result of either (1) an exchange line between the core area (Denmark/Scania) and a western periphery in which weapons were of great importance, and another connection between the core area and a northern periphery, in which flanged axes were most significant, or (2) a two-step procedure: from the core to the western peripheral centre and from this area to the northern centre. While rare and luxury weapons were consumed and used in the social competition in central Västergötland, the more ordinary flanged axes were passed on to Uppland.

The differences recorded for the areas discussed in this paper are the results of social, economic and political processes in society, where metalwork of certain types and forms, differently related to the productive and reproductive spheres (Larsson 1986: Figure 3), was actively used to express and symbolise phenomena like group affiliation, age, sex, wealth, and power. Different types of artefacts had different symbolic meaning. While a sword may have been related to the reproduction of the power structure, it is quite possible that a flanged axe and a palstave of a particular type were exponents of a larger group (e.g. tribe). Differences in form and decoration of axes were thus more related to ethnic expressions, while weapons indicated a social élite.

Note

This paper is a modified version of Chapters 6.2.1., and 6.2.2., of *The Bronze Age Metalwork in Southern Sweden: Aspects of Social and Spatial Organization 1800-500 B.C.* by the author (Larsson 1986).

A morphological study of biconical Late Bronze Age urns

By Carsten U. Larsen — Danish National Museum

In connection with my master's thesis at the Institute of Archaeology, University of Copenhagen (1984), I experimented with numerical methods for the division of pottery vessels into morphological types. The results of these experiments were included in the thesis as a basis for the archaeological treatment of biconical Late Bronze Age urns.

In the following, I shall briefly outline the analytical strategy applied to the problem and the nature and value of the results obtained.

PREREQUISITES TO THE MORPHOLOGICAL STUDY

Even though a vessel is a three-dimensional object, it is customary in archaeology to treat it in two dimensions only. The normal angle of view is from the side, with the vessel standing in an upright position. Although we sometimes use a view from the top or from the bottom, if special features of the vessel are better seen from these angles, when measurements are taken, we always view the vessel from the side.

Vertical measurements are taken parallel to the rotational axis of the vessel. Horizontal measurements are taken perpendicular to it. The rotational axis is not necessarily a true symmetry axis. Obliquity from the hands of the potter, faults from firing, and bad refitting in the hands of the conservator, make most vessels asymmetrical with respect to both vertical and horizontal measurements. In order to cope with this skewness, it is often necessary to use several different views from the side and average the measurements from these.

By vessel outline is meant the outer demarcation of the vessel to one side of the rotational axis as seen only from the side. Along the vessel outline a number of defining points are found, which can be categorised into four types. The bottom point is where the outline touches the horizontal plane on which the vessel stands. The rim point is equal to the upper termina-

tion of the outline. A vertical tangent point is a point where the outline changes direction from outward to inward (outer vertical tangent point) or vise versa (inner vertical tangent point). A tangent redirection point is a point where the tangent values change from rising to falling or from falling to rising. Any vessel can have only one bottom point and one rim point, but may have more than one vertical tangent point or tangent redirection point.

The defining points may be used to divide the vessel into a set of horizontal zones, always counted from the bottom up. Thus the pottery vessels from Denmark's Late Bronze Age can have the following zones: The bottom is the horizontal plane on which the vessel rests. The foot or concave lower body is the zone between the bottom and the first tangent redirection point (I), if such a point be present before a vertical tangent point (an inner vertical tangent point (F) may co-occur with the tangent redirection point). The body is the zone from the bottom or from F or I, if these be present, to the first outer vertical tangent point (B). The shoulder is the zone from B to the following tangent redirection point (S). The neck is the zone from B or S to the next inner vertical tangent point (H), or if this be lacking, to the terminal point of the outline (R). The rim is the zone from H (if present) to R.

From these definitions it follows that a vessel may have as many as five parts in all (foot/concave lower body, body, shoulder, neck and rim) not counting the bottom. A one-part vessel has only the body which is terminated by point R. A two-part vessel in the actual material always has the combination body and neck. A three-part vessel may have the combinations: 1) foot/concave lower body, body and neck, 2) body, shoulder, and neck, 3) body, neck and rim. The four-part vessel turns up with the combinations: 1) foot/concave lower body, body, shoulder and neck, 2) foot/concave lower body, body, neck and rim, 3) body, shoulder, neck and rim. A five-part vessel has all the combinations.

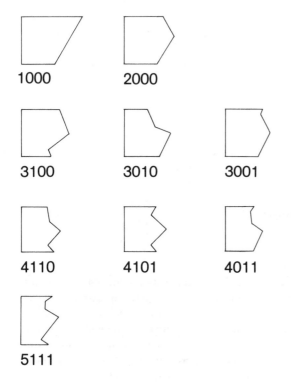

Figure 1. The basic formal division of the vessels studied.

A four-cipher code may be used to designate these various forms. The first cipher gives the number of vessel parts present (1–5), the second cipher gives the presence (1) or absence (0) of a foot or an concave lower body, the third cipher gives the presence/absence of a shoulder, and the fourth and final cipher gives the presence/absence of a rim. As all vessels with more than one part by definition have both body and neck, there is no reason for these parts to be presented by a cipher. The different forms and their codes are seen in Figure 1.

The data for the morphological study come from 21 museums and one private collection. A total of 1818 vessels were measured, and in addition other information concerning the vessels was noted: specifically their combinations with datable artifacts, and whether the vessels are mentioned by either Broholm (1946, 1949) or Baudou (1960), with the dating given in those publications.

ANALYTICAL METHODS

In the present study, a combination of K-means Clustering and Principal Component Analysis is used (for the latter see Madsen this volume). K-means Clustering or Non-hierarchical Clustering works as a divisive method, whereby larger clusters are split into minor clusters following predefined criteria. The aim of the method is to obtain a pre-specified number of clusters – K – in which the mean distance from the individual members of a cluster (the vessels) to the cluster centre reaches a minimum, based on certain distance criteria using the measured variables, at the same time as the distance between the centres of the individual clusters reaches a maximum. The solution is reached iteratively by continuously moving and exchanging members from cluster to cluster, and either accepting or rejecting the transfer according to whether the cluster criteria are improved or not. The clustering result obtained by this method is not absolute. It depends on the way in which an initial configuration of K trial clusters is reached, and on which strategy one chooses for exchanging members between the clusters – 're-assignment pass' or 'hill-climbing pass' (Doran & Hodson 1975:180 ff.).

Nearly all applied cluster analyses in archaeology aim to stipulate how many clusters it is reasonable to divide a material into, and which members should be allocated to which clusters as a base for archaeological conclusions.

The K-means Cluster method does not produce information to indicate the optimal number of clusters. It gives only the optimal clustering of a prespecified number of clusters. How then can one arrive at both the optimal number of clusters and the optimal clustering for that number?

The strategy chosen is to divide the material into a number of clusters – here 20 – that may safely be assumed to be larger than the optimal number. These clusters are then analysed as units in a PCA with the mean values of the measured (standardised) variables in each cluster as input variables.

Subsequently the factors relating to the first two principal axes in the PCA are plotted against one another to reveal the relative closeness of the clusters. This plot, as well as a useful dendrogram that can be constructed to show the movements of members in the successive splitting of the material into the (20) clusters, is then used to lump together again clusters into types representing an 'optimal' division of the material.

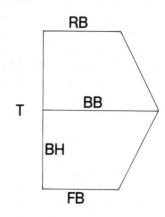

Figure 2. The measurements of form 2000 used in the analyses.

	T	T/BH	T/FB	T/BB	T/RB	BB/FB	BB/RB	1 Comp.	2 Comp.
T	1.000							0.817	-0.033
T/BH	0.355	1.000						0.555	0.082
T/FB	0.703	0.269	1.000					0.853	0.119
T/BB	0.582	0.244	0.660	1.000				0.710	-0.644
T/RB	0.642	0.459	0.696	0.710	1.000			0.930	-0.136
BB/FB	0.202	0.082	0.455	-0.341	0.025	1.000		0.231	0.918
BB/RB	0.439	0.462	0.448	0.184	0.814	0.321	1.000	0.735	0.342

Table 1. Correlation matrix between seven variables measured on 251 vessels (left), and the loadings for the first two components of a PCA of this matrix (right). The explanation percentages of the two components are 52.4% and 20.2% respectively.

Finally the members of the individual types are cross-correlated with attributes not included in the analyses as well as with associated find information to produce more 'visual' type definitions and to outline their regional and chronological background.

THE TYPE DIVISION OF VESSEL–FORM 2000

To exemplify the analytical method and the results obtained by its application, we will go through the analysis of vessel form 2000 in the following. Relevant measurements for this form are given in Figure 2.

Form 2000 consists of a total of 251 vessels. Initially a PCA was run with the 251 vessels described by 7 variables, being mostly indexes of the measurements shown in Figure 2 (e.g. T, T/BH, T/FB, T/BB, T/RB, BB/FB, BB/RB). In Table 1, the correlation matrix and the factor loadings for the two first components are given. In Figure 3 the loadings and in Figure 4 the scores of the two first components are plotted against one another. From this information it appears that variable T/RB (the index of total height to rim diameter) dominates the 1st component, and the variable BB/FB (the index of belly diameter to foot diameter) the 2nd component, where it is in opposition to variable T/BB (the index of total height to belly diameter). From Figure 3 it can be seen that it is the latter two variables that play the dominating role in the division of the vessels into types: whether a vessel is low and broad or high and narrow or whether it is wide or narrow at the bottom. It is immediately possible to see one type separated on this basis in Figure 4. The group of points in the upper left corner represents vessels that would normally be considered to be bowls.

Next, the 251 vessels were run through a K-means Cluster analysis with a K of 20, and with the same seven variables as in the first analysis. The mean value of each variable for each of the 20 clusters is given in Table 2. A dendrogram showing the successive separations of clusters as K is raised from 1 to 20, as well as the movements of vessels among clusters, is shown in Figure 5. It can be seen from this dendrogram that the actual exchanging of vessels among clusters takes place only for Ks less than

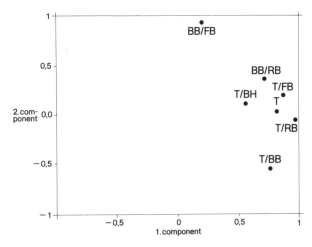

Figure 3. Factor loadings for seven variables on the two first components in a PCA of 251 vessels. For explanation of variables, see text.

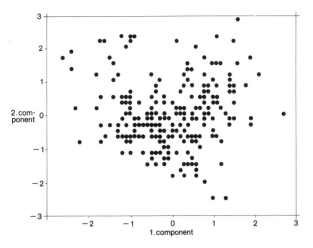

Figure 4. Factor scores for 251 vessels on the two first components in a PCA of seven variables.

four. For larger Ks the separation is purely hierarchical.

Finally the 20 clusters were analysed in a PCA with input data as given in Table 2. In Table 3 the factor loadings for the first three components are given, and in Figure 6 the loadings of the 1st component are seen plotted against the loadings of the 2nd and 3rd components respectively. More important, however, are the factor scores for the 20 clusters given in Table 4, and the plots of the scores from the 1st and 2nd

	T	T/BH	T/FB	T/BB	T7RB	BB/FB	BB/RB
1	30.8000	2.0390	2.9623	1.2301	2.9420	2.4353	2.4011
2	17.3000	2.3408	1.4500	0.6068	0.7376	2.4070	1.1944
3	28.1167	2.9592	1.9957	1.3495	1.9967	1.5152	1.4930
4	31.6333	1.7155	2.4985	1.6428	1.9022	1.5302	1.1585
5	19.0238	1.9251	1.7285	1.0093	1.2996	1.7224	1.2965
6	36.5500	1.7595	3.9930	1.8925	2.6625	2.1335	1.3780
7	30.3600	2.5291	2.4820	1.1225	1.8185	2.2224	1.6265
8	23.4480	1.8802	2.2195	1.2512	1.5656	1.7788	1.2530
9	24.6875	2.2924	2.0225	1.2026	2.2363	1.6860	1.8560
10	21.1944	1.4340	1.7488	0.9751	1.1204	1.7994	1.1531
11	21.3111	1.5651	1.7981	0.7363	0.8686	2.4802	1.1773
12	36.0833	2.0233	2.4865	1.2830	2.5273	1.9430	1.9700
13	24.2476	2.2135	1.8805	1.2752	1.7100	1.4844	1.3433
14	14.0542	1.5574	1.4247	0.9297	1.0279	1.5390	1.1068
15	23.3733	1.4709	2.1427	1.3304	1.4835	1.6206	1.1162
16	30.6308	2.0302	2.5936	1.2594	1.8218	2.0809	1.4437
17	12.0500	1.4912	1.2567	0.5614	0.6662	2.2427	1.1642
18	32.1000	2.0161	3.3283	1.3201	2.0448	2.5488	1.5472
19	30.2500	1.6653	2.1989	1.2183	1.4884	1.8087	1.2240
20	25.2500	1.9652	2.4012	1.1149	2.1359	2.1676	1.9151

Table 2. The mean values of the seven measurement variables according to the 20 clusters separated by a K-means Clustering.

Var	1. Comp.	2. Comp.	3. Comp.
T/BH	0.416	0.251	0.781
T/FB	0.873	-0.072	-0.427
T/BB	0.774	-0.606	-0.116
T/RB	0.981	-0.048	0.046
BB/FB	0.140	0.841	-0.473
BB/RB	0.744	0.480	0.215

Table 3. Factor loadings for the first three components of a PCA on the data in Table 2 (excluding T). The explanation percentages are 51.2%, 22.9% and 18.0% for the three components respectively.

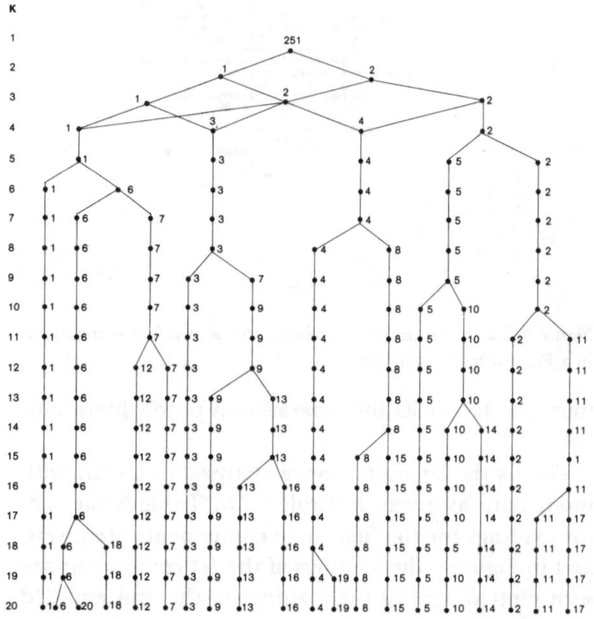

Figure 5. Dendrogram showing the successive separation of clusters as K moves from 1 to 20.

1	1.053	1.223	1.755
2	-1.865	0.553	0.881
3	-0.233	2.098	-1.611
4	0.995	-0.868	-1.339
5	-0.669	-0.018	-0.586
6	2.510	-1.071	0.265
7	-0.144	1.180	0.520
8	0.076	-0.355	-0.553
9	0.032	1.376	-0.555
10	-0.556	-1.137	-0.251
11	-1.057	-1.030	1.371
12	0.666	0.845	0.251
13	-0.171	0.568	-1.391
14	-0,897	-0.800	-0.942
15	0.298	-1.248	-0.880
16	0.344	0.005	0.242
17	-1.651	-0.924	0.898
18	0.947	-0.224	1.462
19	0.087	-0.787	-0.384
20	0.233	0.613	0.844

Table 4. Factor scores for the first three components of a PCA on the data in Table 2 (excluding T).

component against each other (Figure 7), the 1st and 3rd component against each other (Figure 8) and the 2nd and 3rd component against each other (Figure 9). These may be used directly to separate the final types. A closer inspection of the three plots would tend to suggest four types, one of which is the bowls. The other three we may refer to as types A, B and C.

The most marked break in the plot concerns clusters 2, 5, 10, 11, 14 and 17. They are clearly separated from the rest when the 1st component is plotted against the 2nd component (Figure 7). Further, clusters 2, 11 and 17 are clearly separated from clusters 5, 10 and 14 when the 1st component is plotted against the 3rd component (Figure 8). The former three clusters represent the bowls, the latter three I will term type C. Clusters 1, 3, 7, 9, 12, 13

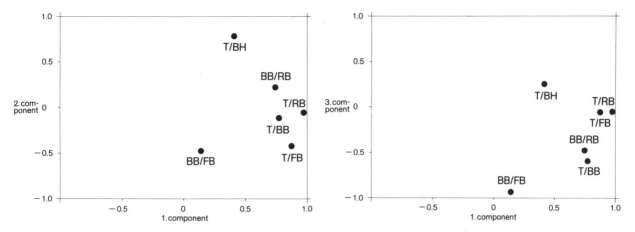

Figure 6. Factor loadings for six variables on the 1st component plotted against the loadings on the 2nd component (left) and the 3rd component (right) from a PCA of 20 clusters obtained through K-mean clustering. For explanation of variables, see text.

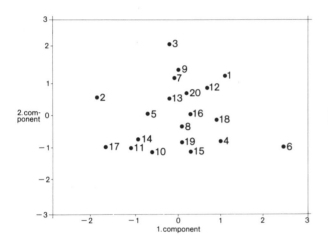

Figure 7. Factor scores for the two first components in a PCA of the data in Table 2 (excluding T). The numbers refer to the numbering of clusters.

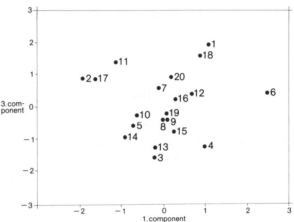

Figure 8. Factor score for the 1st and 3rd components in a PCA of the data in Table 2 (excluding T). The numbers refer to the numbering of clusters.

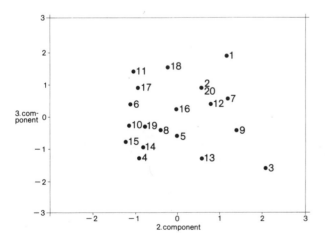

Figure 9. Factor scores for the 2nd and 3rd components in a PCA of the data in Table 2 (excluding T). The numbers refer to the numbering of clusters.

and 20 may also clearly be separated from the rest in the plot of the 1st against the 2nd component (Figure 7). This is further supported if we look at the 2nd component plotted against the 3rd component (Figure 9). These clusters together with cluster 16, which has an intermediate position, I will name type A. The remaining clusters (4, 6, 8, 15, 18, 19) I call type B. The bowls will not be considered further in this study.

We may now turn to a more formal description of the three types separated. Type A is characterized by vessels with a small bottom radius (FB), a relatively (compared to FB) wide belly (BB) and a low to medium belly height (BH). Type B has a rather large belly height (BH) and a rim radius (RB) that is not much smaller than the belly radius (BB) resulting in rather open vessels. Type C has a very large belly height (BH) and a rim radius (RB) only slightly smaller than the belly radius (BB). This gives very open vessels with a form not very different from the bowls.

	Type A	Type B	Type C
Period IV (III)	15	4	1
Period IV (V)	4	3	2
Period IV or V	2	1	2
Period V (IV)	1	2	1
Period V	1	4	3
Period VI	0	6	0

Table 5. Number of datable objects for each of the three vessel types, categorised according to approximate dating.

If we cross-correlate the three types with the datable objects found together with them (Table 5) we find that type A is clearly the oldest, and that it is gradually replaced by type B, whereas type C seems to have a more intermediate though generally late position.

It is beyond the scope of the present paper to describe the individual types and their context. However, one important aspect of the chronology should be emphasized. Apart from the surface moulding, type A has no elements in common with the Pre-roman Iron Age pottery. With type B this is often the case, and with type C there is a regular correspondence with the Iron Age pottery. From this viewpoint type C thus seems to be the latest type.

The purpose of the present study was to make a meaningful type division of two-part (biconical) Bronze age urns through a numerical analysis of basic measurements taken on the vessels. The method chosen was a combination of a K-means Cluster Analysis and Principal Component Analysis to lump together those vessels sufficiently alike to be considered beyond doubt to stem from the same type. The number of clusters had to be chosen sufficiently large (here 20) to ensure that any cluster would never contain vessels from more than one 'natural type'. The next step was to aggregate the clusters into types according to their inter-distances. For this purpose a Principal Component Analysis was chosen. The result was four types, of which one consisted of bowls. The three other types of truely biconical vessels named A, B and C could finally be shown to be chronologically significant, and thus clearly useful.

Some attempts to relate ancient land use to soil properties by means of statistics

By Henry Freij — University of Stockholm

It is obviously of great interest to determine how the land was utilised during the past. A possible method is to analyse certain chemical-physical properties of the soils and draw conclusions from the results. Thus phosphate content, colour and consistency of soil have been used for many years to indicate settlements, but often with low precision.

A method based on a combination of a number of significant soil properties would give better results. Even if the individual measured variables have a low significance, it is possible that the combined information is acceptable. In order to construct such a method, a sequence of measured soil properties has to be linked to known land use in the past.

The main problem is that true knowledge of how the land was used, independently of the chemical-physical soil properties, is very rare. Archaeologists try to draw conclusions from artefacts in the strata. Thus Janzon (1974, and personal communication) has categorised the strata at the Pitted Ware cemetery at Ire on Gotland as surface soil, culture soil and sand. By help of combinations of measured soil properties, it was possible to connect isolated soil samples from the same area to these categories. It was also possible to define a fourth category probably stemming from a settlement.

Within human geography, the interpretation of land use is based on fence systems in connection with settlements, field patterns visible as field ridges, plough-marks and general theories concerning the development of infields over the years. Windelhed (1976, and personal communication) has conducted extensive research on the cultural landscape at Vinarve on Gotland, and has categorised the strata as follows: settlement soil, extensively used soil (slash-and-burn), intensively used soil and intensively used mature soil. Samples were collected from these strata as well as from enriched soil and the sterile sand below. A total of 51 soil samples were analysed for the following parameters: phosphate content according to the citric-acid method, darkness of the soil measured with a photoelectric meter, weight per volume unit to decide organic content, and magnetic susceptibility in order to determine firing activity. Most soils contain non-magnetic iron oxides. When heated together with organic material, these oxides are partly reduced to oxides with higher magnetic susceptibility (Aitken 1959:32).

The complete data matrix is shown in the left part of Table 1. Observe that the classification by the human geographer has the headline 'assumed category', and that some classifications are uncertain or alternative. A definite class determination is counted as two observations and an uncertain or alternative determination as one observation, when mean values and standard deviations are calculated. The mean values and standard deviations are shown in Figure 1, where the heavy lines include plus/minus one standard deviation. It can be seen that if only one variable is taken into consideration, it is difficult to determine which category a sample belongs to. By combining two or more variables, the reliability increases. For instance, it is possible to pick out extensively used soil samples using high weight in combination with dark appearance. Thus, in order to classify the soil samples properly, we have to combine two or more measured variables. A method for this purpose is outlined in the following.

To explain the basic idea, let us start with soil samples with only two measured properties. These can be presented in a two-dimensional coordinate system with the original measurement units used for the division of the axes (ie. g/cm^3 and darkness). A number of samples, assumed to be of, say, the category extensively used soil, can be presented as in Figure 2. The scale for each axis is optional and dependent only on the paper size. The data in Figure 2 show two properties without common variation, and indeed in order for the method to work, a generally low co-variation among the variables is required.

However, to make a more appropriate comparison between variables, it is desirable that they be measured on comparable scales. If the measured variables are approximately normally distributed, a nor-

No.	Assumed category	PHOS	MAGN	DARK	WEIG	SAND	ENRI	EXUS	INUS	INUM	SETT	SAND	ENRI	EXUS	INUS	INUM	SETT
1	INUM	21	7.0	88	0.99	0	0	0	0	30	48	6	-1	-21	11	70	19
2	INUS	45	6.4	75	1.30	5	0	87	12	2	6	-4	6	54	15	14	-3
3	ENRI ?	67	5.1	62	1.43	57	18	28	0	0	0	11	21	60	-5	-2	-1
4	INUM	18	5.2	72	1.16	1	0	1	0	27	4	-14	14	30	9	52	1
5	ENRI ?	42	3.9	48	1.40	95	72	7	0	0	0	41	22	27	2	-4	1
6	INUM	39	9.6	78	1.17	1	0	1	63	10	26	-5	9	26	23	26	15
7	EXUS	42	4.1	68	1.33	19	0	89	1	0	1	-4	13	60	8	16	-8
8	SAND/ENRI ?	64	4.3	40	1.44	95	39	1	0	0	0	82	19	-1	0	-1	-5
9	INUM	36	5.6	89	1.10	0	0	0	11	57	60	11	-12	16	29	49	-11
10	EXUS	42	3.8	68	1.33	19	0	87	1	0	1	-5	13	61	8	17	-9
11	SAND/ENRI ?	67	4.9	45	1.43	98	87	4	0	0	0	62	21	14	1	0	-5
12	SETT	70	7.4	72	1.04	0	0	0	0	0	82	1	-6	14	-12	-1	82
13	SAND	127	2.9	42	1.38	12	1	1	0	0	0	74	10	-9	1	-7	18
14	SETT	82	24.2	93	0.98	0	0	0	0	0	85	1	10	-19	18	-4	95
15	EXUS	100	3.1	77	1.27	2	0	21	0	0	10	-9	5	97	12	-2	4
16	ENRI ?	115	3.7	47	1.42	31	12	2	0	0	0	51	24	21	-1	2	-3
17	EXUS	64	3.7	68	1.33	21	0	94	0	0	1	-5	14	72	7	9	-5
18	EXUS	76	3.0	65	1.35	31	0	76	0	0	0	-3	18	76	3	5	-3
19	SAND	91	4.8	47	1.43	78	69	3	0	0	0	55	24	20	0	2	-8
20	EXUS/INUM ?	21	5.3	77	1.16	0	0	1	0	59	12	-11	9	29	17	51	-7
21	ENRI	21	5.0	50	1.37	63	39	8	0	0	0	33	22	25	4	11	3
22	SAND	30	3.7	35	1.41	66	6	1	0	0	0	93	16	-6	-3	4	3
23	INUM ?	28	6.2	73	1.10	0	0	0	0	84	6	-13	12	23	2	46	23
24	ENRI/EXUS ?	55	6.0	48	1.39	99	32	10	0	0	0	50	19	19	4	3	-2
25	SAND	45	5.3	37	1.39	92	20	2	0	0	0	92	13	-7	-2	4	-1
26	INUM ?	36	6.2	89	1.00	0	0	0	8	30	54	14	-10	-11	16	51	23
27	INUS ?	52	9.7	88	1.06	0	0	0	34	2	78	8	-5	7	27	25	31
28	EXUS	97	6.6	89	1.36	0	0	26	0	0	27	-6	-4	13	-11	1	-3
29	INUS	39	9.7	87	1.07	0	0	0	70	11	72	4	0	3	26	37	23
30	SAND/INUS ?	42	10.3	85	1.10	0	0	0	96	5	69	1	2	11	27	30	23
31	SAND ?	64	39.4	68	1.20	0	0	0	0	0	3	59	-4	0	12	7	0
32	SETT	127	20.9	92	1.02	0	0	0	0	0	96	1	-2	8	23	-20	80
33	SETT	345	20.1	90	1.06	0	0	0	0	0	13	8	1	-2	3	0	97
34	EXUS	79	10.5	82	1.40	3	0	30	0	0	12	0	1	68	-5	-11	24
35	SAND/EXUS ?	100	10.8	55	1.32	33	0	10	0	0	0	42	14	20	7	8	-9
36	INUS/SETT ?	48	12.9	90	1.11	0	0	0	29	0	86	8	-2	3	38	20	31
37	EXUS ?	42	9.0	82	1.34	3	0	66	36	0	17	5	-7	41	14	0	15
38	SAND	45	6.7	47	1.45	95	3	3	0	0	0	64	19	9	3	-6	0
39	SETT ?	227	30.9	98	0.96	0	0	0	0	0	28	-3	-3	5	-1	3	63
40	EXUS ?	52	10.8	78	1.39	5	0	47	4	0	6	8	-2	39	7	-15	31
41	SAND	45	7.0	48	1.47	90	1	2	0	0	0	64	19	8	2	-11	2
42	SETT	30	8.7	88	1.00	0	0	0	3	22	58	6	-1	-17	14	53	31
43	EXUS	27	4.4	65	1.35	23	3	61	0	0	0	1	14	48	8	16	-5
44	SAND	36	4.3	37	1.41	83	26	1	0	0	0	88	17	-4	-1	3	1
45	SETT ?	36	7.3	83	1.33	2	0	65	9	2	19	5	-10	44	13	9	2
46	EXUS	24	4.8	67	1.39	18	4	45	0	0	0	4	9	46	3	7	0
47	SAND	39	4.2	37	1.44	81	15	1	0	0	0	92	18	-7	0	-1	-1
48	SETT	139	32.4	92	1.42	0	0	0	0	0	18	0	2	3	2	8	92
49	SETT	82	54.9	90	1.07	0	0	0	0	0	19	-4	1	1	18	-4	101
50	EXUS/SETT ?	97	18.0	92	1.28	0	0	0	0	0	69	3	-1	40	29	-11	48
51	SAND	48	5.4	42	1.53	58	0	0	0	0	0	90	21	-7	-6	-16	2

PHOS : Phosphate
MAGN : Magnetic susceptibility
DARK : Darkness
WEIG : Weight

SAND : Sand
ENRI : Enriched soil
EXUS : Extensively used soil
INUS : Intensively used soil
INUM : Intensively used matured soil
SETT : Settlement soil

Table 1. Information on the soil samples. The left part of the table shows sample numbers and classifications according to the human geographer, followed by the measured soil properties. The centre part of the table shows the calculated category scores according to the method suggested here. The right part of the table shows the category scores according to the multiple regression analysis of Siven.

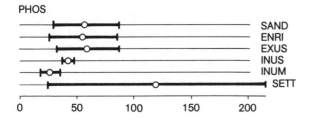

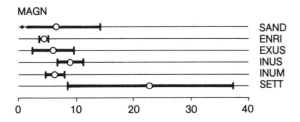

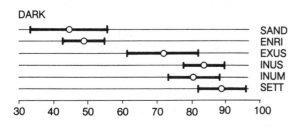

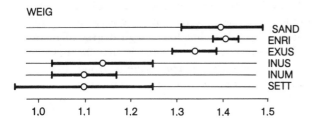

Figure 1. Mean values and standard deviations of measured properties according to assumed soil categories. Labels refer to Table 1.

malisation of the data may be carried out (each measurement of a variable being divided by the standard deviation after subtraction of the mean). It may of course be doubted whether measurements of phosphate and magnetic susceptibility follow a normal distribution, but in the test material used here, a plotting of the variables on cumulative probability paper seems to justify the assumption that they are approximately normally distributed.

As all samples in Figure 2 - according to the human geographer - belong to the same class or category, we can now define this category in terms of the measurements of two variables. We choose to do this geometrically by drawing a circle with a radius of one standard deviation and a centre in the mutual mean of the variables (Figure 3). We may term this a category cluster. It is also possible to express how far the individual samples are situated from the category centre in terms of the unit standard deviation. This may be calculated simply using the theorem of Pythagoras (Figure 4).

Up till now, only two variables have been considered. If more variables are included, it is necessary only to add more dimensions to the two-dimensional expression, and expand the theorem of Pythagoras. A soil category will then be presented as a cluster in a multidimensional space (Abler et al. 1972:166). For the four properties in the Vinarve analysis, we would simply have to add two further variable terms to the two under the square root sign in Figure 4.

A four-dimensional space is hard to visualise, but if one of the variables is removed, a fully understandable three-dimensional space remains. We can view a three-dimensional space in terms of three two by

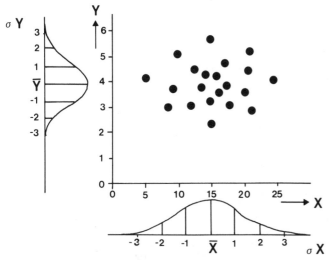

Figure 2. A two-dimensional scattergram for a single soil category, with each of the two measured properties approximately normally distributed and with a low co-variation.

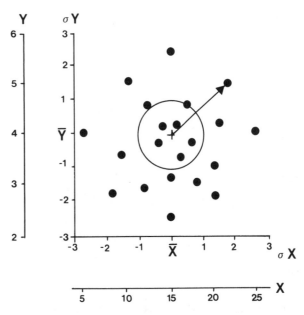

Figure 3. Normalised representation of Figure 2. The category is defined by a circle with a radius of one standard deviation and a centre in the common mean of the variables.

141

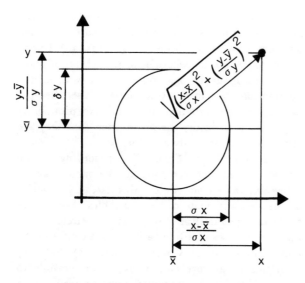

Figure 4. The Theorem of Pythagoras used to calculate the distance from a specific soil sample to a category centre.

two plots of the variables. In a four-dimensional space we have to use six such projections to give an equivalent knowledge of the content. Figure 5 shows, as an example, two of the six possible projections of the four-dimensional space.

When operating within a four-dimensional space, it is complicated to calculate how many per-cent of a category are more distant from the category centre than a specific sample. To simplify the calculation, a computer simulation with a large number (160) of pretended samples was made. Four 'property values'

from a table of normally distributed random numbers were allocated to each 'sample', and the distance to the cluster centre was calculated using Pythagoras. The result presented in rank order is shown in Figure 6, and this was used to determine the category of a real sample.

On evaluation of the result, one has to remember that the categories are defined by mean values and standard deviations. A consequence is that a sample with an extremely high phosphate content shows less affinity to the settlement category than does a sample with lower phosphate content, but greater similarity to the category average. However, the extreme phosphate content will also make the sample distant from all other categories, and thus prevent it from joining any of these. As the tails of the normal distribution asymptotically approach zero, a consequence is that every category is more or less a part of all other categories. In principle, a category can be entirely covered by another category. This corresponds with the real situation, since, for instance, most of the iron-enriched soil can be classified as a sub-group within sterile sand.

The final result, expressed in percentage membership of the six categories, is shown in the centre part of Table 1. If the membership score indicates that a sample is peripheral to the category suggested by the human geographer, but has a high degree of membership with another category, it may be possible that his hypothetical interpretation is wrong. In most cases a check on the find circumstances did reveal that the sample was taken close to strata boundaries.

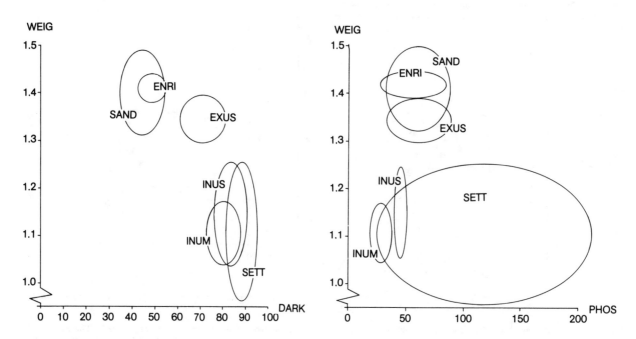

Figure 5. Category clusters represented in two two-dimensional projections showing weight, darkness and phosphate content. Labels refer to Table 1.

Distance from category centre

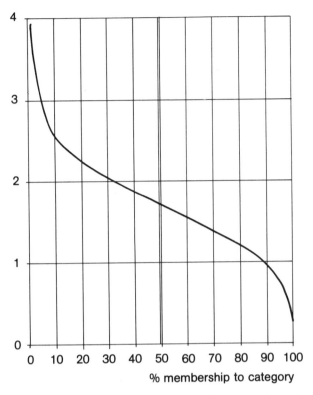

Figure 6. Diagram to determine category membership of a sample.

Having by this method defined the soil categories of a site in terms of objective measurement data, it is now possible to treat isolated samples from the same general locality and classify them according to soil category by means of the same basic measurements. However, the described method can usually be used locally only. Differences in the allover pattern of mineral content in the soil from area to area normally override the differences between soil categories. A target for further research is thus to find a more general method, based on a relative difference between the utilised topsoil categories and the underlying mineral soil.

From the beginning, the samples were defined as belonging to certain categories, and the measurement data on the samples were then used to define the characteristics and consistencies of these categories.

However, it may indeed be questioned whether the measured properties themselves indicate the existence of groups, and if groups do exist, how well they fit the classification of the human geographer. To answer this question, an average linkage cluster analysis was applied to the sample data (Abler et al. 1972:158).

Due to the limited computer memory available, I was compelled to use the rank number of each measured value as a substitute for the real value. Objections can be raised against the use of ordinal scales in cluster analysis, and this of course has to be kept in mind when the results are evaluated. Yet

the resulting clusters do show a reasonable agreement with the classification of the human geographer (Figure 7).

Siven (personal communication) has applied a third method, multiple regression analysis, to the same sample data. He used the computer programme Yale TSP, accessible in the QZ data centre in Stockholm (Peck 1977). As the dependent variable, he used the classification of the human geographer in the way that he rated the samples 1 for membership of a category, 0 for non-membership, and 0.5 for uncertain membership. As the independent variables, he used the measured soil properties. For each category, the computer used the least square method to find the second degree polynomial giving the best fit between the dependent and independent variables. These equations are subsequently used to calculate the probabilities for the membership of a given sample of a specific category. The result of this analysis is given in the right part of Table 1. The

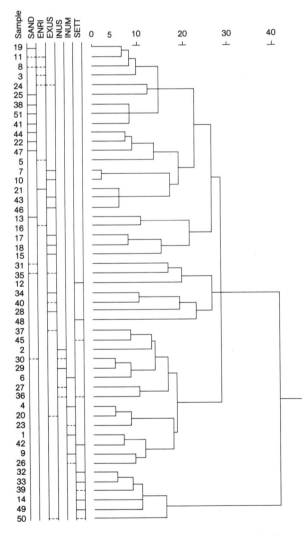

Figure 7. Result of average linkage cluster analysis compared with the assumed category membership.

143

actual figures have a different meaning than those reached by the method presented in this paper, but the overall agreement is nevertheless astonishing.

The method suggested in this paper has here been applied to soil analysis, but can probably be used for artefact typologies as well. The method gives a multidimensional view to the classification problem, where each class may also be part of all other classes, dependent on the specific dimension in focus.

References

Abler, Ronald, John S. Adams and Peter Gould

1972 *Spatial Organization. The Geographer's View of the World.* Prentice/Hall International Inc: London.

Aitken, M.J.

1959 Magnetic prospecting II. *Archaeometry* Vol 2:32-36

Albrectsen, Erling

1968 *Fynske Jernaldergrave III. Yngre Romersk Jernalder.* Odense.

Andersen, Niels H.

1981 Sarup. Befæstede neolitiske anlæg og deres baggrund. *KUML Årbog for Jysk Arkæologisk Selskab* 1980:63-103.

Andersen, Niels H. og Torsten Madsen.

1978 Skåle og bægre med storvinkelbånd fra yngre stenalder. Overgangen mellem tidlig- og mellemneolitikum. *KUML Årbog for Jysk Arkæologisk Selskab* 1977:131-160.

Andreassen, Reidun Laura

1985 *Yngre steinalder på Sørøy: økonomi og samfunn 4000 - 1000 f. Kr.* Unpublished Magistergrad thesis in archaeology, University of Tromsø.

Aner, Ekkehard

1956 Grab und Hort. Ein Beitrag zur Deutung der altbronzezeitlichen Hortsitte. *Offa* 15:31-42.

Barth, Friedrich

1969 *Ethnic groups and boundaries. The social organization of culture difference.* Universitetsforlaget: Oslo.

Baudou, Evert

1953 De svenska holkyxorna under bronsåldern. *Fornvännen. Tidsskrift för Svensk Antikvarisk Forskning* 48:241-261.

1956 Regionala grupper i Norden under yngre bronsåldern. *Fornvännen. Tidsskrift för Svensk Antikvarisk Forskning* 51:19-36.

1960 *Die regionale und chronologische Einteilung der jüngeren Bronzezeit im Nordischen Kreis.* Almqvist & Wiksell: Stockholm.

Becker, C.J.

1954 Die Mittel-Neolitischen Kulturen in Südskandinavien. *Acta Archaeologica* Vol. XXV:49-150.

1955 Stenalderbebyggelsen ved Store Valby i Vestsjælland. Problemer omkring Tragtbægerkulturens ældste og yngste fase. *Aarbøger for Nordisk Oldkyndighed og Historie* 1954:127-197.

1960 Stendyngegrave fra Mellem-Neolitisk tid. *Årbøger for Nordisk Oldkyndighed og Historie* 1959:1-90.

1963 Kompliceret jordfæstelse. *Skalk* 1963 Nr 3:3-7.

1966 The interrelationship of the TRB and Battle axe cultures in Denmark. *Palaeohistoria* XII:33-41.

1967 Gådefulde jyske stenaldergrave. *Nationalmuseets Arbejdsmark* 1967:19-30.

1969 Grav eller tempel? En kultbygning fra yngre stenalder ved Herrup, Vestjylland. *Nationalmuseets Arbejdsmark* 1969:17-28.

1973 »Problems of the Megalithic 'Mortuary Houses' in Denmark« in *Megalithic Graves and Ritual. Papers presented at the III Atlantic Colloquium, Moesgård 1969.* Edited by Glyn Daniel and Poul Kjærum, pp. 75-79. Jutland Archaeological Society, Publications XI.

Berg, H.

1951 *Klintebakken. En boplads fra yngre stenalder på Langeland.* Meddelelser fra Langelands Museum, Rudkbing.

Bertelsen, Reidar

1979 Farm Mounds in North Norway. A Review of Recent Research. *Norwegian Archaeological Review.* 12 No 1:48-56.

1984 Farm Mounds of the Harstad Area. Quantitative Investigations of Accumulation Characteristics. *Acta Borealia.* Vol. 1:7-25.

1985 Artifact Pattern and Stratificational Units. *American Archaeology* Vol 5. No 1:16-20.

Bertelsen, Reidar & P. Urbanczyk

1985a *The Soløy farm mound. Excavations and methods of stratigraphical analysis.* Tromura Hum. series no 4. University of Tromsø.

1985b Polsko-Norweskie wykopaliska w Soløy. Prosba analizy stratygraficznej. *Sprawozdania Archeologiczne* T. XXXVII:217-250.

Bibby, T.G.

1969 *Looking for Dilmun.* Alfred A. Knopf: New York.

Binford, Lewis R.

1972a »Contemporary model building: paradigms and the current state of Palaeolithic research« in *Models in Archaeology.* Edited by David L. Clarke, pp. 109-166. Methuen & Co Ltd: London.

1972b *An Archaeological Perspective.* Seminar Press: New York.

1983 *In Pursuit of the Past. Decoding the Archaeological Record.* Thames and Hudson: London.

Bloch, Maurice

1983 *Marxism and Anthropology.* Clarendon Press: Oxford.

Broholm, Hans Christian

1944 *Danmarks Bronzealder II.* Nyt Nordisk Forlag: København.

1946 *Danmarks Bronzealder III.* Nyt Nordisk Forlag: København.

1949 *Danmarks Bronzealder IV*. Nyt Nordisk Forlag: København.

Brøgger, A.W.

1931 *Nord-Norges bosetningshistorie*. Instituttet for sammenlignende Kulturforskning, serie CII-4.

Bølviken, Erik

n.d. *Reduction of multiway tables via bivariate association: Multicanonical analysis as scaling method*. Unpublished manuscript from 1983.

Bølviken, Erik, Ericka Helskog, Knut Helskog, Inger Marie Holm-Olsen, Leiv Solheim and Reidar Bertelsen

1982 Correspondence analysis: an alternative to principal components. *World Archaeology* Volume 14 No. 1:41-60.

Bølviken, Erik and Tore Schweder

1983 *An introduction to correspondence analysis and other exploratory statistical methods, set in an archaeological context*. University of Tromsø, Institute of Mathematical and Physical Sciences. Statistics Reports.

Chapman, R.

1981 »The emergence of formal disposal areas and the 'problem' of megalithic tombs in prehistoric Europe« in *The archaeology of death*. Edited by Robert Chapman, Ian Kinnes and Klavs Randsborg, pp. 71-82. Cambridge University Press: Cambridge.

Childe, V. Gordon

1956 *Piecing Together the Past. The Interpretation of Archæological Data*. Routledge & Keagan: London.

Conkey, M.W.

1978 »Style and Information in Cultural Evolution: Towards a Predictive Model for the Palaeolithic« in *Social Archaeology. Beyond Subsistence and Dating*. Edited by Charles L. Redman et. al., pp. 61-85. Studies in Archaeology. Academic Press: New York.

1980 »Context, structure and efficacy in Palaeolithic art and design« in *Symbol as sense*. Edited by M.L. Foster and S.H. Brandes, pp. 225-248. Academic Press: New York.

1982 »Boundedness in art and society« in *Symbolic and structural archaeology*. Edited by Ian Hodder, pp. 115-128. New directions in Archaeology. Cambridge University Press: Cambridge.

Cullberg, Carl

1968 *On artifact analysis. A study in the systematics and classification of a Scandinavian early Bronze Age material with metal analysis and chronology as contributing factors*. Acta Archaeologica Lundensia. Series in 4^0. No.7. Rudolf Habelt Verlag: Bonn. CWK Gleerups Förlag: Lund.

Davidsen, Karsten

1978 *The final TRB culture in Denmark. A settlement study*. Arkæologiske Studier V. Akademisk Forlag: København.

David, Nicholas and Hennig, Hilke

1972 *The etnography of Pottery: A Fulani Case seen in Archaeological Perspective*. Module 21. Addison-Wesley Modular Publications.

Doran, J.E. and F.R. Hodson

1975 *Mathematics and Computers in Archaeology*. Edinburgh University Press: Edinburgh.

Ebbesen, Klaus

1975 *Die jüngere Trichterbecherkultur auf den dänischen Inseln*. Arkæologiske Studier II. Akademisk Forlag: København.

1978 *Tragtbægerkultur i Nordjylland. Studier over jættestuetiden*. Nordiske Fortidsminder, Serie B - in quarto, bind 5. Det kongelige nordiske Oldskriftselskab, København.

1979 *Stordyssen i Vedsted. Studier over tragtbægerkulturen i Sønderjylland*. Arkæologiske Studier VI. Akademisk Forlag: København.

Ebbesen, Klaus og Ditlev Mahler.

1980 Virum. Et tidligneolitisk bopladsfund. *Aarbøger for Nordisk Oldkyndighed og Historie* 1979:11-61.

Eggert, Manfred K. H.

1982 »Comment I: On Form and Content« in *Theory and Explanation in Archaeology. The Southampton Conference*. Edited by Colin Renfrew, Michael J. Rowlands and Barbara Abbot Segraves, pp. 139-150. Academic Press: New York, London.

Engelstad, Ericka

1984 Diversity in Arctic maritime adaptions: An example from the Late Stone Age of Arctic Norway. *Acta Borealia* 1(2):3-24.

1985 The Late Stone Age of Arctic Norway: A Review. *Arctic Anthropology* 22(1):79-96.

Eriksen, Palle

1984 Det neolitiske bopladskompleks ved Fannerup. *KUML Årbog for Jysk Arkæologisk Selskab* 1984:9-76.

Faber, Ole

1977 Endnu et kulthus. Et stenaldertempel ved Engedal i Midtjylland. *Antikvariske studier* 1:35-46.

Fischer, Christian

1976 Tidlig-neolitiske anlæg ved Rustrup. *KUML Årbog for Jysk Arkæologisk Selskab* 1975:29-72.

Flannery, Kent V.

1982 The Golden Marshalltown: A Parable for the Archaeology of the 1980's. *American Anthropologist* 84:265-278.

Forsberg, Lars

1984 »A multivariate analysis of hunting and fishing sites on the river Umälv, Northern Sweden« in *Papers in Northern Archaeology*. Edited by Evert Baudou, pp. 31-44. Archaeology and Environment 2. University of Umeå.

1985 *Site Variability and Settlement Patterns*. Archaeology and Enviroment 5. University of Umeå.

Forssander, J.

1936 Skånsk megalitkeramik och kontinentaleuropeisk stenålder. *Meddelanden från Lunds Universetets Historiska Museum* 1936:1-77.

Foster, Georg M.

1959 Life-expectancy of utilitarian pottery in Tzintzuntzan, Michoacan, Mexico. *American Antiquity* vol 25, 4:606-609.

Franzén, Gösta

1982 *Ortnamn i Östergötland*. Stockholm.

Friedman, Jonathan and Michael Rowlands

1977 »Notes towards an epigenetic model of the evolution of 'civilization' « in *The Evolution of Social Systems*. Edited by Jonathan Friedman and Michael Rowlands, pp. 201-276. Duckworth: London.

Fritz, John M. and Fred T. Plog

1970 The Nature of Archaeological Explanation. *American Antiquity* Vol. 35, No.4:405-412.

Gebauer, Anne Birgitte

1977 Review of Klaus Ebbesen 1975, Die jüngere Trichterbecherkultur auf den dänischen Inseln. *Kontaktstencil* 13:73-84.

1979 Mellemneolitisk tragtbægerkultur i Sydvestjylland. En analyse af keramikken. *KUML Årbog for Jysk Arkæologisk Selskab* 1978:117-159.

1984 The meaning of material culture. *Kontaktstencil* 26-27:53-89.

Gjessing, Gutorm

1942 *Yngre steinalder i Nord-Norge*. Institutt for Sammenlignende Kulturforskning Serie B, Skrifter XXXIX.

Goldmann, Klaus

1972 Zwei Methoden chronologischer Gruppierung. *Acta Praehistorica et Archaeologica* 3:1-34.

Gower, J. C.

1971 A general coefficient of similarity and some of its properties. *Biometrics* 27:857-874.

Greenacre, Michael J.

1984 *Theory and Applications of Correspondence Analysis*. Academic Press: New York.

Gregory, C.A.

1982 *Gifts and Commodities. Studies in Political Economy*. Academic Press: London.

Gräslund, Bo

1974 Relativ datering. Om kronologisk metod i nordisk arkeologi. *TOR. Tidsskrift för nordisk fornkunskap* Vol. XVI:9-248.

Hansen, Ulla Lund

1976 Das Gräberfeld bei Harpelev, Seeland. Studien Zur Jüngeren Römischen Kaiserzeit in der Seeländischen Inselgruppe. *Acta Archaeologica* vol. 47:91-160.

Harris, E.C.

1975a The Stratigraphic Sequence: a Question of Time. *World Archaeology* Volume 7:109-121

1975b Stratigraphic Analyses and the Computer. *Computer Applications in Archaeology* 1975:109-121.

1977 Units of Archaeological Stratification. *Norwegian Archaeological Review* Vol 10:84-94.

1979 *Principles of Archaeological Stratigraphy*. London.

Hawkes, Jaquetta

1968 The Proper Study of Mankind. *Antiquity* XLII:255-262.

Helskog, Ericka

1983 *The Iversfjord locality: A study of behavioral patterning during the Late Stone Age of Finmark, North Norway*. Tromsø Museums Skrifter XIX.

Helskog, Knut

1974 Two tests of the prehistoric cultural chronology of Varanger, North Norway. *Norwegian Archaeological Review* 7(2):98-103.

1978a Late Holocene sea-level changes seen from prehistoric settlements. *Norsk geografisk Tidsskrift* 32:111-119.

1978b Varangers forhistorie i lys av 14C dateringer. *Paper read at the Symposium in honour of the 25th anniversary of the Radiocarbon Laboratory in Trondheim, May 8-10, 1978*.

1980 The chronology of the younger Stone Age in Varanger, North Norway. Revisited. *Norweigian Archaeological Review* 13(1):47-60.

1984 Younger Stone Age settlements in Varanger, North Norway. *Acta Borelia* 1(1):39-70.

Helskog, Knut and Tore Schweder

n.d. The number of contemporaneous houses seen from radiocarbon dates. *American Antiquity* in press.

Hill, M.O.

1974 Correspondence Analysis: A Neglected Multivariate Method. *Applied Statistics* 23, No 3:340-354.

Hodder, Ian

1974 Regression analysis of some trade and marketing patterns. *World Archaeology* No.6:172-189.

1979 Social and economic stress and material culture patterning. *American Antiquity* 44(3):446-454.

1982a *The present past*.

1982b »Sequences and structural change in the Dutch Neolithic« in *Symbolic and structural archaeology*. Edited by Ian Hodder, pp. 162-177. New directions in Archaeology. Cambridge University Press: Cambridge.

1982c *Symbols in Action. Ethnoarchaeological studies of material culture*. New Studies in Archaeology. Cambridge University Press: Cambridge.

1984 »Burials, houses, women and men in the European neolithic« in *Ideology, Power and Prehistory*. Edited by D. Miller and C. Tilley. New directions in Archaeology. Cambridge University Press: Cambridge,

Holm-Olsen, Inger Marie

1979 »Gårdshaugsstratigrafi. En diskusjon med utgangspunkt i Helgøyprosjektets undersøkelser« in *På leiting etter den eldste garden*. Edited by Fladby and Sandnes. Universitetsforlaget: Oslo.

1981 Economy and Settlement Pattern 1350-1600 AD., based on Evidence from Farm Mounds. *Norwegian Archaeological Review* Vol 14,2:86-101.

1983 Gårdshaugene og gårdene. *Foreningen til Norske Fortidsminnesmerkers Bevaring, Årbok 1983*:37-45

1985 Farm Mounds and Land Registers in Helgøy, North Norway: An Investigation of Trends in Site Location by Correspondence Analysis. *American Archaeology*. Vol 5. No 1:27-34.

Hyenstrand, Åke

1979a *Arkeologisk regionindelning av Sverige*. Riksantikvarieämbetet, Stockholm.

1979b *Ancient Monuments and Prehistoric Society*. Riksantikvarieämbetet, Stockholm.

Højlund, Flemming

1979 Symboler i materiel kultur. *hikuin* 5:5-6

1983   The 2nd mill. settlements on Failaka, Kuwait. Unpublished paper given at the *Rencontre Assyriologique Internationale* in Leiden 1983, and at the *Seminar for Arabian Studies* in London 1983.

1986   »The chronology of City II and III at Qal'at al- Bahrain« in *Bahrain through the Ages: the Archaeology*. Edited by S.H.A. al Khalifa & M. Rice. Paul Keagan International Ltd: London.

1987   *The Bronze Age Pottery. Failaka/Dilmun. The Second Millennium Settlements. Danish Archaeological Investigations on Failaka, Kuwait* Vol. 2. Jutland Archaeological Society Publications XVII:2.

n.d.   Some new evidence of Harappan influence in the Arabian Gulf. *South Asian Archaeology 1985. Proceedings of the 8th International Conference of the Association of South Asian Archaeologists in Western Europe*.

Iversen, Mette og Ulf Näsman

1977   Smykkefund fra Eketorp-II. *KUML Årbog for Jysk Arkæologisk Selskab* 1977: 85-104.

Janzon, Gunborg O.

1974   *Gotlands mellanneolitiska gravar*. Acta Universitatis Stockholmiensis. Studies in North-European Archaeology 6. Almqvist og Wiksell: Stockholm.

Jensen, Jørgen

1982   *The Prehistory of Denmark*. Methuen: London.

Johansen, Else and Knut Odner

1968   Arkeologiske undersøkelser på Mortensnes ved Varangerfjorden. *Viking* XXXII:57-85.

Jöreskog, K.G., J.E. Klova and R.A.Reyment.

1976   *Geological Factor Analysis*. Elsevir Scientific Publishing Company: Amsterdam.

Jørgensen, Erik

1973   Magtpolitik i yngre stenalder. *Skalk* 1973(4):3-10.

1977a   *Hagebrogård - Vroue - Koldkur. Neolithische Gräberfelder aus Nordwest Jütland*. Arkæologiske Studier IV. Akademisk Forlag: København.

1977b   Brændende langdysser. *Skalk* 1977(5):7-13.

1985   Brydningstid. *Skalk* 1985(2):3-8.

Jørgensen, R.

1984   *Bleik. En økonomisk/økologisk studie av grunnlaget for jernaldergården på Andøya i Nordland*. Thesis, University of Tromsø.

Kendall, David G.

1970   A mathematical approach to seriation. *Phil. Trans. Roy. Soc. Lond.* A.269:125-135.

1971   »Seriation from abundance matrices« in *Mathematics in the Archaeological and Historical Sciences*. Edited by F.R.Hodson, D.G.Kendall and P.Tautu pp. 215-253. Edingburgh University Press: Edingburgh.

Kjærum, Poul

1955   Tempelhus fra stenalder. *KUML Årbog for Jysk Arkæologisk Selskab* 1955:7-36.

1966   The chronology of the passage graves in Jutland. *Palaeohistoria* XII:323-333.

1967   Mortuary Houses and Funeral Rites in Denmark. *Antiquity* XLI:190-196.

1970   Jættestuen Jordhøj. *KUML Årbog for Jysk Arkæologisk Selskab* 1969:9-66.

1980   Seals of 'Dilmun-Type' from Failaka, Kuwait. *Proceedings of the Seminar for Arabian Studies* vol. 10.

1983   *The Stamp and Cylinder Seals. Plates and Catalogue Descriptions. Failaka/Dilmun. The Second Millennium Settlements* vol. 1:1. Jutland Archaeological Society Publications XVII:1.

1986   Architecture and settlement patterns in 2nd mill. Failaka. *Proceedings of the Seminar for Arabian Studies* vol. 16.

Kleppe Johansen, Else

1974   *Samiske jernalderstudier ved Varangerfjorden*. Unpublished magistergrad thesis in archaeology, University of Bergen, Bergen.

Klindt-Jensen, O.

1978   *Slusegårdgravpladsen I og II*. Jysk Arkæologisk Selskabs Skrifter XIV.

Koch, Jan og Anne Birgitte Gebauer

1976   En dysse fra Aal sogn - om anlægget og dets keramik. *Mark og Montre* 1976:12-24.

Kristiansen, Kristian

1978   »The Consumption of Wealth in Bronze Age Denmark. A Study in the Dynamics of Economic Processes in Tribal Societies« in *New Directions in Scandinavian Archaeology* 1. Edited by Kristian Kristiansen and Carsten Paludan-Müller, pp. 158-190. Nationalmuseet: København.

1982   »The formation of tribal systems in later European prehistory: Northern Europe 4000-500 B.C« in *Theory and Explanation in Archaeology. The Southhampton Conference*. Edited by Colin Renfrew, Michael J. Rowlands and Barbara Abbot Segraves. pp. 241-280. Academic Press.

1984   »Ideology and material culture: an archaeological perspective« in *Marxist Perspectives in Archaeology*. Edited by Matheu Spriggs, pp. 72-100. New directions in Archaeology. Cambridge University Press: Cambridge.

Langballe, Hans

1985   Foulum huset - tempel eller bolig. *MIV* 13:6-35.

Larsen, Carsten U.

1984   *Form, dekoration, tid og rum for toledede urner i Danmarks yngre bronzealder*. Unpublished thesis, Institute of Archaeology, University of Copenhagen.

Larsson, Thomas B.

1984   »Multi-level exchange and cultural interaction in late Scandinavian Bronze Age« in *Settlement and Economy in Later Scandinavian Prehistory*. Edited by Kristian Kristiansen, pp. 63-83. B.A.R. International Series 211, Oxford.

1986   *The Bronze Age Metalwork in Southern Sweden: Aspects of Social and Spatial Organization 1800-500 B.C.* Archaeology and Environment 6. University of Umeå.

Liversage, David

1981   Neolithic monuments at Lindebjerg, Northwest Zealand. *Acta Archaeologica* 51:85-152.

Mackeprang, Mogens B.

1943   *Kulturbeziehungen im Nordischen Raum des 3.-5. Jahrhunderts*. Leipzig.

Madsen, Bo og Poul Otto Nielsen

1977   To tidlig-neolitiske jordgrave. *Antikvariske Studier* 1:27-34.

Madsen, Torsten

1976 Stendyngegrave ved Fjelsø. *KUML Årbog for Jysk Arkæologisk Selskab* 1975:73-82.

1979 Earthen Long Barrows and Timber Structures: Aspects of the Early Neolithic Mortuary Practice in Denmark. *Proceedings of the Prehistoric Society* 45:301-320.

1982 Settlement Systems of Early Agricultaral Societies in East Jutland, Denmark: A Regional Study of Change. *Journal of Anthropological Archaeology* vol.1:197-236.

1985 *Numerisk dataanalyse for arkæologer.* Institute of Archaeology, University of Århus.

Malmer, Mats P.

1962 *Jungneolithische Studien.* Acta Archaeologica Lundensia. Series in 8⁰ No.2. Rudolf Habelt Verlag: Bonn. CWK Gleerups Förlag: Lund.

1963 *Metodproblem inom järnålderens konsthistoria.* Acta Archaeologica Lundensia. Series in 8⁰ No 3. Rudolf Habelt Verlag: Bonn, CWK Gleerups Förlag: Lund.

1984 Arkeologisk positivism. *Fornvännen. Tidsskrift för Svensk Antikvarisk Forskning Årgång* 79:260-268

Marquardt, William H.

1978 »Advances in Archaeological Seriation« in *Advances in Archaeological Method and Theory* Volume 1, Edited by Michael B. Schiffer, pp. 257-314. Academic Press: New York, San Francisco, London.

Marseen, Oscar

1960 Ferslev-huset. En kultbygning fra jættestuetid. *KUML Årbog for Jysk Arkæologisk Selskab* 1960:36-55.

Mathiassen, Therkel

1939 Bundsø. En yngre Stenalders boplads på Als. *Aarbøger for Nordisk Oldkyndighed og Historie* 1939:1-56.

1944 The Stone Age Settlement at Trelleborg. *Acta Archaeologica* XV:77-98.

McBurney, C.B.M.

1967 *The Haua Fteah (Cyrenaica) and the Stone Age of the South-East Mediterranean.* Cambridge University Press: London, New York.

Meinander, C.F.

1962 Smikarr. *Finskt Museum* LXIX:5-38.

Moberg, Carl-Axel

1956 Till frågan om samhällsstrukturen i Norden under bronsåldern. *Fornvännen. Tidsskrift för Svensk Antikvarisk Forskning* 1956:65-79.

Montelius, Oscar

1917 *Minnen från vår Forntid.* Stockholm.

Munch, G. Stamsø.

1966 Gårdshauger i Nord-Norge. *Viking* 30:25-59.

Narroll, R.

1964 Ethnic unit classification. *Current Anthropology* Vol.5, No.4

Neustupny, E.

1973 »Factors determining the variability of the Corded Ware culture« in *The Explanation of Culture Change. Models in Prehistory.* Edited by Colin Renfrew, pp. 725-730. Duckworth: London.

Nicolaissen, O.M.

1893 Undersøgelser i Nordlands Amt 1892. *Aarsberetning fra Foreningen til Norske Fortidsminnesmerkers Bevaring* 1892:1-13.

Nie, Norman H., C. Hadlai Hull, Jean G. Jenkins, Karin Steinbrenner and Dale H. Bent

1975 *SPSS. Statistical Package for the Social Sciences.* McGraw-Hill: New York.

Nielsen, Eva Koch

1983 *Tidligneolitiske keramikfund.* Unpublished thesis. Institute of Archaeology, University of Copenhagen.

Nielsen, Karen Høilund

1984a *Bornholm - Sydskandinavien - Europa i yngre germansk jernalder.* Unpublished thesis. Institute of Archaeology, University of Aarhus

1984b Kronologiske forhold i ældre germansk jernalder med udgangspunkt i det jyske materiale. *Lag* 1:7-68.

1988 Zur chronologie der jüngeren Germanischen Eisenzeit auf Bornholm. Untersuchungen zu Schmuckgarnituren. *Acta Archaeologica* Volume 57 1987:47-86.

Nielsen, Poul Otto

1979 De tyknakkede flintøksers kronologi. *Aarbøger for Nordisk Oldkyndighed og Historie* 1979:5-71.

1982 Review of Klaus Ebbesen. 1978. Tragtbægerkultur i Nordjylland. Nordiske Fortidsminder, Serie B - in quarto, vol. 5. *Journal of Danish Archaeology* vol. 1:152-153.

Nielsen, S. Vestergaard

1952 Stendyngegrave fra jættestuetid. *KUML Årbog for Jysk Arkæologisk Selskab* 1952:109-118.

Nummedal, Anders

1937 Yngre stenaldersfund fra Nyelv og Karlebotn i Østfinnmark. *Universitetets Oldsaksamlings Årbok* 1935-36:69-131.

1938 Yngre stenaldersfund fra Nyelv og Karlebotn i Østfinnmark II. *Universitetets Oldsakssamlings Årbok* 1937:1-25.

Odner, Knut and Povl Simonsen

1963 »Tillæg: undersøgelser i 1960« in *Varangerfunnene III.* By Povl Simonsen. Tromsø Museums Skrifter VII(3).

Oldeberg, Andreas

1974 *Die ältere metallzeit in Schweden I.* Kungliga Vitterhets Historie och Antikvitets Akademien, Stockholm.

1976 *Die ältere metallzeit in Schweden II.* Kungliga Vitterhets Historie och Antikvitets Akademien, Stockholm.

Olsen, Bjørnar

1984 *Stabilitet og endring: Produksjon og samfunn i Varanger 800 f.kr. - 1700 e.Kr.* Unpublished Magistergrad thesis in archaeology, University of Tromsø.

O'Shea, John

1981 »Social configurations and the archaeological study of mortuary practices: a case study« in *The archaeology of death.* Edited by Robert Chapman, Ian Kinnes and Klavs Randsborg, pp. 39-52. Cambridge University Press: Cambridge.

Peck, J.K.

1977 *Yale Time series processor Ver. 4.8* Dep. of Economics, Yale University, New Haven, Connecticut.

Renfrew, Colin

1973   *Before civilisation. The Radiocarbon Revolution and Prehistoric Europe.* Jonathan Cape: London.

1976   »Megaliths, territories and populations« in*Acculturation and continuity in Atlantic Europe mainly during the Neolithic period and the Bronze Age.* Edited by Sigfried J. De Laet, pp. 198-220. De Tempel: Brugge.

1984   *Approaches to Social Archaeology.* Edingburgh University Press: Edingburgh.

Renfrew, Colin & Gene Sterud

1969   Close-proximity analysis: a rapid method for the ordering of archaeological materials. *American Antiquity* Vol. 34, No. 3:265-277.

Renouf, M.A. Priscilla

1981   *Prehistoric coastal economy in Varangerfjord, North Norway.* Unpublished Ph.D. dissertation, University of Cambridge: Cambridge.

1984   Northern coastal hunter-fishers: an archaeological model. *World Archaeology* 16(1): 18-27.

Rey, Piere Philipe

1977   Contradiction de classe dans les societes lineagires. *Dialectique* No. 21

Robinson, W.S.

1951   A method for Chronologically Ordering Archaeological Deposits. *American Antiquity* Volume XVI, no 4.

Rummel, R.J.

1970   *Applied Factor Analysis.* Northwestern University.

Schanche, Kjeiski

1985   »Registrering og kartleggning av fornminner på Mortensnes, sommeren 1984« in *Arkeologisk Feltarbeid i Nord-Norge 1984.* Edited by Ericka Engelstad and I.M. Holm-Olsen, pp. 147-150. Tromura. Kulturhistorie nr. 5.

Shanks, Michael and Christopher Tilley

1982   »Ideology, symbolic power and ritual communication: a reinterpretation of Neolithic mortuary practices« in *Symbolic and Structural Archaeology.* Edited by Ian Hodder, pp. 129-154. New Directions in Archaeology, Cambridge University Press: Cambridge.

Schiffer, M. B.

1972   Archaeological Context and Systemic Context. *American Antiquity* Vol. 37, No. 2:156-165.

1976   *Behavioural Archaeology.* Academic Press, New York.

Schwabedissen, Herman

1953   Fruchtschalen aus Schleswig-Holstein und ihre Zeit. *Offa* 12:14-66.

Service, E.R.

1962   *Primitive social organisation.* Random House: New York.

Simonsen, Povl

1956   Nye fund af stenalderbopladser i Troms. *Acta Borealia* B, nr. 4.

1961   *Varanger-Funnene II. Fund og udgravninger på fjordens sydkyst.* Tromsø Museums Skrifter VII(2).

1963   *Varanger-Funnene III. Fund og udgravninger i Pasvikdalen og ved den østlige fjordstrand.* Tromsø Museums Skrifter VII (3).

1965   »Settlement and occupations in the Younger Stone Age« in *Hunting and Fishing.* Edited by H. Hvarfner, pp. 397-406. Norrbottens Museum.

1968   Steinalder på Sørøy. *Ottar* 55(1).

1972   »The transition from food-gathering to pastoralism in north Scandinavia and its impact on settlement patterns« in*Man, Settlement and Urbanism.* Edited by P.J. Ucko, R. Tringham and G.W. Dimbleby, pp. 187-192. Duckworth: London.

1973   Fra livet i Finmark i steinalderen: om de arkeologiske utgravninger på Sørøy. *Forsknings Nytt* 18(2):6-12.

1974   *Veidemenn på Nordkalotten, hefte 1.* Institutt for samfunnsvitenskap, Universitetet i Tromsø, Stensilserie: B - historie nr. 1.

1975a »When and why did occupational specialization begin at the Scandinavian north coast« in *Prehistoric Maritime Adaptations in the Circumpolar Zone.* Edited by W. Fitzhugh, pp. 75-85. Mouton: The Hague.

1975b *Veidemenn på Nordkalotten, hefte 2. Yngre steinalder.* Universitetet i Tromsø, institut for Samfunnsvitenskap, Stensilserie B - historie, Nr.4.

1976   Steinalderens hustyper i Nord-Norge. *ISKOS* 1:23-25

1979   *Veidemenn på Norkalotten, hefte 3: Yngre steinalder og overgang til metaltid.* Universitetet i Tromsø, Institut for Samfunsvitenskap, Stensilserie B - historie, Nr.17.

Sjøvold, Thorleif

1962   *The Iron Age Settlement of Arctic Norway I.* Tromsø Museums Skrifter vol. X, 1.

1974   *The Iron Age Settlement of Arctic Norway II.* Tromsø Museums Skrifter vol. X, 2.

Skjelsvik, Elizabeth

1978   Registrering av fornminner for det Økonomiske kartverket i Norge 1963-1977. *Fornvännen. Tidsskrift för Svensk Antikvarisk Forskning* 73:134-141.

Sokal, Robert R. and Peter Sneath

1963   *Principles of Numerical Taxonomy.* W. H. Freeman and Company: San Francisco.

Solheim, Leiv

1981   *Multidimensional data analysis. Data reducing methods implemented on CYBER 171, written in the GENSTAT language.* University of Tromsø, Institute of Mathematical and Physical Sciences. Statistical Reports.

n.d.   *New ideas in correspondence analysis: discrimination and aggregation subjects.* University of Tromsø, Institute of Mathematical and Physical Sciences. Statistical Reports.

Spiegel, Murray R.

1972   *Theory and problems of statistics.* Schaum's outline Series. McGraw-Hill Book Company

Stephenson, W.

1953   *The study of Behavior.* The University Press of Chicago: Chicago.

Storli, Inger

1986   A Review of Archaeological Research on Sami Prehistory. *Acta Borealia* 1986, nr. 1:43-63.

Søbstad, Tom

1981   The Helgøy Project: Housegrounds of the 'Gamme' Type and the Sami Settlement. *Norwegian Archaeological Review* 14 (2):102-106.

Tainter, J.A.

1978 Mortuary Practices and the Study of Prehistoric Social Systems. *Advances in Archaeological Method and Theory* volume 1:105-141.

Thompson, Raymond H.

1956 The Subjective Element in Archaeological Inference. *Southwestern Journal of Anthropology* 12, No.3:327-332.

Thorvildsen, Knud

1946 Grønhøj ved Horsens. En Jættestue med Offerplads. *Aarbøger for Nordisk Oldkyndighed og Historie* 1946:73-120.

Tilley, Christopher

1984 »Ideology and the legitimation of power in the middle neolithic of southern Sweden« in *Ideology, Power and Prehistory*. Edited by D. Miller and C. Tilley, pp. 111-146. New directions in Archaeology. Cambridge University Press: Cambridge.

Vandkilde, Helle

1986 *En typologisk og kronologisk klassifikation af flad- og randlisteøkserne i Danmark og Slesvig på baggrund af en kronologisk analyse af relationerne mellem den tidligste metalkultur i Sydskandinavien.* Unpublished thesis. Institute of Prehistoric Archaeology, University of Aarhus.

Watson, Patty Jo, Steven A. Leblanc and Charles L. Redman.

1972 *Explanation in Archaeology. An Explicitly Scientific Approach.* Columbia University Press: New York, London.

Vedel, E.

1886 *Bornholms Oldtidsminder og Oldsager.*

1890 Bornholmske undersøgelser med særligt hensyn til den senere jernalder. *Aarbøger for Nordisk Oldkyndighed og Historie* 1890:1-104.

1897 *Efterskrift til Bornholms Oldtidsminder og Oldsager.*

Welinder, Stig

1977 *Ekonomiska processer i förhistorisk expansion.* Acta Archaeologica Lundensia. Series in 8^0 Minore No 7. Rudolf Habelt Verlag: Bonn. CWK Gleerups Förlag: Lund.

Whallon, Robert

1982 »Variables and Dimensions: The Critical Step in Quantitative Typology« in *Essays on archaeological typology*. Edited by Robert Whallon and James A. Brown. Center for American Archaelogy. Kampsville Seminars in Archaeology, Volumen 1. Evanston.

Wiesner, Polly

1984 Reconsidering the Behavioral Basis for Style: A Case Study among the Kalahari San. *Journal of Anthropological Archaeology* vol. 3:190-234.

Windelhed, Bengt

1976 Kulturgeografiska undersökningar vid Vinarve i Rone. *Gotländskt Arkiv* 1976:133-134.

Winther, J.

1926 *Lindø I. En Boplads fra Danmarks Yngre Stenalder.* Rudkøbing.

1928 *Lindø II. En Boplads fra Danmarks Yngre Stenalder.* Rudkøbing.

1935 *Troldebjerg I. En Bymæssig Bebyggelse fra Danmarks Yngre Stenalder.* Rudkøbing.

1938 *Troldebjerg II. En Bymæssig Bebyggelse fra Danmarks Yngre Stenalder. Tillæg.* Rudkøbing.

1943 *Blandebjerg (Fyldekalk imellem Troldebjerg og Lindø).* Rudkøbing.

Winther, Th.

1877 Om den saakaldte 'arktiske Gruppe' af Stensager, med specielt Hensyn til de i Tromsø Museum opbevarede. *Foreningen til Norske Fortidsminnesmerkers Bevaring, Aarsberetning* 1877:105-146.

Voss, J.

1982 *A study of western TRB social organisation.* Berichten van de Rijksdienst voor het Oudheidkundige Bodemonderzock. Amersfoort.

Ørsnes, Mogens

1966 *Form og stil i Sydskandinaviens Yngre Germanske Jernalder.* Nationalmuseet, København.

Åberg, Niels

1923 *Kalmar läns förhistoria.* Uppsala.